◣SCHOLASTIC

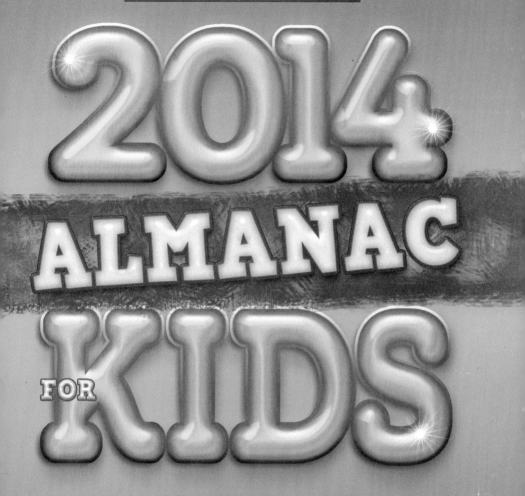

2014 ALMANAC FOR KIDS

Scholastic Inc.

Scholastic 2014 Almanac for Kids is produced by J. A. Ball Associates, Inc., 1200 Westlake Ave. North, Seattle, WA 98109.

Editorial Director: Jacqueline A. Ball
Manager, Design & Production: Mathew McInelly
Designer, Chapter Openers: Ron Leighton
Writers: Lynn Brunelle, Jim Brunelle, Delia Greve, Monique Peterson
Research: Brianne McInelly

ISBN 978-0-545-56264-5

10 9 8 7 6 5 4 3 2 1   13 14 15 16 17

Printed in the U.S.A.   40
First printing, September 2013
Cover design by Kay Petronio

Due to the publication date, statistics are current as of June 2013.

CONTENTS

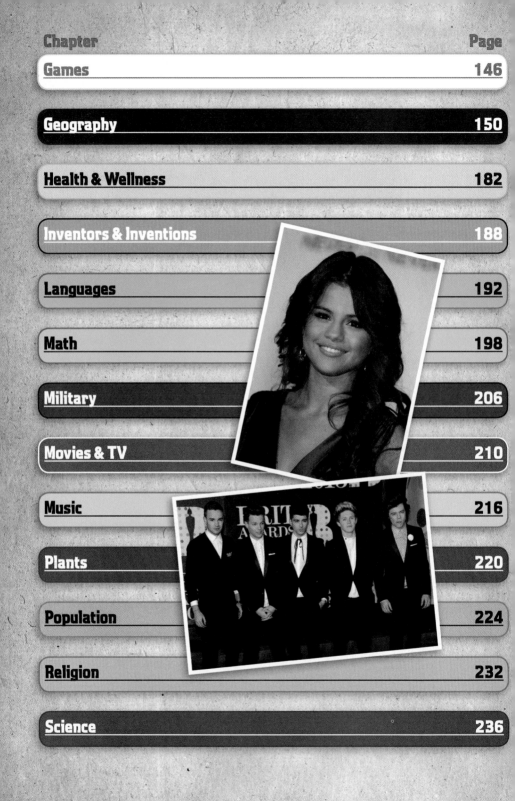

In 2013, environmental groups sued the U.S. government to get more protection for the endangered loggerhead turtle. Read more about animals in trouble on p. 28.

Animals

DO SOMETHING!

A popped balloon looks a lot like a jellyfish to a hungry sea turtle, and that's a problem. The balloon can get lodged in the turtle's throat and cause it to choke. Don't release balloons outdoors! Go to www.nps.gov/bisc/naturescience/how-you-can-help-protect-sea-turtles.htm for other ways to help.

THE ANIMAL KINGDOM
Detailed Classification

- Porifera — SPONGES
- Cnidaria — COELENTERATES
- Platyhelminthes — FLATWORMS
- Nematoda — ROUNDWORMS
- Mollusca — MOLLUSKS
- Annelida — TRUE WORMS

- Hydrozoa — HYDRAS, HYDROIDS
- Scyphozoa — JELLYFISH
- Anthozoa — SEA ANEMONES, CORAL

- Turbellaria — FREE-LIVING FLATWORMS
- Monogenea — PARASITIC FLUKES
- Trematoda — PARASITIC FLUKES
- Cestoda — TAPEWORMS

- Polyplacophora — CHITONS
- Gastropoda — SNAILS, SLUGS
- Bivalvia — CLAMS, SCALLOPS, MUSSELS
- Cephalopoda — OCTOPUSES, SQUID

- Polychaeta — MARINE WORMS
- Oligochaeta — EARTHWORMS, FRESHWATER WORMS
- Hirudinea — LEECHES

- Insecta — INSECTS
- Chilopoda — CENTIPEDES
- Diplopoda — MILLIPEDES
- Symphyla — SYMPHYLANS, PAUROPODS

Collembola, SPRINGTAILS
Thysanura, SILVERFISH, BRISTLETAILS
Ephemeroptera, MAYFLIES
Odonata, DRAGONFLIES
Isoptera, TERMITES
Orthoptera, LOCUSTS, CRICKETS, GRASSHOPPERS
Dictyptera, COCKROACHES, MANTIDS
Dermaptera, EARWIGS
Phasmida, STOCK INSECTS, LEAF INSECTS
Psocoptera, BOOK LICE, BARK LICE
Diplura, SIMPLE INSECTS

Protura, TELSONTAILS
Plecoptera, STONE FLIES
Grylloblattodea, TINY MOUNTAIN INSECTS
Strepsiptera, TWISTED-WINGED STYLOPIDS
Trichoptera, CADDIS FLIES
Embioptera, WEBSPINNERS
Thysanoptera, THRIPS
Mecoptera, SCORPION FLIES
Zoraptera, RARE TROPICAL INSECTS
Hemiptera, TRUE BUGS
Anoplura, SUCKING LICE

Mallophaga, BITING LICE, BIRD LICE
Homoptera, WHITEFLIES, APHIDS, SCALE INSECTS, CICADAS
Coleoptera, BEETLES, WEEVILS
Neuroptera, ALDERFLIES, LACEWINGS, ANT LIONS, SNAKEFLIES, DOBSONFLIES
Hymenoptera, ANTS, BEES, WASPS
Siphonaptera, FLEAS
Diptera, TRUE FLIES, MOSQUITOES, GNATS
Lepidoptera, BUTTERFLIES, MOTHS

Insectivora, INSECTIVORES (e.g., shrews, moles, hedgehogs)
Chiroptera, BATS
Dermoptera, FLYING LEMURS
Edentata, ANTEATERS, SLOTHS, ARMADILLOS
Pholidota, PANGOLINS
Primates, PROSIMIANS (e.g., lemurs, tarsiers, monkeys, apes, humans)

Rodentia, RODENTS (e.g., squirrels, rats, beavers, mice, porcupines)
Lagomorpha, RABBITS, HARES, PIKAS
Cetacea, WHALES, DOLPHINS, PORPOISES
Carnivora, CARNIVORES (e.g., cats, dogs, weasels, bears, hyenas)
Pinnipedia, SEALS, SEA LIONS, WALRUSES
Tubulidentata, AARDVARKS

Hyracoidea, HYDRAXES
Proboscidea, ELEPHANTS
Sirenia, SEA COWS (e.g., manatees, dugongs)
Perissodactyla, ODD-TOED HOOFED ANIMALS (e.g., horses, rhinoceroses, tapirs)
Artiodactyla, EVEN-TOED HOOFED ANIMALS (e.g., hogs, cattle, camels, hippopotamuses)

Animals

KEY

These colors show the classification groupings in the chart.

- PHYLUM
- SUBPHYLUM
- SUPERCLASS
- CLASS
- SUBCLASS
- INFRACLASS
- ORDER

(For a simpler way to classify animals, turn the page.)

Arthropoda **ARTHROPODS**

Minor Phyla

Echinadermata **ECHINODERMS**

Chordata **CHORDATES**

- Ctenophora, COMB JELLIES
- Mesozoa, MESOZOANS
- Rotifera, ROTIFERS
- Tardigrada, WATER BEARS
- Bryozoa, BRYOZOANS
- Brachiopoda, LAMPSHELLS
- Hemichordata, ACORN WORMS

Uniramia **UNIRAMIANS**

Crustacea **CRUSTACEANS**

Chelicerata **CHELICERATES**

Urochordata **SEA SQUIRTS**

Cephalochordata **AMPHIOXUS**

Vertebrata **VERTEBRATES**

Crinoidea **SEA LILIES, FEATHER STARS**

Stelleroidea **STARFISH, BRITTLE STARS, BASKET STARS**

Echinoidea **SEA URCHINS, HEART URCHINS, SAND DOLLARS**

Holothuroidea **SEA CUCUMBERS**

Arachnida **SPIDERS, SCORPIONS, MITES, TICKS**

Pycnogonida **SEA SPIDERS**

Merostomata **HORSESHOE CRABS**

Gnathostomata **VERTEBRATES WITH JAWS**

Agnatha **VERTEBRATES WITHOUT JAWS**

Malacostraca **LOBSTERS, CRABS, SHRIMPS, WOOD LICE**

Cirripedia **BARNACLES**

Branchiopoda **FAIRY SHRIMPS, WATER FLEAS**

Cyclostomata **LAMPREYS, HAGFISH**

Mammalia **MAMMALS**

Osteichthyes **BONY FISHES**

Chondrichthyes **CARTILAGINOUS FISHES** (e.g., sharks, skates, rays)

Reptilia **REPTILES**

Amphibia **AMPHIBIANS**

Aves **BIRDS**

Prototheria **PRIMITIVE MAMMALS**

Theria **ADVANCED MAMMALS**

Lepidosauria **LEPIDOSAURIANS**

Anapsida **ANAPSIDS**

Archosauria **ARCHOSAURIANS**

Anura **FROGS, TOADS**
Urodela **SALAMANDERS, NEWTS**
Apoda **CAECILIANS**

Monotremata **EGG-LAYING MAMMALS**

Eutheria **PLACENTAL MAMMALS**

Metatheria **NONPLACENTAL MAMMALS**

Squamata **LIZARDS, SNAKES**
Rynocephalia **TUATARA**

Chelonia **TURTLES, TORTOISES, TERRAPINS**

Crocodilia **CROCODILES, ALLIGATORS, GHARIAL**

Marsupia **UCHED MAMMALS, NGAROOS, KOALAS, OPOSSUMS**

Struthioniformes, OSTRICHES
Rheiformes, RHEAS
Causariformes, CASSOWARIES, EMUS
Apterygiformes, KIWIS
Tinamiformes, TINAMOUS
Sphenciformes, PENGUINS
Gaviiformes, LOONS
Podicipediformes, GREBES
Procellariiformes, PETRELS, ALBATROSSES, SHEARWATERS, FULMARS
Pelecaniformes, PELICANS, GANNETS, BOOBIES, CORMORANTS, SHAGS, DARTERS, FRIGATE BIRDS
Ciconiiformes, HERONS, BITTERNS
Anseriformes, DUCKS, GEESE, SWANS, SCREAMERS

Falconiformes, FALCONS, VULTURES, KITES, EAGLES, BUZZARDS, HAWKS, KESTRELS, OSPREYS, SECRETARY BIRDS
Galliformes, TURKEYS, PHEASANTS, PARTRIDGES, GROUSE, PEAFOWL
Gruiformes, CRANES, RAILS, COOTS, BUSTARDS
Charadriiformes, JACANAS, OYSTERCATCHERS, AVOCETS, COURSERS, PLOVERS, LAPWINGS, SNIPE, SKUAS, GULLS, TERNS, SKIMMERS, AUKS
Pteroclidiformes, SAND GROUSE
Columbiformes, DOVES, PIGEONS
Psittaciformes, PARROTS, PARAKEETS, LORIES, LORIKEETS, COCKATOOS, MACAWS
Cuculiformes, CUCKOOS, TURACOS, HOATZIN

Strigiformes, OWLS
Caprimulgiformes, NIGHTJARS, NIGHTHAWKS, FROGMOUTHS, OILBIRDS, POTOOS
Apodiformes, SWIFTS, HUMMINGBIRDS
Coliiformes, MOUSEBIRDS
Trogoniformes, TROGONS
Coraciiformes, KINGFISHERS, TOADIES, MOTMOTS, BEE EATERS, ROLLERS, HOOPOES, HORNBILLS
Piciformes, WOODPECKERS, BARBETS
Passeriformes, PERCHING BIRDS (e.g., larks, swallows, shrikes, wrens, thrushes, warblers, sunbirds, honey eaters, buntings, blackbirds, finches, weavers, sparrows, starlings, birds of paradise, crows)

9

Show Some Spine

The simplest way to classify animals is to divide them into two groups: those with spinal columns, or backbones, and those without backbones. The bones in the spinal column are called vertebrae, so animals with backbones are called vertebrates. There are at least 40,000 species of vertebrates. There are many millions of species of invertebrates, or animals without backbones.

All mammals, fish, birds, reptiles, and amphibians are vertebrates. Invertebrates include everything else: sponges, jellyfish, insects, spiders, clams, snails, worms, and many, many others.

Vertebrates

Invertebrates

Animals with Most Known Species

Mollusks
100,000

Fish
24,000

Worms
20,000

Birds
9,600

Reptiles
8,700

Mammals
5,000

Insects and
Other Arthropods
1,000,000+

10 Longest Animal Life Spans

Animal	Maximum age (years)
uahog (marine clam)	400
Giant tortoise	150
Human	122
Sturgeon	100
Killer whale	90
Blue whale	80
Golden eagle	80
Elephant	75
Sea anemone	70
Crocodile	60

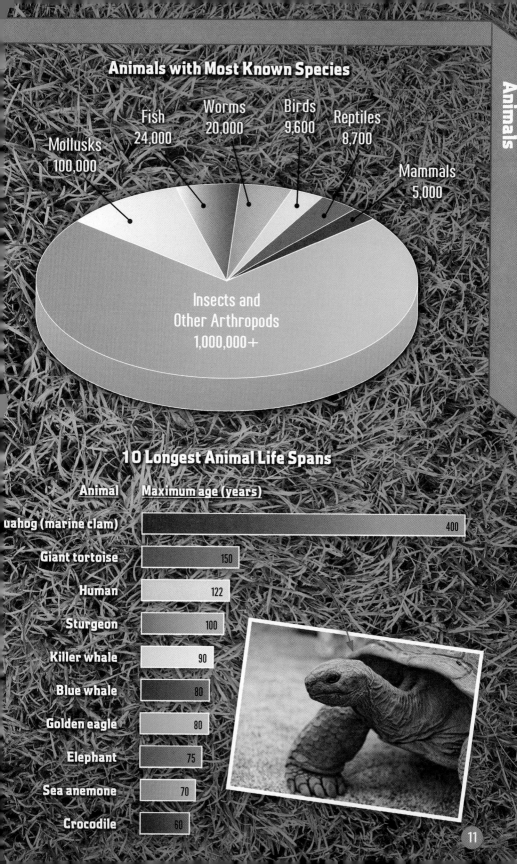

For the better part of 200 million years, dinosaurs ruled the world. Yet until the 19th century, they didn't even have a name. In 1842, English scientist Sir Richard Owen concluded that recently discovered fossils of huge jaws and teeth must belong to reptiles unlike any living animals. He named them *Dinosauria* ("terribly great lizards"). Some dinosaurs *were* great. *Supersaurus* could grow to a length of 130 feet (40 m)—as long as a 13-story building is tall—and weigh as much as 10 elephants. But other dinosaurs were the size of chickens. Most dinosaurs were herbivores, and most lived on land. They coexisted peacefully with mammals, most of which were small rodents.

- *Apatosaurus* 75–80 ft. (23–24 m)
- *Tyrannosaurus rex* 40 ft. (12 m)
- *Stegosaurus* 30 ft. (9 m)
- *Ankylosaurus* 25 ft. (7.6 m)
- *Triceratops* 25 ft. (7.6 m)

Animals

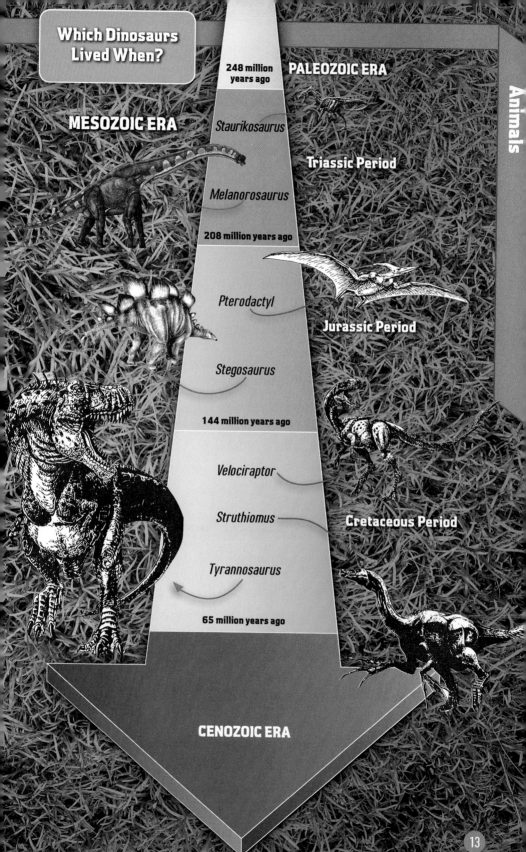

Which Dinosaurs Lived When?

Animals

PALEOZOIC ERA

MESOZOIC ERA

248 million years ago

Staurikosaurus

Triassic Period

Melanorosaurus

208 million years ago

Pterodactyl

Jurassic Period

Stegosaurus

144 million years ago

Velociraptor

Struthiomus

Cretaceous Period

Tyrannosaurus

65 million years ago

CENOZOIC ERA

Sauropods were the giants of the prehistoric world. The *apatosaurus*, *diplodocus*, and *seismosaurus* were all sauropods. These dinosaurs had long necks, long tails, and huge stomachs and chests. Big as they were, the sauropods were peaceful plant eaters.

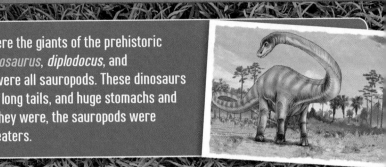

Theropods were the only meat-eating dinosaurs. One of the fiercest was *Tyrannosaurus rex*, but the *velociraptor* was equally ferocious. It slashed and sliced prey to pieces with the razor-sharp curved claws on its feet.

Stegosaurs' plates and spikes may have done more than keep away enemies. Scientists think blood flowing through the spikes could have been warmed or cooled by the air moving over the stegosaur's back, controlling body temperature.

Ankylosaurs were built for survival. Heavy, bony plates protected their bodies like armor on a tank. Some types had a mass of bone on their tails that they could use as a club.

Ceratopsians looked like rhinoceroses. They had horns on their faces and a curved collar of bone around their neck. Horns over a *triceratops*'s eyes could reach 3 feet (90 cm) long.

Animals

What Really Killed the Dinosaurs?

For millions and millions of years, dinosaurs dominated. Then they were gone—forever. What happened? In March 2010, after years of debate, an international panel of scientists concluded that an asteroid was to blame. They said an enormous asteroid about 6 miles (9.6 km) wide struck Earth with an impact more powerful than a billion atomic bombs.

The crash caused worldwide earthquakes, tsunamis, landslides, and fires. It sent millions of tons of sulfur, dust, and soot into the atmosphere, blocking sunlight for months. Plants died, and plant-eating dinosaurs starved to death. The meat-eating dinosaurs that fed on the plant eaters starved, too.

However, in February 2013, a modified theory surfaced. Some scientists now think that although an asteroid may have delivered the final death blow, dinosaurs had been dying off for years due to climate changes from volcanic eruptions. The newer research pinpointed the date of extinction to slightly over 66 million years ago.

CHECK IT OUT !

Little Dino, Big News

Not all dinosaurs were big, but in 2012 scientists discovered remains of a dinosaur that was less than 12 inches (30 cm) long—about the size of a blue jay. It had feathers like a bird, too. However, because of its small wingspan and other factors, scientists say it probably never got off the ground.

The newest dinosaur was discovered in northeastern China and dates from the Jurassic period, from about 199.6 million to 145.5 million years ago. Scientists say the discovery is another clue that dinosaurs and birds were relatives way, way back when.

Insects

Insects come in an amazing number of shapes and colors, but all you have to do is count to three to tell them apart from other creatures. All insects have three pairs of legs and three body parts: the head, the thorax, and the abdomen. Scorpions, ticks, centipedes, and many other creatures that look like insects are not the real thing.

Insects come in an amazing number of species, too. There are about four times as many insects as every other kind of animal, combined. Why so many? Insects have adapted to survive.

They can live in the hottest, coldest, wettest, and driest places. Their small size lets them survive in tiny spaces with practically no food. Many insects give birth to millions of young at once, so there's always a new generation to keep the species alive. Most have wings to fly away from danger.

Bugs may bug us, but only about 1 percent of insects are harmful. On the other hand, bees, wasps, and butterflies help keep us supplied with fruits and vegetables and help keep our world beautiful by pollinating plants and flowers.

Top 10 Most Common Insects

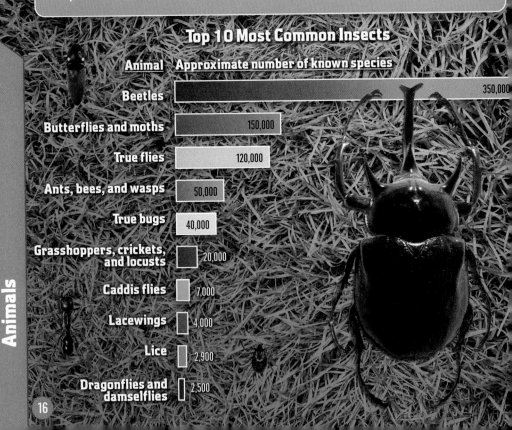

Animal	Approximate number of known species
Beetles	350,000
Butterflies and moths	150,000
True flies	120,000
Ants, bees, and wasps	50,000
True bugs	40,000
Grasshoppers, crickets, and locusts	20,000
Caddis flies	7,000
Lacewings	4,000
Lice	2,900
Dragonflies and damselflies	2,500

To hide from predators, walking sticks can blend into the twigs and branches on which they live. The largest kinds of walking sticks live in Asia and can grow to be more than 22 inches (56 cm) with their legs fully extended.

Insect eyes can have up to 30,000 lenses. Each lens lets in a separate piece of the scene, and then the parts combine to form a whole picture.

Grasshoppers have about 900 muscles—over 200 more muscles than humans. Many insects can lift or pull objects 20 times their weight.

Scientists say the dragonfly is the fastest-flying insect, capable of reaching 38 miles per hour (61 kph).

Fruit farmers love ladybugs because they eat the aphids that destroy crops. Predators hate their gross taste, which comes from a liquid produced from joints in their legs when threatened.

Mammals

There are more than 4,500 kinds of mammals, including the species you see when you look in the mirror: human. Mammals are different from all other animals in two important ways:

- Babies feed on their mother's milk.

- They have hair or fur.

Most mammals eat only plants, but big cats like the leopard and lion are exclusively meat eaters. Humans and some other species are omnivores. They have flat teeth to grind plants, sharp teeth to pierce animal flesh, and the digestive systems to handle both kinds of food.

All mammals are warm-blooded. Their body temperature stays the same no matter how cold or warm it gets around them. They also have large brains compared to their body size. Scientists say this lets certain mammals, like humans, chimps, and dolphins, learn more than other animals. In February 2010, a panel of scientists declared that dolphins are second only to humans in intelligence and are so bright they should be considered "nonhuman persons."

Unlike kangaroos, koalas, and other marsupials, the opossum does not have a pouch.

Flying squirrels don't really fly. They stretch out a fold of skin between their forelimbs and hind limbs and glide from tree to tree.

What do an armadillo's bony shell and a rhinoceros's thick hide have in common? They both protect against sharp-clawed predators.

The echidna and the platypus are the only mammals that don't give birth to live young. They're *monotremes* that lay eggs with leathery shells.

Many scientists say that a bear's winter sleep isn't true *hibernation* because the animal's body temperature falls only slightly. Other mammals, such as chipmunks and woodchucks, undergo a sharp temperature drop when they take their seasonal snooze.

Heaviest Land Mammals

Mammal	Weight
African elephant	15,000 lb. (6,804 kg)
Hippopotamus	9,920 lb. (4,500 kg)
White rhinoceros	5,000 lb. (2,268 kg)
Giraffe	3,000 lb. (1,361 kg)
Asian water buffalo	2,600 lb. (1,179 kg)
Arabian camel (dromedary)	1,520 lb. (689 kg)
Grizzly bear	1,500 lb. (680 kg)
Gorilla	500 lb. (227 kg)
Siberian tiger	400 lb. (181 kg)

Heaviest Marine Mammals

Mammal	Weight
Blue whale	150 tons
Fin whale	80 tons
Right whale	70 tons
Sperm whale	60 tons
Humpback whale	40 tons
Sei whale	40 tons
Gray whale	15 tons
Baird's beaked whale	14 tons
Killer whale	10 tons

Smallest Mammals

Mammal	Weight
Kitti's hog-nosed bat	1.2 in. (3.2 cm)
Pipistrelle bat	1.4 in. (3.6 cm)
Masked shrew	1.8 in. (4.6 cm)
Common (Eurasian) shrew	2.0 in. (5.1 cm)
Harvest mouse	2.0 in. (5.1 cm)
Southern blossom bat	2.0 in. (5.1 cm)
House mouse	2.5 in. (6.4 cm)

Fastest Mammals

Mammal	Maximum speed
Cheetah	70 mph (113 kph)
Pronghorn antelope	61 mph (98 kph)
Springbok	55 mph (89 kph)
Blue wildebeest	50 mph (80 kph)
Lion	50 mph (80 kph)
Brown hare	48 mph (77 kph)
Red fox	30 mph (48 kph)

Birds

If you see an animal with feathers, you can be sure it's a bird. Only birds have them, and they have lots! Scientists say birds have between about 1,000 and 25,000 feathers, which they shed once a year as new ones grow in. Feathers keep birds warm, help them fly, and give them their remarkable variety of colors and markings.

Like mammals, birds are warm-blooded vertebrates. A bird's skeleton is strong because many of the bones are fused together. In humans and other animals, they're separate. At the same time, bird skeletons are lightweight because many of the bones are hollow.

Scientists believe that birds evolved from ancient reptiles—specifically, meat-eating dinosaurs such as *Tyrannosaurus rex* and the *velociraptor*. They say at one time these ferocious dinosaurs may have had feathers!

The feathers of this mallard and of all birds are made of keratin, the same substance that covers a rhinoceros's bony horn and makes up human hair and nails.

Hummingbirds are the only birds that can fly backward. A hummingbird's heart beats 1,000 times a minute.

Parrots have a large cerebrum, the part of the brain that controls learning. Scientists say that may be why they can learn to talk.

Do you have eyes like a hawk? Not a chance! Hawks can see about eight times as well as humans.

Arctic terns migrate the farthest of any bird. Every year they travel about 22,000 miles (35,400 km) from the Arctic to their Antarctic winter home and back again.

All birds have wings, but not all birds can fly. Ostriches, the largest living birds, walk or run. Penguins swim, using their wings as flippers.

When a woodpecker digs for insects in the bark of a tree, it makes a loud hammering sound. It makes the same sound when trying to attract a mate or to claim territory from other birds. Some woodpeckers can make holes large enough to damage trees or even break them in half.

Fish and Other Marine Life

Not every animal that spends its life in the water is a fish—even if its name is *fish*! Jellyfish and starfish are not true fish. Clams, crabs, and scallops are called shellfish, but they're not really fish, either. Why not? None of these animals has a backbone. True fish are vertebrates. In fact, they were the first animals on Earth to have a backbone.

Fish are cold-blooded, which means their body temperature changes to match the temperature of their surroundings. Fish breathe through gills, which filter oxygen out of the water. Almost all fish have fins, which they use for swimming.

Most fish have skeletons made of bone, and most of these bony fish have an inflatable sac called a swim bladder below their backbone. The bladder gives them the buoyancy they need to stay afloat without moving. Sharks, rays and some other fish have skeletons made of cartilage. These types of fish don't have a swim bladder. When they stop swimming, they sink.

There are more than 24,000 species of fish, with scientists discovering more all the time.

Most fish swim horizontally, but the sea horse swims vertically.

Barracudas and piranhas have razor-sharp teeth that can strip the flesh from a large mammal in minutes.

The whale shark is the largest fish. It grows to more than 50 feet (15.2 m) in length and may weigh several tons. The smallest fish—as well as the smallest vertebrate—is the paedocypris, which is less than one-third of an inch (7.9 mm) long.

Sharks have excellent eyesight, especially in the darkness. Bright colors such as yellow and orange seem to attract them. Based on documented attacks, the five most dangerous species of shark are the great white, bull shark, tiger shark, grey nurse shark, and lemon shark.

Clown fish stay safe from predators by hiding inside the poisonous stinging tentacles of certain sea anemones. Why aren't the clown fish stung? Scientists say they may be protected by a layer of slime on their skin.

Reptiles & Amphibians

Reptiles and amphibians have a lot in common. They're both vertebrates. They're both cold-blooded, and they've both been around for millions of years. However, there are important differences. Most amphibians hatch from eggs laid in water and then spend their adult lives on land. Reptiles are primarily land animals, although some, like sea turtles and sea snakes, spend their whole life in the water.

Another difference is their skin. A reptile's skin is dry and scaly. Most amphibians have moist skin, which is often kept that way by a slimy coating of mucus.

Lizards and snakes are the most common reptiles—there are thousands of different kinds. Alligators, crocodiles, and turtles are also reptiles. Frogs, toads, and salamanders are the most common amphibians.

Since about the 1980s, the population of some frog species has been declining. Scientists don't fully understand why. However, because frogs and all amphibians absorb gases and other chemicals directly through their skin, there is some worry that disappearing frogs could be an indication of serious environmental problems.

The Gila monster has a poisonous bite, but most reptiles are harmless to humans.

The gray tree frog can freeze solid without harming itself. A substance in its blood works like antifreeze to protect its organs and tissues.

One way to tell a frog from a toad is to look at its skin. A frog's skin is smooth and moist. A toad's is bumpy and dry.

For many years, scientists thought a chameleon changed colors to blend into its surroundings for protection from predators. Now some scientists think that chameleons change colors to stand out to other chameleons. Brighter colors are used to show dominance and attract mates, while drab colors signal surrender.

Animals in Trouble

According to the World Wildlife Fund (WWF), the Amur leopard of the eastern mountains of Russia is one of the most critically endangered animals in the world. Less than 40 of these beautiful rare cats are said to exist. In 2012, to try to save the species, the government of Russia created the 650,000-acre Land of the Leopard National Park, protecting the leopard's breeding areas and more than half its remaining habitat.

The 14 animals below are also on the WWF's Critically Endangered list, identified as the species at the highest risk for extinction. Visit www.worldwildlife.org to read more about these species and learn what you can do to help.

Black rhino	South China tiger
Cross River gorilla	Sumatran elephant
Hawksbill turtle	Sumatran orangutan
Javan rhino	Sumatran rhino
Leatherback turtle	Sumatran tiger
Mountain gorilla	Vaquita
Saola (SOW-la)	Western Lowland gorilla

Habitat loss, environmental changes, poaching, and hunting are some critical threats to these animals' survival.

Names of Male, Female, and Young Animals

Animal	Male	Female	Young
Bear	Boar	Sow	Cub
Cat	Tom	Queen	Kitten
Cow	Bull	Cow	Calf
Chicken	Rooster	Hen	Chick
Deer	Buck	Doe	Fawn
Dog	Dog	Bitch	Pup
Donkey	Jack	Jenny	Foal
Duck	Drake	Duck	Duckling
Elephant	Bull	Cow	Calf
Fox	Dog	Vixen	Kit
Goose	Gander	Goose	Gosling
Horse	Stallion	Mare	Foal
Lion	Lion	Lioness	Cub
Rabbit	Buck	Doe	Bunny
Sheep	Ram	Ewe	Lamb
Swan	Cob	Pen	Cygnet
Swine	Boar	Sow	Piglet
Tiger	Tiger	Tigress	Cub
Whale	Bull	Cow	Calf
Wolf	Dog	Bitch	Pup

Animals

Animals

Animal Multiples

ants: colony

bears: sleuth, sloth

bees: grist, hive, swarm

birds: flight, volery

cats: clutter, clowder

cows: drove

chicks: brood, clutch

clams: bed

cranes: sedge, seige

crows: murder

doves: dule

ducks: brace, team

elephants: herd

elks: gang

finches: charm

fish: school, shoal, drought

foxes: leash, skulk

geese: flock, gaggle, skein

gnats: cloud, horde

goats: trip

gorillas: band

hares: down, husk

hawks: cast

hens: brood

hogs: drift

horses: pair, team

hounds: cry, mute, pack

kangaroos: troop

kittens: kindle, litter

larks: exaltation

lions: pride

locusts: plague

magpies: tidings

mules: span

nightingales: watch

oxen: yoke

oysters: bed

parrots: company

partridges: covey

peacocks: muster, ostentation

pheasants: nest, bouquet

pigs: litter

ponies: string

quail: bevy, covey

rabbits: nest

seals: pod

sheep: drove, flock

sparrows: host

storks: mustering

swans: bevy, wedge

swine: sounder

toads: knot

turkeys: rafter

turtles: bale

vipers: nest

whales: gam, pod

wolves: pack, route

woodcocks: fall

29

Popular Pets in the United States

The American Pet Products Association (APPA) reported that nearly seven in ten U.S. households included at least one pet in 2012, representing a record-high level of pet ownership.

Animal	Percent of households owning
Any pet	68%
Dog	46.7%
Cat	37.3%
Freshwater fish	11.8%
Bird	5.7%
Small animal	5.7%
Reptile	4.6%
Horse	2.3%
Saltwater fish	1.5%

Top 10 Registered U.S. Dog Breeds

Labrador retriever

German shepherd

Golden retriever

Beagle

Bulldog

Yorkshire terrier

Boxer

Poodle

Rottweiler

Dachshund

Top 10 Registered U.S. Cat Breeds

Persian

Exotic

Maine coon

Ragdoll

Abyssinian

Sphynx

American shorthair

British shorthair

Siamese

Devon Rex

31

Birthdays

PEOPLE Tiny gold medal–winning gymnast Kyla Ross ("Mighty Mouse") turns 18 on October 24, 2014, giving her the right to vote in U.S. elections. In 2013, Argentina lowered its voting age to 16. Should American 16-year-olds be able to vote?

> **Milestone Birthdays 2014**

> Zachary Gordon........16......February 15
> Elle Fanning...............16......April 9
> Malia Obama.............16......July 4
> Abigail Breslin..........18......April 14
> Victoria Justice........21......February 19
> Miranda Cosgrove....21......May 14

January

1 Paul Revere, American patriot, 1735

2 Kate Bosworth, actor, 1983

3 J. R. R. Tolkien, author, 1892

4 Doris Kearns Goodwin, historian, 1943

5 Diane Keaton, actor, 1946

6 Joan of Arc, military leader and saint, around 1412

7 Blue Ivy Carter, daughter of Beyoncé and Jay-Z, 2012

8 Stephen Hawking, physicist, 1942

9 Kate Middleton, Duchess of Cambridge, wife of William, Prince of Wales, 1982

10 George Foreman, boxer, 1949

11 John MacDonald, first Canadian prime minister, 1815

12 Jack London, author, 1876

13 Orlando Bloom, actor, 1977

14 Albert Schweitzer, scientist and humanitarian, 1875

15 Drew Brees, football player, 1979

16 Kate Moss, model, 1974

17 Michelle Obama, U.S. First Lady, 1964

18 Kevin Costner, actor, 1955

19 Edgar Allan Poe, author, 1809

20 Edwin "Buzz" Aldrin, astronaut, 1930

21 Plácido Domingo, operatic tenor, 1941

22 Sir Francis Bacon, explorer, 1561

23 Edouard Manet, painter, 1832

24 Maria Tallchief, ballerina, 1925

25 Alicia Keys, musician, 1981

26 Ellen Degeneres, TV personality, 1958

27 Wolfgang Amadeus Mozart, composer, 1756

28 Jackson Pollock, artist, 1912

29 Oprah Winfrey, media personality, 1954

30 Christian Bale, actor, 1974

31 Justin Timberlake, entertainer, 1981

February

1 Langston Hughes, writer, 1902

2 Christie Brinkley, model, 1954

3 Norman Rockwell, painter, 1894

4 Rosa Parks, civil rights activist, 1913

5 Cristiano Ronaldo, soccer player, 1985

6 Babe Ruth, baseball player, 1895

7 Ashton Kutcher, actor, 1978

8 Jules Verne, author, 1828

9 Alice Walker, author, 1944

10 George Stephanopoulos, TV news personality, 1961

11 Thomas Edison, inventor, 1847

12 Judy Blume, author, 1938

13 Chuck Yeager, test pilot, 1923

14 Jack Benny, radio and TV entertainer, 1894

15 Susan B. Anthony, suffragist and civil rights leader, 1820

16 Ice-T, rap musician and actor, 1958

17 Michael Jordan, basketball player, 1963

18 John Travolta, actor, 1954

19 Victoria Justice, actor, 1993

20 Gloria Vanderbilt, fashion designer, 1924

21 W. H. Auden, poet, 1907

22 Edward Kennedy, U.S. senator, 1932

23 Dakota Fanning, actor, 1994

24 Steve Jobs, cofounder of Apple Computers, 1955

25 Sean Astin, actor, 1971

26 Johnny Cash, singer and songwriter, 1932

27 Chelsea Clinton, U.S presidential daughter, 1980

28 Frank O. Gehry, architect, 1929

29 Jimmy Dorsey, orchestra leader, 1904

March

1 Ron Howard, actor and director, 1954

2 Dr. Seuss (Theodor Geisel), author, 1904

3 Jessica Biel, actor, 1982

4 Knute Rockne, football star, 1888

5 Eva Mendes, actor, 1974

6 Michelangelo, painter, 1475

7 Rachel Weisz, actor, 1970

8 Freddie Prinze Jr., actor, 1976

9 Juliette Binoche, actor, 1964

10 Shannon Miller, gymnast, 1977

11 Terrence Howard, actor, 1969

12 Amelia Earhart, aviator, 1897

13 Abigail Fillmore, U.S. First Lady, 1798

14 Billy Crystal, actor, 1948

15 Ruth Bader Ginsburg, Supreme Court justice, 1933

16 Jerry Lewis, entertainer, 1926

17 Mia Hamm, soccer player, 1972

18 Queen Latifah, entertainer, 1970

19 Wyatt Earp, U.S. western lawman, 1848

20 Lois Lowry, author, 1937

21 Matthew Broderick, actor, 1962

22 Bob Costas, sportscaster, 1952

23 Wernher von Braun, rocket scientist, 1912

24 Peyton Manning, football player, 1976

25 Danica Patrick, race car driver, 1982

26 Sandra Day O'Connor, U.S. Supreme Court justice, 1930

27 Fergie, singer, 1975

28 Lady Gaga, singer, 1986

29 Jessica Chastain, actor, 1981

30 Vincent van Gogh, painter, 1853

31 René Descartes, philosopher, 1596

April

1. Lon Chaney, Sr., horror movie star, 1883
2. Dana Carvey, entertainer, 1955
3. Jane Goodall, anthropologist, 1934
4. Maya Angelou, poet, 1928
5. Booker T. Washington, inventor, 1856
6. Zach Braff, actor, 1975
7. Jackie Chan, actor, 1954
8. Kofi Atta Annan, UN secretary-general, 1938
9. Elle Fanning, actor, 1998
10. Frances Perkins, first female member of U.S. presidential cabinet (secretary of labor), 1880
11. Viola Liuzzo, U.S. civil rights activist, 1925
12. Tom Clancy, author, 1947
13. Samuel Beckett, playwright, 1906
14. Adrien Brody, actor, 1973
15. Emma Watson, actor, 1990
16. Wilbur Wright, aviator, 1867
17. John Pierpoint Morgan, industrialist, 1837
18. Conan O'Brien, TV personality, 1963
19. Kate Hudson, actor, 1979
20. Don Mattingly, baseball player, 1961
21. John Muir, environmentalist, 1838
22. Jack Nicholson, actor, 1937
23. William Shakespeare, poet and playwright, 1564
24. Kelly Clarkson, singer, 1982
25. Renée Zellweger, actor, 1969
26. John James Audubon, naturalist, 1785
27. Samuel Morse, inventor, 1791
28. Jay Leno, TV personality, 1950
29. Duke Ellington, jazz musician, 1899
30. Kirsten Dunst, actor, 1982

May

1. Tim McGraw, country singer, 1967
2. David Beckham, soccer player, 1975
3. James Brown, singer and songwriter, 1933
4. Will Arnett, actor, 1970
5. Adele, singer and songwriter, 1988
6. Willie Mays, baseball player, 1931
7. Tim Russert, TV news personality, 1950
8. Adrian Gonzalez, baseball player, 1982
9. Howard Carter, archaeologist, 1873
10. Fred Astaire, actor, 1899
11. Salvador Dalí, painter, 1904
12. Yogi Berra, baseball player, 1925
13. Robert Pattinson, actor, 1986
14. Miranda Cosgrove, actor, 1993
15. Madeleine Albright, U.S. secretary of state, 1937
16. Adrienne Rich, poet, 1929
17. Craig Ferguson, TV personality, 1962
18. Tina Fey, actor and writer, 1975
19. Nora Ephron, author and director, 1941
20. Bono, musician, 1960
21. Al Franken, entertainer and U.S. senator, 1951
22. Apolo Anton Ohno, speed skater, 1982
23. Jewel, singer and songwriter, 1974
24. Victoria, Queen of England, 1819
25. Mike Myers, actor, 1963
26. Sally Ride, astronaut, 1951
27. Henry Kissinger, U.S. diplomat, 1923
28. Kylie Minogue, singer, 1968
29. Carmelo Anthony, basketball player, 1984
30. Wynonna Judd, country singer and songwriter, 1964
31. Clint Eastwood, actor and director, 1930

June

1. Heidi Klum, model and TV host, 1973
2. Martha Washington, first U.S. First Lady, 1731
3. Rafael Nadal, tennis player, 1986
4. Angelina Jolie, actor, 1975
5. Mark Wahlberg, actor, 1971
6. Alexander Pushkin, author, 1799
7. Dean Martin, singer and actor, 1917
8. Kanye West, rapper, singer, record producer, 1977
9. Natalie Portman, actor, 1981
10. Maurice Sendak, author, 1928
11. Shia LaBeouf, actor, 1986
12. Anne Frank, Holocaust diarist, 1929
13. Ashley and Mary-Kate Olsen, actors, 1986
14. Donald Trump, businessman, 1946
15. Courteney Cox, actor, 1971
16. Joyce Carol Oates, author, 1938
17. Venus Williams, tennis player, 1981
18. Paul McCartney, musician, 1942
19. Guy Lombardo, band leader, 1902
20. Shefali Chowdhury, actor, 1988
21. Prince William of Wales, British royal, 1982
22. John Dillinger, bank robber, 1903
23. Randy Jackson, TV personality, 1956
24. Mick Fleetwood, musician, 1942
25. Sonia Sotomayor, U.S. Supreme Court justice, 1954
26. Babe Didrikson Zaharias, athlete, 1911
27. Helen Keller, deaf-blind author and activist, 1880
28. John Cusack, actor, 1966
29. George Washington Goethals, chief engineer of the Panama Canal, 1858
30. Michael Phelps, swimmer, 1985

July

1 Benjamin Oliver Davis, first African American general in the U.S. Army, 1877
2 Lindsay Lohan, actor, 1986
3 Tom Cruise, actor, 1962
4 George Steinbrenner, New York Yankees owner, 1930
5 P. T. Barnum, showman and entertainer, 1810
6 50 Cent, rap musician, 1976
7 Michelle Kwan, ice skater, 1980
8 Anna Quindlen, author, 1952
9 Tom Hanks, actor, 1956
10 Jessica Simpson, actor and singer, 1980
11 Sela Ward, actor, 1956
12 Henry David Thoreau, author and philosopher, 1817
13 Harrison Ford, actor, 1942
14 Crown Princess Victoria, Swedish monarch, 1977
15 Rembrandt, painter, 1606
16 Will Ferrell, actor, 1967
17 Erle Stanley Gardner, mystery writer
18 Nelson Mandela, South African political leader, 1918
19 Edgar Degas, painter, 1834
20 Gisele Bundchen, model, 1980
21 Brandi Chastain, soccer player, 1968
22 Selena Gomez, singer and actor, 1992
23 Daniel Radcliffe, actor, 1989
24 Jennifer Lopez, actor and singer, 1969
25 Matt LeBlanc, actor, 1967
26 Sandra Bullock, actor, 1964
27 Alex Rodriguez, baseball player, 1975
28 Beatrix Potter, author, 1866
29 Martina McBride, country singer, 1966
30 Emily Brontë, author, 1818
31 J. K. Rowling, author, 1965

August

1 Francis Scott Key, writer of "The Star-Spangled Banner," 1779
2 James Baldwin, author, 1924
3 Martha Stewart, lifestyle spokesperson and TV personality, 1941
4 Jeff Gordon, race car driver, 1971
5 Neil Armstrong, astronaut, 1930
6 Lucille Ball, actor, 1911
7 Ralph Bunche, Nobel Peace Prize winner, 1903
8 Roger Federer, tennis player, 1981
9 John Dryden, poet, 1631
10 Betsey Johnson, fashion designer, 1942
11 Suzanne Collins, author of The Hunger Games, 1962
12 Pete Sampras, tennis player, 1971
13 Annie Oakley, Wild West entertainer, 1860
14 Tim Tebow, football player, 1987
15 Napoleon Bonaparte, emperor, 1769
16 Angela Bassett, actor, 1958
17 Davy Crockett, frontiersman, 1786
18 Roberto Clemente, baseball player, 1934
19 Gene Roddenberry, creator of Star Trek, 1921
20 Al Roker, TV meteorologist, 1954
21 Wilt Chamberlain, basketball player, 1936
22 Tori Amos, musician, 1963
23 Kobe Bryant, basketball player, 1978
24 Anna Lee Fisher, chemist and astronaut, 1949
25 Leonard Bernstein, conductor and composer, 1918
26 Branford Marsalis, musician, 1960
27 Mother Teresa, nun and humanitarian, 1910
28 Shania Twain, country singer, 1965
29 Michael Jackson, entertainer, 1958
30 Mary Shelley, author of Frankenstein, 1797
31 Richard Gere, actor, 1949

September

1 Gloria Estefan, singer, 1957
2 Keanu Reeves, actor, 1964
3 Shaun White, snowboarder, 1986
4 Beyoncé Knowles, singer and actress, 1981
5 Kim Yu-Na, figure skater, 1990
6 John Dalton, scientist, 1766
7 Michael DeBakey, pioneer heart surgeon, 1908
8 Pink, singer, 1979
9 Adam Sandler, actor, 1966
10 Colin Firth, actor, 1960
11 William Sydney Porter ("O. Henry"), short story writer, 1862
12 Yao Ming, basketball player, 1980
13 Milton Hershey, chocolate magnate, 1857
14 Amy Winehouse, singer and songwriter, 1983
15 Prince Henry ("Harry") of Wales, British royal, 1984
16 Alexis Bledel, actor, 1981
17 William Carlos Williams, poet, 1883
18 Lance Armstrong, bicycle racer, 1971
19 Trisha Yearwood, country singer, 1964
20 Sophia Loren, actor, 1934
21 Stephen King, author, 1947
22 Joan Jett, singer, 1960
23 Bruce Springsteen, musician, 1949
24 Jim Henson, creator of the Muppets, 1936
25 Will Smith, actor, 1968
26 Serena Williams, tennis player, 1981
27 Avril Lavigne, singer, 1984
28 Caravaggio, painter, 1571
29 Enrico Fermi, physicist and atom bomb developer, 1901
30 Elie Wiesel, author and Holocaust survivor, 1928

October

1 Vladimir Horowitz, pianist, 1904
2 Groucho Marx, comedian, 1890
3 Gwen Stefani, singer, 1969
4 Alicia Silverstone, actor, 1976
5 Maya Lin, architect, 1959
6 George Westinghouse, inventor, 1846
7 Yo-Yo Ma, cellist, 1955
8 Rev. Jesse Jackson, African American leader, 1941
9 John Lennon, singer and songwriter, 1940
10 Brett Favre, football player, 1969
11 Eleanor Roosevelt, U.S. First Lady and diplomat, 1884
12 Hugh Jackman, actor, 1968
13 Margaret Thatcher, British prime minister, 1925
14 Usher, rap singer, 1979
15 Emeril Lagasse, chef, 1959
16 John Mayer, singer, 1977
17 Mae Jemison, first African American female astronaut, 1956
18 Lindsey Vonn, skier, 1984
19 Peter Max, artist, 1937
20 Bela Lugosi, actor who played Dracula, 1882
21 Alfred Nobel, scientist, 1883
22 Deepak Chopra, self-help writer, 1946
23 Pelé, soccer player, 1940
24 Kevin Kline, actor, 1947
25 Katy Perry, singer, 1984
26 Hilary Rodham Clinton, U.S. First Lady, U.S. senator, and secretary of state, 1947
27 Captain James Cook, explorer, 1728
28 Bill Gates, founder of Microsoft, 1955
29 Gabrielle Union, actor, 1972
30 Nastia Liukin, gymnast, 1989
31 Chiang Kai-Shek, Nationalist Chinese leader, 1887

November

1 Toni Collette, actor, 1972
2 Daniel Boone, frontiersman, 1734
3 Vincenzo Bellini, composer, 1801
4 Walter Cronkite, TV news personality, 1916
5 Roy Rogers, TV cowboy, 1911
6 James A. Naismith, inventor of basketball, 1861
7 Marie Curie, chemist, 1867
8 Margaret Mitchell, author, 1900
9 Carl Sagan, scientist, 1934
10 Miranda Lambert, singer and songwriter, 1983
11 Leonardo DiCaprio, actor, 1974
12 Elizabeth Cady Stanton, suffragist, 1815
13 Louis Brandeis, U.S. Supreme Court justice, 1856
14 Georgia O'Keeffe, painter, 1887
15 Kevin Eubanks, musician and TV personality, 1957
16 Shigeru Miyamoto, video game designer, 1952
17 Danny DeVito, actor, 1944
18 Wilma Mankiller, first female Chief of the Cherokee Nation, 1945
19 Calvin Klein, fashion designer, 1942
20 Edwin Hubble, scientist, 1889
21 Ken Griffey Jr., boxer, 1969
22 Mark Ruffalo, actor, 1967
23 Miley Cyrus, singer and actor, 1992
24 Scott Joplin, composer, 1868
25 Andrew Carnegie, industrialist, 1883
26 Charles Schulz, cartoonist, 1922
27 Anders Celsius, scientist, 1701
28 Jon Stewart, TV personality, 1965
29 Mariano Rivera, baseball player, 1969
30 Mark Twain, author, 1835

December

1 Woody Allen, actor and director, 1935
2 Britney Spears, singer, 1981
3 Ozzy Osbourne, musician and performer, 1948
4 Jay-Z, rap singer and songwriter, 1969
5 Walt Disney, producer and animator, 1901
6 Ira Gershwin, lyricist, 1896
7 Willa Cather, author, 1873
8 Eli Whitney, inventor, 1765
9 Clarence Birdseye, frozen food pioneer, 1886
10 Emily Dickinson, poet, 1830
11 Mo'Nique, actor, 1967
12 Frank Sinatra, singer and actor, 1915
13 Taylor Swift, singer, 1989
14 Vanessa Hudgens, actor, 1988
15 Gustave Eiffel, designer of the Eiffel Tower, 1832
16 Jane Austen, author, 1775
17 Milla Jovovich, actor, 1975
18 Steven Spielberg, director, 1946
19 Edith Piaf, singer, 1915
20 Harvey Samuel Firestone, tire manufacturer, 1868
21 Kiefer Sutherland, actor, 1966
22 Diane Sawyer, TV news personality, 1945
23 Madame C. J. Walker, inventor and businesswoman, 1867
24 Stephenie Meyer, author, 1973
25 Clara Barton, founder, American Red Cross, 1821
26 Chris Daughtry, musician, 1979
27 Louis Pasteur, chemist, 1822
28 Denzel Washington, actor, 1954
29 Charles Goodyear, inventor, 1800
30 LeBron James, basketball player, 1984
31 Henri Matisse, painter, 1869

There's nothing wimpy about Diary of a Wimpy Kid book sales. As of early 2013, the seven books in the core series have sold more than 75 million copies all over the world. The first ebooks came out in October 2012 and even have their own name: Wimp-E-Books. The eighth Wimpy Kid book is due out in late 2013, and the fourth Wimpy Kid movie, *The Ugly Truth*, should be in theaters in early 2014. Wimps rule!

❯ Wimpy Kid Series

DIARY of a Wimpy Kid
THE THIRD WHEEL

Jeff Kinney

Books &
Literature

10 Top-Selling New Young Adult Books of 2012 (Hardcover)

Title	Author
The Mark of Athena	Rick Riordan
The Third Wheel	Jeff Kinney
The Serpent's Shadow	Rick Riordan
Tales from a Not-So-Graceful Ice Princess	Rachel Renée Russell
Insurgent	Veronica Roth
Tales from a Not-So-Smart Miss Know-It-All	Rachel Renée Russell
Middle School: Get Me Out of Here!	James Patterson and Chris Tebbetts
Hidden	P. C. Cast and Kristin Cast
"Who Could That Be at This Hour?"	Lemony Snicket
Big Nate Goes for Broke	Lincoln Peirce

Top-Selling Young Adult Series of 2012

Title	Author
The Hunger Games	Suzanne Collins
Percy Jackson & the Olympians, Heroes of Olympus	Rick Riordan
Diary of a Wimpy Kid	Jeff Kinney
Maximum Ride and other series	James Patterson
Dork Diaries	Rachel Renée Russell
Divergent (first two books)	Veronica Roth
Big Nate	Lincoln Peirce
Twilight	Stephenie Meyer

10 Top-Selling Ebooks of 2012

Title	Author
The Hunger Games	Suzanne Collins
Catching Fire	Suzanne Collins
Mockingjay	Suzanne Collins
The Mark of Athena	Rick Riordan
Divergent	Veronica Roth
Insurgent	Veronica Roth
Artemis Fowl	Eoin Colfer
War Horse	Michael Morpurgo
The Serpent's Shadow	Rick Riordan
The Fault in Our Stars	John Green

2013 Children's Book Award Winners

Caldecott Medal: *This Is Not My Hat*, Jon Klassen

Newbery Medal: *The One and Only Ivan*, Katherine Applegate

National Book Award, Young People's Literature:
Goblin Secrets, William Alexander*

Printz Award: *In Darkness*, Nick Lake

Coretta Scott King Book Award (Author):
Andrea Pinkney, *Hand in Hand: Ten Black Men Who Changed America*

Coretta Scott King Book Award (Illustrator):
Bryan Collier, *I, Too, Am America*

Scott O'Dell Award for Historical Fiction: *Chickadee*, Louise Erdrich

Teen Choice Book of the Year:
Clockwork Prince: The Infernal Devices, Book Two, Cassandra Clare

*2012 winner

2013 Nickelodeon Kids' Choice Awards Book Winner

Favorite Book: The Hunger Games series

Buildings & Landmarks

BREAKING RECORDS

The Singapore Flyer is the world's tallest "observation" wheel—for now. New York City announced plans to start building an even bigger wheel in 2014.

Big Wheels

- New York City (planned) .... 625 feet (190.5 m)
- Singapore Flyer .... 541 feet (165 m)
- Star of Nanchang .... 525 feet (160 m)
- London Eye .... 443 feet (135 m)
- Original Ferris Wheel .... 264 feet (80.4 m)
  —*Chicago, IL, 1893*

Milestones in Modern Architecture Timeline

First modern metal-frame skyscraper, Chicago's ten-story Home Insurance Company Building, is designed by U.S. architect William Jenney (1832–1907). It features a metal skeleton of cast-iron columns and nonsupporting curtain walls, which become characteristic of modern design.

1884

U.S. architect Frank Lloyd Wright (1867–1959) becomes famous for designing houses in the Prairie style, characterized by low, horizontal lines and use of natural earth colors. Wright believes buildings should complement settings.

1900

Walter Gropius (1883–1969) founds Bauhaus, a German school of design, to combine art and architecture with modern industrial technology. Bauhaus styles are notable for geometric lines and use of steel, glass, and concrete.

1919

Noted American architect (Richard) Buckminster Fuller (1895–1983) designs a self-contained "4-D" prefabricated house. Fuller becomes known for his "Dymaxion" principle of trying to get the most from the least amount of material and energy.

1928

1937

Ludwig Mies van der Rohe (1886–1969) emigrates to the United States and becomes a leader in glass-and-steel architecture. He pioneers rectangular lines in design, including cubelike brick structures, uncovered steel columns, and large areas of tinted glass.

1948

Petronas Twin Towers in Kuala Lumpur, Malaysia, are built and become the world's tallest buildings at a height of 1,483 feet (452 m). In 2003, the towers lose their title to the Taipei 101 Tower in Taiwan. Taipei 101 measures 1,667 feet (508 m) tall.

Finnish-born American architect Eero Saarinen (1910–1961) becomes known for innovative designs for various buildings in the United States. His sweeping style features soaring rooflines, extensive use of glass, and curved lines.

1996

2009

Taipei 101's title falls to Burj Khalifa in Dubai, United Arab Emirates, 2,717 feet (828 m) tall.

Construction of Important Earthworks, Dams, and Canals Timeline

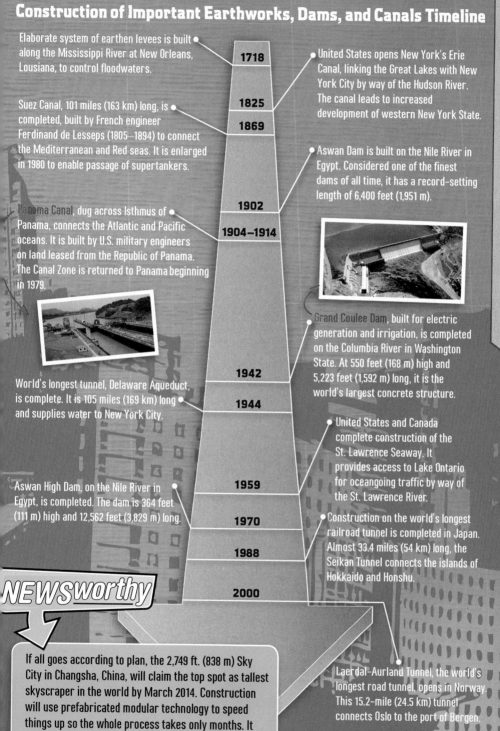

Elaborate system of earthen levees is built along the Mississippi River at New Orleans, Lousiana, to control floodwaters.

1718

United States opens New York's Erie Canal, linking the Great Lakes with New York City by way of the Hudson River. The canal leads to increased development of western New York State.

1825

Suez Canal, 101 miles (163 km) long, is completed, built by French engineer Ferdinand de Lesseps (1805–1894) to connect the Mediterranean and Red seas. It is enlarged in 1980 to enable passage of supertankers.

1869

Aswan Dam is built on the Nile River in Egypt. Considered one of the finest dams of all time, it has a record-setting length of 6,400 feet (1,951 m).

1902

Panama Canal, dug across Isthmus of Panama, connects the Atlantic and Pacific oceans. It is built by U.S. military engineers on land leased from the Republic of Panama. The Canal Zone is returned to Panama beginning in 1979.

1904–1914

Grand Coulee Dam, built for electric generation and irrigation, is completed on the Columbia River in Washington State. At 550 feet (168 m) high and 5,223 feet (1,592 m) long, it is the world's largest concrete structure.

1942

World's longest tunnel, Delaware Aqueduct, is complete. It is 105 miles (169 km) long and supplies water to New York City.

1944

United States and Canada complete construction of the St. Lawrence Seaway. It provides access to Lake Ontario for oceangoing traffic by way of the St. Lawrence River.

1959

Aswan High Dam, on the Nile River in Egypt, is completed. The dam is 364 feet (111 m) high and 12,562 feet (3,829 m) long.

1970

Construction on the world's longest railroad tunnel is completed in Japan. Almost 33.4 miles (54 km) long, the Seikan Tunnel connects the islands of Hokkaido and Honshu.

1988

2000

NEWSworthy

If all goes according to plan, the 2,749 ft. (838 m) Sky City in Changsha, China, will claim the top spot as tallest skyscraper in the world by March 2014. Construction will use prefabricated modular technology to speed things up so the whole process takes only months. It took 5 years to finish Burj Khalifa.

Laerdal-Aurland Tunnel, the world's longest road tunnel, opens in Norway. This 15.2-mile (24.5 km) tunnel connects Oslo to the port of Bergen.

The Seven Wonders of the Modern World

Wonder/Location

Description

Channel Tunnel
England and France

The 31-mile (50-km) Channel Tunnel (Chunnel) is actually three concrete tubes, each 5 feet (2 m) thick, which burrow under the English Channel. They enter the earth at Coquelles, France, and reemerge at Folkstone, England, behind the white cliffs of Dover.

CN Tower
Toronto

The world's third-tallest freestanding tower soars 1,815 feet (553 m) above Toronto, Canada. The CN Tower was designed to withstand 260-mph (418-kph) gusts.

Empire State Building
New York City

At 1,434 feet (437 m), the Empire State Building is the best-known skyscraper in the world. For more than 40 years it was the tallest building in the world. Construction took only one year and 45 days.

Netherlands North Sea Protection Works
Netherlands

This is not just one structure but a complex system of dams, floodgates, storm surge barriers, and other engineered works that protect the country against destructive floods.

Golden Gate Bridge
San Francisco

Once the world's tallest suspension bridge, the Golden Gate Bridge hangs from two 746-foot (227-m) towers and is supported by enough cable to circle Earth three times.

Itaipu Dam
Brazil and Paraguay

Five miles (8 km) wide and as high as a 65-story building, the main dam is made of concrete while the flanking wings are earth and rock fill. The dam generates enough energy to power most of California.

Panama Canal
Panama

To build the Panama Canal, 42,000 workers dredged, blasted, and excavated from Colón to Balboa. They moved enough earth and rubble to bury the island of Manhattan to a depth of 12 feet (4 m)—or enough to open a 16-foot (5-m) tunnel to Earth's center.

The Seven Wonders of the Ancient World

Wonder/Location	Description
Colossus of Rhodes Harbor of Rhodes, in Aegean Sea, off coast of Turkey	This huge bronze statue of the sun god, Helios, took 12 years to build and stood about 105 feet (32 m) tall. It was destroyed by an earthquake in 225 BCE.
Hanging Gardens of Babylon Ancient city of Babylon (now near Baghdad, Iraq)	The hanging gardens were a series of landscaped terraces along the banks of the Euphrates River, planted with trees, flowers, and shrubs. The gardens were probably built by King Nebuchadnezzar II for his wife.
Pharos (lighthouse) Pharos Island, off coast of Alexandria, Egypt	Built around 270 BCE, this was the world's first important lighthouse. It stood in the harbor for 1,000 years until it was destroyed by an earthquake. It served as a prototype for all other lighthouses built by the Roman Empire.
Mausoleum of Halicarnassus Ancient city of Halicarnassus, now Turkish town of Bodrum	This monumental marble tomb was built by the widow of Mausolus, king of Anatolia, in 353 BCE. 
Statue of Zeus Olympia, Greece	This huge, ornate statue of the god on his throne was almost 60 feet (18 m) tall.
Pyramids of Egypt Giza, Egypt	The oldest pyramid was built with more than two million limestone blocks and stands more than 480 feet (146 m) high. This is the only one of the ancient wonders still in existence.
Temple of Artemis Ancient Greek city of Ephesus, now in Turkey near Selçuk	Built in the sixth century BCE to honor the goddess Artemis, this was one of the largest Greek temples ever built. It was famous for the artistic decoration and use of marble.

World's 10 Tallest Dams

Name	Country	Height above lowest formation
Rogun	Tajikistan	1,099 ft. (335 m)
Bakhtiari	Iran	1,033 ft. (315 m)
Jinping	China	1,001 ft. (305 m)
Nurek	Tajikistan	984 ft. (300 m)
Xiaowan	China	958 ft. (292 m)
Grande Dixence	Switzerland	935 ft. (285 m)
Xiluodu	China	912 ft. (278 m)
Inguri	Georgia	892 ft. (272 m)
Vajont	Italy	859 ft. (262 m)
Manuel M. Torres (also known as Chicoasén)	Mexico	856 ft. (261 m)

*Planned or under construction as of mid-2013

Top 10 Longest Suspension Bridges in North America

Name/Location	Completed	Length of main span
Verrazano-Narrows Lower New York Bay, NY	1964	4,260 ft. (1,298 m)
Golden Gate San Francisco Bay, CA	1937	4,200 ft. (1,280 m)
Mackinac Lakes Michigan and Huron, MI	1957	3,800 ft. (1,158 m)
George Washington Hudson River at New York City, NY	1931	3,500 ft. (1,067 m)
Tacoma Narrows II Puget Sound at Tacoma, WA	1950, 2007	2,800 ft. (853 m)
Carquinez (Alfred Zampa Memorial) Carquinez Strait, CA	2003	2,388 ft. (728 m)
San Francisco-Oakland Bay San Francisco Bay, CA	1936	2,310 ft. (704 m)
Bronx-Whitestone East River, New York City, NY	1939	2,300 ft. (701 m)
Pierre Laporte Quebec City, QC	1970	2,190 ft. (668 m)
Delaware Memorial (twin) Delaware River near Wilmington, DE	1951, 1968	2,150 ft. (655 m)

Top 10 Longest Road Tunnels in the World

Name/Location	Completed	Tunnel length
Laerdal-Aurland Norway	2000	15.2 mi. (24.5 km)
Zhongnanshan China	2007	11.2 mi. (18 km)
St. Gotthard Switerland	1980	10.5 mi. (16.9 km)
Arlberg Austria	1978	8.7 mi. (14.0 km)
Fréjus France/Italy	1980	8.0 mi. 12.9 km)
Hsuehshan Taiwan	2007	8.0 mi. 12.9 km)
Maijishan China	2009	7.6 mi. (12.3 km)
Mont Blanc France/Italy	1991	7.3 mi. (11.7 km)
Gudvanga Norway	2001	7.1 mi. (11.4 km)
Folgefonn (tie) Norway	1991	7.0 mi. (11.2 km)
Baojishan (tie) China	2009	7.0 mi. (11.2 km)

Buildings & Landmarks

Top 10 "Tallest" Cities in the World

City	Towers 700–999 ft. (213–304.5 m)	Towers 1000+ ft. (304.8+ m)
Dubai, United Arab Emirates	26	14
Hong Kong, China	32	6
New York, New York, United States	33	4
Shanghai, China	24	4
Chicago, Illinois, United States	14	5
Shenzhen, China	16	2
Singapore, Singapore	16	0
Tokyo, Japan	12	2
Houston, Texas, United States	9	1
Los Angeles, California, United States	9	1

Top 10 Tallest Completed Buildings in the World

Name/Location	Height
Burj Khalifa Dubai, United Arab Emirates	2,717 ft. (828 m)
Makkah Clock Royal Tower Hotel Mecca, Saudi Arabia	1,971 ft. (601 m)
Taipei 101 Taipei, Taiwan	1,667 ft. (508 m)
Shanghai World Financial Center Shanghai, China	1,614 ft. (492 m)
International Commerce Centre Hong Kong, China	1,585 ft. (483 m)
Petronas Tower 1 Kuala Lumpur, Malaysia	1,483 ft. (452 m)
Petronas Tower 2 Kuala Lumpur, Malaysia	1,483 ft. (452 m)
Zifeng Tower Nanjing, China	1,476 ft. (450 m)
Willis (formerly Sears) Tower Chicago, Illinois, United States	1,451 ft. (442 m)
Kingkey 100 Shenzhen, China	1,450 ft. (442 m)

Rankings on this page based on structures completed as of 2013.

Exploring Museums

Museums are buildings that preserve and display important pieces of history, culture, and human knowledge. They let us explore everything from Renaissance paintings to baseball cards, from mummies to lightning. Read about these famous museums and learn a little of what's inside each one. Visit them online if you can't get there in person.

British Museum

Location: London, England

What's Inside: This London landmark holds seven million objects representing civilizations and cultures from prehistory to modern times. World-famous exhibits include the Rosetta Stone, an ancient (196 BCE) Egyptian tablet that helped us understand Egyptian hieroglyphics.

Website: www.britishmuseum.org

The Exploratorium

Location: San Francisco, California, United States

What's Inside: "Don't touch" is definitely NOT the rule here. This hands-on museum has hundreds and hundreds of interactive exhibits to let visitors explore sound, light, motion, electricity, perception, the weather, and so much more up close.

Website: www.exploratorium.edu

Guggenheim Museum Bilbao

Location: Bilbao, Spain

What's Inside: This museum has an impressive collection of art from all over the world, mostly from the last half of the twentieth century. However, equally impressive is the spectacular titanium and glass building itself, designed by famous architect Frank Gehry.

Website: www.guggenheim.org/bilbao

The Louvre

Location: Paris, France

What's Inside: The most-visited museum in the world, the Louvre is home to 35,000 art objects dating from ancient times to the 19th century. Visitors flock to da Vinci's *Mona Lisa* and the famous sculptures *Winged Victory* and *Venus de Milo*.

Website: www.louvre.fr

Buildings & Landmarks

Metropolitan Museum of Art

Location: New York, New York, United States

What's Inside: "The Met" is so gigantic that its Egyptian art section contains an entire temple, which was shipped to America as a gift. The massive museum contains art from every period in history and every part of the world. In the Newbery Award—winning novel *From the Mixed-up Files of Mrs. Basil E. Frankweiler*, two kids hide out at the Met for days after running away from home.

Website: www.metmuseum.org

Museum of Modern Art

Location: New York, New York, United States

What's Inside: This New York City landmark holds one of the world's best collections of modern art, including van Gogh's *Starry Night*, Monet's *Water Lilies*, and Warhol's *Campbell's Soup Cans*.

Website: www.moma.org

National Baseball Hall of Fame and Museum

Location: Cooperstown, New York, United States

What's Inside: This popular upstate New York attraction is the center of the world of baseball, past and present. There are thousands of clippings, photos, and baseball cards and special displays to Babe Ruth, Jackie Robinson, and women's baseball. Thirty glass-enclosed lockers, one for each Major League team, contain team jerseys and other items.

Website: www.baseballhall.org

Smithsonian Institution

Location: Washington, DC, United States

What's Inside: The Smithsonian is the largest museum complex in the world, composed of 19 different museums and the National Zoo. Within the complex you can check out Dorothy's red slippers from *The Wizard of Oz*, the lunar landing "dune buggy" from the Apollo moon missions—and millions of other items and displays.

Website: www.si.edu

NEWSworthy

On February 22, 2012, the Smithsonian broke ground for the National Museum of African American History and Culture (http://nmaahc.si.edu), planned as the largest cultural showcase of the African American experience in the country. Exhibits, programs, and thousands of items, including Harriet Tubman's hymnbook and a Spirit of Tuskegee World War II biplane, will help visitors have a closer look at the struggles and accomplishments of black people throughout history. The museum is scheduled to open in 2015.

SAVE THE DATE On June 19, 1865, the last slaves were freed by the Emancipation Proclamation. Now there is a bill in Congress to make June 19 a national holiday. Does your state already celebrate "Juneteenth"? Find out at www.juneteenth.com.

Calendars & Holidays

Periods of Time

annual	yearly
biannual	twice a year
bicentennial	marking a period of 200 years
biennial	marking a period of 2 years
bimonthly	every 2 months; twice a month
biweekly	every 2 weeks; twice a week
centennial	marking a period of 100 years
decennial	marking a period of 10 years
diurnal	daily; of a day
duodecennial	marking a period of 12 years
millennial	marking a period of 1,000 years
novennial	marking a period of 9 years
octennial	marking a period of 8 years
perennial	occurring year after year
quadrennial	marking a period of 4 years
quadricentennial	marking a period of 400 years
quincentennial	marking a period of 500 years
quindecennial	marking a period of 15 years
quinquennial	marking a period of 5 years
semiannual	twice a year
semicentennial	marking a period of 50 years
semidiurnal	twice a day
semiweekly	twice a week
septennial	marking a period of 7 years
sesquicentennial	marking a period of 150 years
sexennial	marking a period of 6 years
thrice weekly	3 times a week
tricennial	marking a period of 30 years
triennial	marking a period of 3 years
trimonthly	every 3 months
triweekly	every 3 weeks; 3 times a week
undecennial	marking a period of 11 years
vicennial	marking a period of 20 years

MAY 9

MAY 1

JULY 10

NOV 5

Months of the Year in Different Calendars

Gregorian	Jewish	Hindu	Muslim
January	Shevat	Magha	Muharram
February	Adar	Phalgun	Safar
March	Nisan	Cait	Rabi I
April	Iyar	Baisakh	Rabi II
May	Sivan	Jyeshtha	Jumada I
June	Tammuz	Asarh	Jumada II
July	Av	Sravan	Rajab
August	Elul	Bhadon	Sha'ban
September	Tishrei	Asvin	Ramadan
October	Cheshvan	Kartik	Shawwal
November	Kislev	Margasira	Dhu'l-Qadah
December	Tevet	Pus	Dhu'l-Hijja

Wedding Anniversary Gift Chart

Anniversary	Traditional	Modern
1st	paper	clocks
2nd	cotton	china
3rd	leather	crystal
4th	fruit/flowers	linen/silk
5th	wood	silverware
6th	iron	wood
7th	wool	desk sets
8th	bronze	linen
9th	pottery	leather
10th	tin	diamond jewelry
11th	steel	fashion jewelry
12th	silk/linen	pearls
13th	lace	textiles
14th	ivory	gold jewelry
15th	crystal	watches
20th	china	platinum
25th	silver	silver
30th	pearls	diamonds
35th	coral	jade
40th	rubies	rubies
45th	sapphires	sapphires
50th	gold	gold
55th	emeralds	emeralds
60th	diamonds	diamonds

Chinese Years, 1900–2019

Rat	Ox	Tiger	Hare (Rabbit)	Dragon	Snake
1900	1901	1902	1903	1904	1905
1912	1913	1914	1915	1916	1917
1924	1925	1926	1927	1928	1929
1936	1937	1938	1939	1940	1941
1948	1949	1950	1951	1952	1953
1960	1961	1962	1963	1964	1965
1972	1973	1974	1975	1976	1977
1984	1985	1986	1987	1988	1989
1996	1997	1998	1999	2000	2001
2008	2009	2010	2011	2012	2013

Horse	Sheep (Goat)	Monkey	Rooster	Dog	Pig
1906	1907	1908	1909	1910	1911
1918	1919	1920	1921	1922	1923
1930	1931	1932	1933	1934	1935
1942	1943	1944	1945	1946	1947
1954	1955	1956	1957	1958	1959
1966	1967	1968	1969	1970	1971
1978	1979	1980	1981	1982	1983
1990	1991	1992	1993	1994	1995
2002	2003	2004	2005	2006	2007
2014	2015	2016	2017	2018	2019

Perpetual Calendar, 1775–2050

A perpetual calendar lets you find the day of the week for any date in any year. The number next to each year below corresponds to one of the 14 calendars that follow.

Year		Year		Year		Year		Year		Year	
1775	1	1821	2	1867	3	1913	4	1959	5	2005	7
1776	9	1822	3	1868	11	1914	5	1960	13	2006	1
1777	4	1823	4	1869	6	1915	6	1961	1	2007	2
1778	5	1824	12	1870	7	1916	14	1962	2	2008	10
1779	6	1825	7	1871	1	1917	2	1963	3	2009	5
1780	14	1826	1	1872	9	1918	3	1964	11	2010	6
1781	2	1827	2	1873	4	1919	4	1965	6	2011	7
1782	3	1828	10	1874	5	1920	12	1966	7	2012	8
1783	4	1829	5	1875	6	1921	7	1967	1	2013	3
1784	12	1830	6	1876	14	1922	1	1968	9	2014	4
1785	7	1831	7	1877	2	1923	2	1969	4	2015	5
1786	1	1832	8	1878	3	1924	10	1970	5	2016	13
1787	2	1833	3	1879	4	1925	5	1971	6	2017	1
1788	10	1834	4	1880	12	1926	6	1972	14	2018	2
1789	5	1835	5	1881	7	1927	7	1973	2	2019	3
1790	6	1836	13	1882	1	1928	8	1974	3	2020	11
1791	7	1837	1	1883	2	1929	3	1975	4	2021	6
1792	8	1838	2	1884	10	1930	4	1976	12	2022	7
1793	3	1839	3	1885	5	1931	5	1977	7	2023	1
1794	4	1840	11	1886	6	1932	13	1978	1	2024	9
1795	5	1841	6	1887	7	1933	1	1979	2	2025	4
1796	13	1842	7	1888	8	1934	2	1980	10	2026	5
1797	1	1843	1	1889	3	1935	3	1981	5	2027	6
1798	2	1844	9	1890	4	1936	11	1982	6	2028	14
1799	3	1845	4	1891	5	1937	6	1983	7	2029	2
1800	4	1846	5	1892	13	1938	7	1984	8	2030	3
1801	5	1847	6	1893	1	1939	1	1985	3	2031	4
1802	6	1848	14	1894	2	1940	9	1986	4	2032	12
1803	7	1849	2	1895	3	1941	4	1987	5	2033	7
1804	8	1850	3	1896	11	1942	5	1988	13	2034	1
1805	3	1851	4	1897	6	1943	6	1989	1	2035	2
1806	4	1852	12	1898	7	1944	14	1990	2	2036	10
1807	5	1853	7	1899	1	1945	2	1991	3	2037	5
1808	13	1854	1	1900	2	1946	3	1992	11	2038	6
1809	1	1855	2	1901	3	1947	4	1993	6	2039	7
1810	2	1856	10	1902	4	1948	12	1994	7	2040	8
1811	3	1857	5	1903	5	1949	7	1995	1	2041	3
1812	11	1858	6	1904	13	1950	1	1996	9	2042	4
1813	6	1859	7	1905	1	1951	2	1997	4	2043	5
1814	7	1860	8	1906	2	1952	10	1998	5	2044	13
1815	1	1861	3	1907	3	1953	5	1999	6	2045	1
1816	9	1862	4	1908	11	1954	6	2000	14	2046	2
1817	4	1863	5	1909	6	1955	7	2001	2	2047	3
1818	5	1864	13	1910	7	1956	8	2002	3	2048	11
1819	6	1865	1	1911	1	1957	3	2003	4	2049	6
1820	14	1866	2	1912	9	1958	4	2004	12	2050	7

Calendar 1

JANUARY
S M T W T F S
1 2 3 4
5 6 7 8 9 10 11
12 13 14 15 16 17 18
19 20 21 22 23 24 25
26 27 28 29 30 31

FEBRUARY
S M T W T F S
1
2 3 4 5 6 7 8
9 10 11 12 13 14 15
16 17 18 19 20 21 22
23 24 25 26 27 28

MARCH
S M T W T F S
1
2 3 4 5 6 7 8
9 10 11 12 13 14 15
16 17 18 19 20 21 22
23 24 25 26 27 28 29
30 31

APRIL
S M T W T F S
1 2 3 4 5
6 7 8 9 10 11 12
13 14 15 16 17 18 19
20 21 22 23 24 25 26
27 28 29 30

MAY
S M T W T F S
1 2 3
4 5 6 7 8 9 10
11 12 13 14 15 16 17
18 19 20 21 22 23 24
25 26 27 28 29 30 31

JUNE
S M T W T F S
1 2 3 4 5 6 7
8 9 10 11 12 13 14
15 16 17 18 19 20 21
22 23 24 25 26 27 28
29 30

JULY
S M T W T F S
1 2 3 4 5
6 7 8 9 10 11 12
13 14 15 16 17 18 19
20 21 22 23 24 25 26
27 28 29 30 31

AUGUST
S M T W T F S
1 2
3 4 5 6 7 8 9
10 11 12 13 14 15 16
17 18 19 20 21 22 23
24 25 26 27 28 29 30
31

SEPTEMBER
S M T W T F S
1 2
3 4 5 6 7 8 9
10 11 12 13 14 15 16
17 18 19 20 21 22 23
24 25 26 27 28 29 30

OCTOBER
S M T W T F S
1 2 3 4
5 6 7 8 9 10 11
12 13 14 15 16 17 18
19 20 21 22 23 24 25
26 27 28 29 30 31

NOVEMBER
S M T W T F S
1
2 3 4 5 6 7 8
9 10 11 12 13 14 15
16 17 18 19 20 21 22
23 24 25 26 27 28 29
30

DECEMBER
S M T W T F S
1 2 3 4 5 6
7 8 9 10 11 12 13
14 15 16 17 18 19 20
21 22 23 24 25 26 27
28 29 30 31

Calendar 2

JANUARY
S M T W T F S
1 2 3 4 5 6
7 8 9 10 11 12 13
14 15 16 17 18 19 20
21 22 23 24 25 26 27
28 29 30 31

FEBRUARY
S M T W T F S
1 2 3
4 5 6 7 8 9 10
11 12 13 14 15 16 17
18 19 20 21 22 23 24
25 26 27 28

MARCH
S M T W T F S
1 2 3
4 5 6 7 8 9 10
11 12 13 14 15 16 17
18 19 20 21 22 23 24
25 26 27 28 29 30 31

APRIL
S M T W T F S
1 2 3 4 5 6 7
8 9 10 11 12 13 14
15 16 17 18 19 20 21
22 23 24 25 26 27 28
29 30

MAY
S M T W T F S
1 2 3 4 5
6 7 8 9 10 11 12
13 14 15 16 17 18 19
20 21 22 23 24 25 26
27 28 29 30 31

JUNE
S M T W T F S
1 2
3 4 5 6 7 8 9
10 11 12 13 14 15 16
17 18 19 20 21 22 23
24 25 26 27 28 29 30

JULY
S M T W T F S
1 2 3 4 5 6 7
8 9 10 11 12 13 14
15 16 17 18 19 20 21
22 23 24 25 26 27 28
29 30 31

AUGUST
S M T W T F S
1 2 3 4
5 6 7 8 9 10 11
12 13 14 15 16 17 18
19 20 21 22 23 24 25
26 27 28 29 30 31

SEPTEMBER
S M T W T F S
1
2 3 4 5 6 7 8
9 10 11 12 13 14 15
16 17 18 19 20 21 22
23 24 25 26 27 28 29
30

OCTOBER
S M T W T F S
1 2 3 4 5 6
7 8 9 10 11 12 13
14 15 16 17 18 19 20
21 22 23 24 25 26 27
28 29 30 31

NOVEMBER
S M T W T F S
1 2 3
4 5 6 7 8 9 10
11 12 13 14 15 16 17
18 19 20 21 22 23 24
25 26 27 28 29 30

DECEMBER
S M T W T F S
1
2 3 4 5 6 7 8
9 10 11 12 13 14 15
16 17 18 19 20 21 22
23 24 25 26 27 28 29
30 31

3

JANUARY · FEBRUARY · MARCH
APRIL · MAY · JUNE
JULY · AUGUST · SEPTEMBER
OCTOBER · NOVEMBER · DECEMBER

4

JANUARY · FEBRUARY · MARCH
APRIL · MAY · JUNE
JULY · AUGUST · SEPTEMBER
OCTOBER · NOVEMBER · DECEMBER

5

JANUARY · FEBRUARY · MARCH
APRIL · MAY · JUNE
JULY · AUGUST · SEPTEMBER
OCTOBER · NOVEMBER · DECEMBER

6

JANUARY · FEBRUARY · MARCH
APRIL · MAY · JUNE
JULY · AUGUST · SEPTEMBER
OCTOBER · NOVEMBER · DECEMBER

7

JANUARY · FEBRUARY · MARCH
APRIL · MAY · JUNE
JULY · AUGUST · SEPTEMBER
OCTOBER · NOVEMBER · DECEMBER

8

JANUARY · FEBRUARY · MARCH
APRIL · MAY · JUNE
JULY · AUGUST · SEPTEMBER
OCTOBER · NOVEMBER · DECEMBER

9

JANUARY · FEBRUARY · MARCH
APRIL · MAY · JUNE
JULY · AUGUST · SEPTEMBER
OCTOBER · NOVEMBER · DECEMBER

10

JANUARY · FEBRUARY · MARCH
APRIL · MAY · JUNE
JULY · AUGUST · SEPTEMBER
OCTOBER · NOVEMBER · DECEMBER

11

JANUARY · FEBRUARY · MARCH
APRIL · MAY · JUNE
JULY · AUGUST · SEPTEMBER
OCTOBER · NOVEMBER · DECEMBER

12

JANUARY · FEBRUARY · MARCH
APRIL · MAY · JUNE
JULY · AUGUST · SEPTEMBER
OCTOBER · NOVEMBER · DECEMBER

13

JANUARY · FEBRUARY · MARCH
APRIL · MAY · JUNE
JULY · AUGUST · SEPTEMBER
OCTOBER · NOVEMBER · DECEMBER

14

JANUARY · FEBRUARY · MARCH
APRIL · MAY · JUNE
JULY · AUGUST · SEPTEMBER
OCTOBER · NOVEMBER · DECEMBER

Fixed Dates

These events are celebrated on the same date every year, regardless of where the date falls in the week.

Event	Date
New Year's Day[1]	January 1
Groundhog Day	February 2
Abraham Lincoln's Birthday	February 12
Valentine's Day	February 14
Susan B. Anthony Day	February 15
George Washington's Birthday	February 22
St. Patrick's Day	March 17
April Fools' Day	April 1
Earth Day	April 22
National Maritime Day	May 22
Flag Day	June 14
Canada Day[2]	July 1
Independence Day[1]	July 4
Citizenship Day	September 17
United Nations Day	October 24
Halloween	October 31
Veterans Day[1,3]	November 11
Remembrance Day[2]	November 11
Christmas	December 25
Boxing Day[2]	December 26
New Year's Eve	December 31

Changing Dates

These events are celebrated on different dates every year, but are always on a certain day of a certain week of a certain month.

Event	Day
Martin Luther King Jr. Day[1]	third Monday in January
Presidents' Day[1]	third Monday in February
Daylight saving time begins	second Sunday in March
Arbor Day	last Friday in April
National Teacher Day	Tuesday of the first full week in May
Mother's Day	second Sunday in May
Armed Forces Day	third Saturday in May
Victoria Day[2]	Monday on or before May 24
Memorial Day[1]	last Monday in May
Father's Day	third Sunday in June
Labor Day[1,2]	first Monday in September
Columbus Day[1]	second Monday in October
Thanksgiving Day (Canada)[2]	second Monday in October
Daylight saving time ends	first Sunday in November
Thanksgiving Day (United States)[1]	fourth Thursday in November

Calendars & Holidays

1. Federal holiday in United States   2. Federal holiday in Canada   3. Also known as Armistice Day

Why we celebrate . . .

New Year's Day

The first record of a new year festival is from about 2,000 BCE in Mesopotamia. The festival took place not in January but in mid-March, with the new moon after the spring equinox.

Martin Luther King Jr. Day

This holiday honors the birthday of the slain civil rights leader who preached nonviolence and led the March on Washington in 1963. Dr. King's most famous speech is entitled "I Have a Dream."

Groundhog Day

According to legend, if a groundhog in Punxsutawney, Pennsylvania, peeks his head out of his burrow and sees his shadow, he'll return to his hole and there will be six more weeks of winter.

Lincoln's Birthday

This holiday honors the 16th president of the United States, who led the nation through the Civil War (1861—1865) and was then assassinated. It was first formally observed in Washington, DC, in 1866, when both houses of Congress gathered to pay tribute to the slain president.

Valentine's Day

This holiday of love originated as a festival for several martyrs from the third century, all named St. Valentine. The holiday's association with romance may have come from an ancient belief that birds mate on this day.

Presidents' Day

This official government holiday was created in observance of both Washington's and Lincoln's birthdays.

Washington's Birthday

This holiday honors the first president of the United States, known as the Father of Our Country. It was first officially observed in America in 1879.

St. Patrick's Day

This holiday honors the patron saint of Ireland. Most often celebrated in the United States with parties and special dinners, the most famous event is the annual St. Patrick's Day parade on Fifth Avenue in New York City.

Mother's Day

First proposed by Anna Jarvis of Philadelphia in 1907, this holiday has become a national time for family gatherings and showing appreciation for mothers.

Memorial Day

Also known as Decoration Day, this legal holiday was created in 1868 by order of General John A. Logan as a day on which the graves of Civil War soldiers would be decorated. Since that time, the day has been set aside to honor all American soldiers who have given their lives for their country.

Flag Day

This holiday was set aside to commemorate the adoption of the Stars and Stripes by the Continental Congress on June 14, 1777. It is a legal holiday only in Pennsylvania but is generally acknowledged and observed in many states each year.

Father's Day

This holiday honors the role of the father in the American family, as Mother's Day honors the role of the mother.

Independence Day

This holiday celebrates the signing of the Declaration of Independence, on July 4, 1776. It has been celebrated nationwide since 1777, the first anniversary of the signing.

Labor Day

First proposed by Peter J. McGuire in New York in 1882, this holiday was created to honor the labor unions and workers who built the nation.

Columbus Day

This holiday commemorates the discovery of the New World by Italian explorer Christopher Columbus in 1492. Even though the land was already populated by Native Americans when Columbus arrived, this discovery marks the beginning of European influence in America.

United Nations Day

This holiday marks the founding of the United Nations, which began in its present capacity in 1945 but had already been in operation as the League of Nations.

Halloween

Also known as All Hallows' Eve, this holiday has its origins in ancient Celtic rituals that marked the beginning of winter with bonfires, masquerades, and dressing in costume to frighten away spirits.

Election Day

Since Congress declared it an official holiday in 1845, this has been the day for presidential elections every four years. Most statewide elections are also held on this day, but election years vary according to state.

Veterans Day

Originally called Armistice Day, this holiday was created to celebrate the end of World War I in 1918. In June 1954, Congress changed the name of the holiday to Veterans Day and declared that the day would honor all men and women who have served in America's armed forces.

Thanksgiving

President Lincoln was the first president to proclaim Thanksgiving a national holiday, in 1863. Most people believe the tradition of reserving a day of thanks began with an order given by Governor Bradford of Plymouth Colony in New England in 1621.

January 1 New Year's Day throughout the Western world and in India, Indonesia, Japan, Korea, the Philippines, Singapore, Taiwan, and Thailand; Founding Day of Republic of China (Taiwan)

January 2 Berchtoldstag in Switzerland

January 3 Genshi-Sai (First Beginning) in Japan

January 5 Twelfth Night (Wassail Eve or Eve of Epiphany) in England

January 6 Epiphany, observed by Catholics throughout Europe and Latin America

Mid-January Martin Luther King Jr.'s Birthday on the third Monday in the Virgin Islands

January 15 Adults' Day in Japan

January 20 St. Agnes Eve in Great Britain

JAN
20

January 26 Republic Day in India; Australia Day in Australia

January–February Chinese New Year and Vietnamese New Year (Tet)

February 3 Setsubun (Bean-throwing Festival) in Japan

February 5 Promulgation of the Constitution Day in Mexico

February 11 National Foundation Day in Japan

February 27 Independence Day in the Dominican Republic

March 1 Independence Movement Day in Korea

March 8 International Women's Day in China, Russia, Great Britain, and the United States

March 17 St. Patrick's Day in Ireland and Northern Ireland

March 19 St. Joseph's Day in Colombia, Costa Rica, Italy, and Spain

March 21 Benito Juarez's Birthday in Mexico

March 22 Arab League Day in Arab League countries

March 23 Pakistan Day in Pakistan

March 25 Independence Day in Greece; Lady Day (Quarter Day) in Great Britain

March 26 Fiesta del Arbol (Arbor Day) in Spain

March 29 Youth and Martyr's Day in Taiwan

March 30 Muslim New Year in Indonesia

March–April Carnival/Lent/Easter: The pre-Lenten celebration of Carnival (Mardi Gras) and the post-Lenten celebration of Easter are movable feasts widely observed in Christian countries

April 1 April Fools' Day (All Fools' Day) in Great Britain and the United States

April 5 Arbor Day in Korea

April 7 World Health Day in UN member nations

April 8 Buddha's Birthday in Korea and Japan; Hana Matsuri (Flower Festival) in Japan

April 14 Pan American Day in the Americas

April 19 Declaration of Independence Day in Venezuela

April 22 Queen Isabella Day in Spain

April 23 St. George's Day in England

April 25 Liberation Day in Italy; ANZAC Day in Australia and New Zealand

April 30 Queen's Birthday in the Netherlands; Walpurgis Night in Germany and Scandinavia

May 3 Constitution Day in Japan

May 1 May Day (Labor Day) in Russia and most of Europe and Latin America

May 5 Children's Day in Japan and Korea; Cinco de Mayo in Mexico; Liberation Day in the Netherlands

May 8 V-E Day in Europe

May 9 Victory over Fascism Day in Russia

MAY
9

Late May Victoria Day on Monday before May 25 in Canada

June 2 Founding of the Republic Day in Italy

June 5 Constitution Day in Denmark

June 6 Memorial Day in Korea; Flag Day in Sweden

June 10 Portugal Day in Portugal

June 12 Independence Day in the Philippines

Mid-June Queen's Official Birthday on second Saturday in Great Britain

June 16 Soweto Day in UN member nations

June 20 Flag Day in Argentina

JUN
2

June 24 Midsummer's Day in Great Britain

June 29 Feasts of Saints Peter and Paul in Chile, Colombia, Italy, Peru, Spain, and Venezuela

July 1 Canada Day in Canada; Half-year Holiday in Hong Kong; Bank Holiday in Taiwan

July 5 Independence Day in Venezuela

July 9 Independence Day in Argentina

July 12 Orangemen's Day in Northern Ireland

July 14 Bastille Day in France

Mid-July Feria de San Fermin during second week in Spain

July 17 Constitution Day in Korea

July 20 Independence Day in Colombia

July 21 National Holiday in Belgium

July 22 National Liberation Day in Poland

July 24 Simon Bolivar's Birthday in Ecuador and Venezuela

July 25 St. James Day in Spain

July 28 Independence Day in Peru

August Holiday on first Monday in Grenada, Guyana, and Ireland

August 1 Lammas Day in England; National Day in Switzerland

August 6 Independence Day in Jamaica

August 9 National Day in Singapore

August 10 Independence Day in Ecuador

August 12 Queen's Birthday in Thailand

August 14 Independence Day in Pakistan

August 15 Independence Day in India and Korea; Assumption Day in Catholic countries

August 16 National Restoration Day in the Dominican Republic

August 17 Independence Day in Indonesia

August 31 Independence Day in Trinidad and Tobago

September Respect for the Aged Day in Japan on third Monday

September 7 Independence Day in Brazil

September 9 Choxo-no-Sekku (Chrysanthemum Day) in Japan

September 14 Battle of San Jacinto Day in Nicaragua

Mid-September Sherry Wine Harvest in Spain

September 15 Independence Day in Costa Rica, Guatemala, and Nicaragua

September 16 Independence Day in Mexico and Papua New Guinea

September 18–19 Independence Day in Chile; St. Gennaro Day in Italy

September 28 Confucius's Birthday in Taiwan

October 1 National Day in People's Republic of China; Armed Forces Day in Korea; National Holiday in Nigeria

October 2 Mahatma Gandhi's Birthday in India

October 3 National Foundation Day in Korea; Day of German Unity in Germany

October 5 Proclamation of the Portuguese Republic Day in Portugal

October 9 Korean Alphabet Day in Korea

October 10 Kruger Day in South Africa; Founding Day of the Republic of China in Taiwan

October 12 Columbus Day in Spain and widely throughout Mexico, and Central and South America

October 20 Revolution Day in Guatemala; Kenyatta Day in Kenya

October 24 United Nations Day in UN member nations

October 26 National Holiday in Austria

October 28 Greek National Day in Greece

November 1 All Saints' Day, observed by Catholics in most countries

November 2 All Souls' Day in Ecuador, El Salvador, Luxembourg, Macao, Mexico (Day of the Dead), San Marino, Uruguay, and Vatican City

November 4 National Unity Day in Italy

November 5 Guy Fawkes Day in Great Britain

November 7–8 October Revolution Day in Russia

November 11 Armistice Day in Belgium, France, French Guiana, and Tahiti; Remembrance Day in Canada

November 12 Sun Yat-sen's Birthday in Taiwan

November 15 Proclamation of the Republic Day in Brazil

November 17 Day of Penance in Federal Republic of Germany

November 19 National Holiday in Monaco

November 20 Anniversary of the Revolution in Mexico

November 23 Kinro-Kansha-no-Hi (Labor Thanksgiving Day) in Japan

November 30 Bonifacio Day in the Philippines

December 5 Discovery by Columbus Day in Haiti; Constitution Day in Russia

December 6 Independence Day in Finland

December 8 Feast of the Immaculate Conception, widely observed in Catholic countries

December 10 Constitution Day in Thailand; Human Rights Day in UN member nations

December 12 Jamhuri Day in Kenya; Guadalupe Day in Mexico

Mid-December Nine Days of Posada during third week in Mexico

December 25 Christmas Day, widely observed in all Christian countries

December 26 St. Stephen's Day in Christian countries; Boxing Day in Canada, Australia, and Great Britain

December 26–January 1 Kwanzaa in the United States

December 31 New Year's Eve throughout the world; Omisoka (Grand Last Day) in Japan; Hogmanay Day in Scotland

NOV 5

DEC 5

WHAT'S YOUR SIGN?

The original zodiac signs are thought to have originated in Mesopotamia as far back as 2000 BCE. The Greeks later picked up some of the symbols from the Babylonians and then passed them on to other ancient cultures. Some other societies that developed their own zodiac charts based on these early ideas include the Egyptians, the Chinese, and the Aztecs.

The positions of the Sun, Moon, and planets in the zodiac on the day you are born determine your astrological sign. **What's yours?**

Aries, the Ram

March 21–April 19

Planet: Mars
Element: Fire
Personality Traits: Independent, enthusiastic, bold, impulsive, confident

Taurus, the Bull

April 20–May 20

Planet: Venus
Element: Earth
Personality Traits: Decisive, determined, stubborn, stable

Gemini, the Twins

May 21–June 21

Planet: Mercury
Element: Air
Personality Traits: Curious, sociable, ambitious, alert, intelligent, temperamental

Cancer, the Crab

June 22–July 22

Planet (Celestial Object): Moon
Element: Water
Personality Traits: Organized, busy, moody, sensitive, supportive

Leo, the Lion

July 23–August 22

Planet (Celestial Object): Sun
Element: Fire
Personality Traits: Born leader, bold, noble, generous, enthusiastic, sympathetic

Virgo, the Virgin

August 23–September 22

Planet: Mercury
Element: Earth
Personality Traits: Analytical, critical, intellectual, clever

Libra, the Scales

September 23–October 23

Planet: Venus
Element: Air
Personality Traits: Affectionate, thoughtful, sympathetic, orderly, persuasive

Scorpio, the Scorpion

October 24–November 21

Planet: Mars
Element: Water
Personality Traits: Intense, fearless, loyal, willful

Sagittarius, the Archer

November 22–December 21

Planet: Jupiter
Element: Fire
Personality Traits: Energetic, good-natured, practical, clever

Capricorn, the Goat

December 22–January 19

Planet: Saturn
Element: Earth
Personality Traits: Serious, domineering, ambitious, blunt, loyal, persistent

Aquarius, the Water Bearer

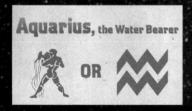

January 20–February 18

Planet: Uranus
Element: Air
Personality Traits: Independent, unselfish, generous, idealistic

Pisces, the Fishes

February 19–March 20

Planet: Neptune
Element: Water
Personality Traits: Compassionate, sympathetic, sensitive, timid, methodical

Crime

Identity thieves steal personal information such as a bank account number to buy things or get money in another person's name. Teens make perfect targets, especially when they're online. Protect yourself!

> Don't share your online passwords with anyone.

> Don't share personal information such as your birthday, address, or phone number on social networks or online game sites.

> Don't leave your smartphone lying around.

Cases Not Yet Cracked

Not every crime can be solved. In these famous cases, the criminals were either never caught or never identified.

1888   Jack the Ripper   London, England
The real identity of one of history's most famous serial killers has never been proved, although there have been many suspects—including Prince Albert Victor, the grandson of Queen Victoria. The killer named himself Jack the Ripper in letters to the police.

1971   D. B. Cooper   Between Seattle, WA, and Portland, OR
After hijacking a plane and receiving $200,000 in ransom money, Cooper boarded another plane and parachuted out a rear door with 20 pounds of cash strapped to his body. Some of the money was later found, and a parachute turned up in 2008, but there has been no trace of Cooper.

1975   Unknown   Detroit, MI
Jimmy Hoffa, former president of the Teamsters Union, disappeared from a Detroit restaurant in July 1975 and was never seen again. He was officially declared dead in 1982, but his body has never been found. Hoffa's ruthless way of doing business made him a lot of enemies, leading to many theories about what happened, who did it, and where Hoffa is buried.

1982   Unknown   Chicago, IL
Seven people died after swallowing Tylenol pain-relieving pills that someone had laced with cyanide, a deadly poison. The criminal was never caught, but the incident led to the institution of tamper-proof seals on medicines.

Innocent Until Proven Guilty

Even if you are suspected of committing a crime, as a citizen of the United States you have rights. You're protected by the 14th amendment of the U.S. Constitution:

> "Nor shall any state deprive any person of life, liberty, or property, without due process of law."

In other words, anyone accused of committing a crime is considered legally innocent until proven guilty. In certain other countries, it's the other way around: You're presumed guilty and have to prove your innocence.

How Due Process Works

Criminal cases are heard in a state or federal court of law, where both sides are represented.

The **defendant** is the person accused of the crime.

The **defense attorney** represents the defendant and presents his or her side of the case.

The **prosecutor** represents the state or federal government in trying to prove the defendant's guilt.

The **judge** presides over the courtroom and determines the sentence.

All the information and evidence is presented to a **jury**, citizens chosen to decide whether or not the defendant has been proven guilty. Their decision is called the **verdict**.

Miranda Rights

The Miranda rights are named for **Ernesto Miranda**, whose 1963 conviction on kidnapping and assault charges was reversed by the U.S. Supreme Court because his confession was obtained without providing him access to a lawyer. Since that court decision, police officers are required to give some form of the following warning to any person being arrested:

"You have the right to remain silent. Anything you say can and will be used against you in a court of law. You have the right to an attorney. If you cannot afford an attorney, one will be appointed to you. Do you understand these rights as they have been read to you?"

BREAKING RECORDS

Hurricane Sandy, which struck the East Coast on October 29, 2012, was the biggest Atlantic hurricane in history and the second-costliest natural disaster in the United States after Hurricane Katrina in 2005. The storm swept a roller coaster out to sea from the boardwalk at Seaside Heights, NJ.

Disasters

What Makes an Earthquake?

At certain places, there are breaks in the rocks that make up Earth's surface. These places are called faults. An earthquake is a shock wave that occurs when the tectonic plates beneath a fault rub or crash together. The U.S. Geological Survey estimates that there are several million earthquakes a year. Most are too small to be detected.

10 Deadliest Earthquakes

Date	Place	Number of Deaths
Jan. 24, 1556	Shaanxi, China	830,000
Jan. 12, 2010	Near Port-au-Prince, Haiti	316,000
Oct. 11, 1737	Calcutta, India	300,000
May 20, 526 CE	Antioch, Syria	250,000
July 28, 1976	Tangshan, China	242,769
Aug. 9, 1138	Aleppo, Syria	230,000
Dec. 26, 2004	Near Sumatra, Indonesia	227,898
Dec. 22, 856 CE	Damghan, Iran	200,000
Dec. 16, 1920	Gansu, China	200,000
March 23, 893 CE	Ardabil, Iran	150,000

NEWSworthy

The California-based Search Dog Foundation (SDF) trains dogs to help humans after disasters. SDF has sent dogs to more than 80 emergencies and disasters, including Hurricane Katrina, the Haiti earthquake, and the Japan earthquake and tsunami of 2011. In Haiti, canine search teams helped bring 12 people to safety. SDF recruits dogs from shelters and rescue groups, looking for young dogs with drive, energy, and focus. The dogs are mostly Labrador retrievers, golden retrievers, border collies, and mixes. SDF hopes to begin building the first national training center for search and rescue dogs in the United States in 2014. Visit www.searchdogfoundation.org to learn more.

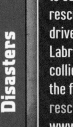

What Makes a Volcano?

A volcano is an opening in Earth's surface that allows hot melted rock, called magma, to escape from below the surface. Scientists say there are about 550 historically active volcanoes.

Gently curved shield volcanoes build up over thousands of years. Mauna Loa is a shield volcano on the island of Hawaii. It rises about 56,000 feet (17 km) above the ocean floor.

Some of the most famous volcanoes in the world are stratovolcanoes, including Mt. Vesuvius, Krakatau, and Mt. Mayon, the most active volcano in the Philippines.

10 Deadliest Volcanic Eruptions

Date	Volcano	Number of Deaths
April 10–12, 1815	Mt. Tambora, Indonesia	92,000
Aug. 26–28, 1883	Krakatau, Indonesia	36,000
May 8, 1902	Mt. Pelee, Martinique	28,000
Nov. 13, 1985	Nevado del Ruiz, Colombia	23,000
Aug. 24, 79 CE	Mt. Vesuvius, Italy	16,000
May 21, 1792	Mt. Unzen, Japan	14,500
1586 (month and day unknown)	Kelut, Indonesia	10,000
June 8, 1783	Laki, Iceland	9,350
May 19, 1919	Mt. Kelut, Indonesia	5,000
Dec. 15, 1631	Mt. Vesuvius, Italy	4,000

What Makes a Tsunami?

A tsunami is a wave that is often caused by an underwater earthquake. The wave travels across the ocean at speeds up to 600 miles per hour (970 kph), then crashes on shore with devastating power. A massive tsunami triggered by an earthquake in the Indian Ocean struck parts of Asia and Africa in December 2004, causing about 225,000 people to lose their lives.

Wild Windstorms

Hurricanes

Hurricanes are huge storms with winds over 74 mph (119 kph) blowing around a center, or eye. Most hurricanes form over the mild waters of the southern Atlantic Ocean, the Caribbean Sea, or the Gulf of Mexico. Equally powerful storms that form over the western Pacific Ocean are called typhoons. If they form over the Indian Ocean, they're called cyclones.

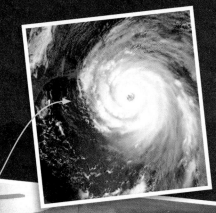

Hurricane Katrina, which hit the Gulf Coast in 2005, was the costliest natural disaster in U.S. history and the third-deadliest hurricane, causing $125 billion in damages and 1,836 deaths.

Tornadoes

Tornadoes are powerful storms with funnels of furious wind spinning from 40 mph (64 kph) to more than 300 mph (482.8 kph). The funnels touch down and rip paths of destruction on land. About 1,500 tornadoes hit the United States every year.

A group of tornadoes is called an outbreak. On April 3, 1974, a group of 148 tornadoes swept through 13 states and parts of Canada in the 1974 Super Outbreak. The storm's path on the ground covered almost 2,500 miles (4,023 km).

Disasters

Major U.S. Natural Disasters

Earthquake **When**: April 18, 1906
Where: San Francisco, California
An earthquake accompanied by a fire
destroyed more than 4 square miles (10 sq km)
and left at least 3,000 dead or missing.

Hurricane **When**: August 27–September 15, 1900
Where: Galveston, Texas
More than 6,000 died from the devastating
combination of high winds and tidal waves.

Tornado **When**: March 18, 1925
Where: Missouri, Illinois, and Indiana
Called the Great Tri-State Tornado, this twister
caused 747 deaths and ripped along a path of
219 miles (352 km) after touching down
near Ellington, Missouri.

Blizzard **When**: March 11–14, 1888
Where: East Coast
Four hundred people died, and 40–50 inches
(101.6–127 cm) of snow fell in the Blizzard of '88.
Damage was estimated at $20 million.

Major U.S. Disasters Caused by Humans

Aircraft **When**: September 11, 2001
Where: New York, New York; Arlington, Virginia; Shanksville, Pennsylvania
Hijacked planes crashed into the World Trade Center, the Pentagon, and a
field in Pennsylvania, causing nearly 3,000 deaths.

Fire **When**: March 25, 1911
Where: New York, New York
The Triangle Shirtwaist Factory caught fire,
trapping workers inside and causing 146 deaths.

Passenger Train **When**: July 9, 1918
Where: Nashville, Tennessee
An inbound and an outbound train collided in a crash
that witnesses heard miles away and took more
than 100 lives. The crash was caused by errors and
misunderstandings by both train crews.

Environmental **When**: April 20, 2010
Where: Gulf of Mexico, 42 miles off the Louisiana coast
The Deepwater Horizon oil rig exploded, killing 11 workers and letting loose
an underwater gush of about 4.9 million barrels of oil over 86 days. The spill
was called the worst environmental disaster in U.S. history. However, after
a massive offshore and onshore cleanup effort, by 2011 Gulf fish, shrimp,
and oysters were deemed safe to eat and most Gulf beaches were open.

SAVE THE DATE For one hour every year, people around the globe show their respect for the earth and concern about climate change by turning out lights in homes, offices, government buildings, and landmarks. In 2014, Earth Hour will take place from 8:30 to 9:30 p.m., your local time, on March 29.

> **Earth Hour Participation**

> 2007: 2.2 million people in Sydney, Australia

> 2008: Over 50 million people around the world

> 2009: About 1 billion people in 1,000 cities

> 2010: About 1.5 billion people in more than 100 countries

> 2011: About 1.8 billion people; 5,251 cities and towns; 135 countries; all 7 continents

> 2012: More than 2 billion people; 7,001 cities and towns; 152 countries; all 7 continents

Paper Power

In 2011, we recycled 52.8 million tons of paper. At the same time, the amount of paper we bought declined. As a result of these two trends, the amount of paper we disposed of in landfills fell 9 percent, or nearly 2 million tons, from 2010. The amount of paper recovered for recycling averaged 338 pounds for each man, woman, and child in the United States.

Paper Products Recycling Rates

Product category	Percent recycled in 2011
Corrugated boxes	90.6
Newsprint	72.7
Paper and paperboard	66.8
Printing and writing papers	56.3

More than 5,000 different products can be made from recycled paper, including lampshades, money, and bandages.

CHECK IT OUT !

Rising Carbon Dioxide Levels

The amount of the main greenhouse gas, carbon dioxide (CO_2), in the atmosphere has been steadily rising for more than a century. Experts say the increase comes mostly from the burning of fossil fuels for energy.

Carbon Dioxide in the Atmosphere, 1903–2009

Year	CO_2 (parts per million)
1903	295
1915	301
1927	306
1943	308
1960	317
1970	326
1980	339
1990	354
2000	367
2005	377
2006	379
2007	381
2008	383
2009	385
2013 (preliminary data)	394

10 Worst Carbon Dioxide–Producing Countries

Country	Millions of Metric Tons Produced Annually
China	8,320.96
United States	5,601.11
India	1,695.62
Russia	1,633.80
Japan	1,164.47
Germany	793.66
South Korea	578.97
Iran	560.33
Canada	548.76
United Kingdom	532.44

Something's in the Air

There are six common air pollutants: ground-level ozone, carbon monoxide, sulfur and nitrogen oxides, lead, and particulate matter such as soot and smoke. The charts on this page show the urban areas with the lowest and highest year-round levels of particle pollution. Find out more at www.lung.org.

Most Polluted U.S. Cities/Urban Areas

Rank	City
1	Bakersfield-Delano, CA
2	Hanford-Corcoran. CA
3	Los Angeles-Long Beach-Riverside, CA
4	Visalia-Porterville, CA
5	Fresno-Madera, CA
6	Pittsburgh-New Castle, PA
7	Phoenix-Mesa-Glendale, AZ
8	Cincinnati-Middletown-Wilmington, OH-KY-IN
9	Louisville-Jefferson County-Elizabethtown-Scottsburg, KY-IN
10	Philadelphia-Camden-Vineland, PA-NJ-DE-MD

Cleanest U.S. Cities/Urban Areas

Rank	City
1	Santa Fe-Espanõla, NM
2	Cheyenne, WY
3	Prescott, AZ
4	Tucson, AZ
5	Albuquerque, NM
6	Redding, CA
7	Colorado Springs, CO
8	Flagstaff, AZ
9	Anchorage, AK
	Boise-Nampa, ID (tie)

Going G-R-R-R-E-E-N!

You won't find *green* spelled that way in any dictionary, but if we all remember the environmental 3 Rs—Reduce, Reuse, Recycle—we can improve the health and life of our planet. Here are simple things everyone can do.

REDUCE

5 Reducing Tips

1. Buy less. Try to purchase only what you need.

2. Use less. For instance, instead of buying two notepads and using only one side of the paper, buy one and use both sides.

3. Buy with minimum packaging in mind. Suggest that your family buy large sizes of cereal, toothpaste, and other things you use all the time to eliminate multiple boxes.

4. Buy longer-lasting products. Compact fluorescent lightbulbs make the same amount of light and use only one-fourth the amount of electricity that incandescent ones use.

5. Make things last longer. Fix your old bike rather than asking for a new one.

What a Waste!
Municipal solid waste (MSW) is trash—the stuff that we dump in landfills by millions of tons every year. What's the best way to reduce waste? Don't make it in the first place!

REUSE

Second Chance
You may be surprised at how many things can be reused. Think before tossing!

5 Reusing Tips

1. Pack your lunch in reusable containers instead of plastic or paper bags. If 25 percent of American homes used 10 fewer plastic bags a month, it would keep 2.5 billion bags out of landfills every year.

2. Use washable cups, travel mugs, and reusable sports bottles for beverages on the go. If you have to use plastic cups or plates, wash and reuse them.

3. Use a sponge to wipe up spills instead of reaching for paper towels.

4. Save wrapping paper and ribbon from gifts and reuse them.

5. Use rechargeable batteries whenever you can. Americans use approximately 2 billion unrechargeable batteries every year, which can release harmful metals into landfills.

Environment

RECYCLE

Around We Go

In the United States, we recycle about 34 percent of our MSW. More than 30 percent of the raw material used in glass production comes from recycled glass. That's good news, but we can do better. Even recycling a tiny amount makes a huge difference:

5 Recycling Stats

1. Recycling one glass bottle saves enough energy to light a 100-watt lightbulb for four hours.

2. If every American household recycled the Sunday newspaper, more than half a million trees would be saved—every week!

3. Recycling one aluminum can saves enough energy to run a TV for three hours.

4. Manufacturing one ton of recycled paper takes about 60 percent of the energy to make a ton of paper from raw pulp.

5. In California in 2004, 12 billion bottles and cans were recycled—enough to power as many as 522,000 homes.

Always Recycle These Items

Acid batteries	Electronic equipment	Newspaper	Steel cans
Aluminum cans	Glass (particularly bottles and jars)	Oil	Tires
Appliances		Paint	Wood
Building materials	Lead	Paper	Writing/copy paper
Cardboard	Magazines	Plastic bags	Yard waste
Chemicals	Metal	Plastic bottles	

Some of these items have special rules for handling or disposal. Look online for your local recycling office. Check out the Environmental Protection Agency (EPA) website at www.epa.gov for a state-by-state list of locations and other helpful information.

Don't turn Earth into a pig*sty*! Avoid Styrofoam. It will stay in landfills forever.

CHECK IT OUT!

Tips to Save Energy and Natural Resources

Close It Up
Close fireplace dampers when there's no fire burning. An open fireplace damper can let 8 percent of the heat from your furnace escape. Close the refrigerator door to keep the cold air inside.

Turn It Up
When it's warm outside, set your home thermostat at 78°F (25.5°C). When no one's home, set it at 85°F (29.4°C). (Check with an adult first.)

Turn It Down
When it's cold, set the thermostat at 68°F (20°C) or lower during the day. Turn it down to 55°F (12.7°C) or turn it off at night. (Again, check with an adult before changing household routines.)

Turn It Off
Save up to 20,000 gallons of water a year by not leaving the faucet running when brushing teeth, washing dishes, or washing the car. Turn off lights, the TV, your computer, radios, and stereos if the room is going to be empty for more than five minutes.

CHECK IT OUT !

Trees, please! If every American family planted just one tree, more than a billion pounds of greenhouse gases would be removed from the atmosphere every year.

Environment

84

Bike It or Hike It!

Every time you travel, you have choices about how you impact the environment. When you go, go green!

Take the bus. A bus carrying 40 passengers takes one-sixth the energy of one car carrying each passenger, while replacing six city blocks' worth of cars.

Skateboard, walk, or ride your bike whenever safety and weather permit. These are the greenest ways to travel, and they're great for your health.

Suggest that the adults in your family drive less, or carpool. Driving 25 fewer miles (40 km) every week can eliminate 1,500 pounds (680 km) of carbon dioxide from the air. Riding with two or more people two days a week can eliminate 1,590 pounds (721 kg) from the air.

CHECK IT OUT !

Shrink Your Carbon Footprint

You can't control the size of your sneakers, but you can control the size of your carbon footprint. Go to www.globalwarming.markey.house.gov/getinvolved to measure your impact on the environment and learn ways to shrink it.

The Panama Canal, which connects the Atlantic and Pacific Oceans, will celebrate its 100th birthday in 2014. Work is underway to allow more ships and bigger ships to pass through. According to a recent Gallup poll, Panama tied with Paraguay as the happiest country in the world. The poll showed that the wealthiest countries are not necessarily the happiest.

FLAGS & FACTS
Countries of the World

Countries of the World

ARCTIC OCEAN

75°N

GREENLAND
(Denmark)

Arctic Cir

ICELAND

CANADA

IRELAND

45°N

UNITED STATES

AZORES
(Portugal)

PORTUGAL

ATLANTIC OCEAN

30°N

CANARY ISLANDS
(Spain)

MOR

WESTERN
SAHARA

MEXICO

BAHAMAS

Tropic of Cancer

CUBA

DOMINICAN
REPUBLIC

CAPE VERDE

MAURITANIA

BELIZE
HONDURAS

HAITI

JAMAICA

SENEGAL

GUATEMALA

NICARAGUA

GAMBIA

EL SALVADOR

COSTA RICA

PANAMA

VENEZUELA

SURINAME

GUINEA-BISSAU

GUINEA

PACIFIC OCEAN

COLOMBIA

FRENCH
GUIANA
(France)

SIERRA LEONE

LIBERIA

COT
(IVO

GUYANA

0°

Equator

ECUADOR

"Equator

S

FRENCH POLYNESIA
(France)

PERU

BRAZIL

15°S

BOLIVIA

PARAGUAY

Tropic of Capricorn

30°S

CHILE

URUGUAY

ARGENTINA

ATLANTIC OCEAN

0	1,000	2,000 Miles
0	1,000	2,000 Kilometers

45°S

FALKLAND ISLANDS
(U.K.)

SOUTH GEORGIA
(U.K.)

60°S

165°W   150°W   135°W   120°W   105°W   90°W   75°W   60°W   45°W   30°W   15°W

Antarctic Circle

ARCTIC OCEAN

ARCTIC OCEAN

FINLAND

ESTONIA
LATVIA
LITHUANIA

BELARUS

UKRAINE
MOLDOVA

ROMANIA

BULGARIA

GREECE

TURKEY

CYPRUS
LEBANON
ISRAEL
JORDAN

SYRIA

IRAQ

EGYPT

SAUDI ARABIA

BAHRAIN
QATAR
U.A.E.

OMAN

YEMEN

SUDAN

ERITREA

DJIBOUTI

SOMALIA

SOUTH
SUDAN

ETHIOPIA

DEMOCRATIC
REPUBLIC OF
THE CONGO

UGANDA

KENYA

RWANDA
BURUNDI

TANZANIA

ZAMBIA

MALAWI

ZIMBABWE

MOZAMBIQUE

BOTSWANA

SWAZILAND

SOUTH
AFRICA

LESOTHO

MADAGASCAR

COMOROS

RUSSIA

KAZAKHSTAN

MONGOLIA

GEORGIA
ARMENIA
AZERBAIJAN

UZBEKISTAN

KYRGYZSTAN

TURKMENISTAN

TAJIKISTAN

IRAN

AFGHANISTAN

KUWAIT

PAKISTAN

NEPAL

BHUTAN

CHINA

NORTH
KOREA

SOUTH
KOREA

JAPAN

PACIFIC OCEAN

INDIA

BURMA

BANGLADESH

LAOS

THAILAND

VIETNAM

CAMBODIA

PHILIPPINES

Tropic of Cancer

NORTHERN
MARIANA ISLANDS
(U.S.)

FEDERATED STATES
OF MICRONESIA

MARSHALL
ISLANDS

SRI
LANKA

MALDIVES

BRUNEI

MALAYSIA

SINGAPORE

PALAU

Equator

KIRIBATI

INDONESIA

PAPUA
NEW GUINEA

SOLOMON
ISLANDS

TUVALU

TIMOR-LESTE

SAMOA

INDIAN OCEAN

Tropic of Capricorn

VANUATU

FIJI

NEW CALEDONIA
(France)

TONGA

AUSTRALIA

NEW
ZEALAND

N
W E
S

30°E   45°E   60°E   75°E   90°E   105°E   120°E   135°E   150°E   165°E   180°

ANTARCTICA

AFGHANISTAN

Capital: Kabul
Population: 31,230,669
Area: 250,001 sq. mi. (647,500 sq km)
Language: Dari (Afghan Persian),
Pashto
Money: Afghani
Government: Islamic republic

CHECK IT OUT

Kite running is a popular sport in
Afghanistan. Kids fly kites, cut them
loose, and then race to recover them.

ALBANIA

Capital: Tirana
Population: 3,011,405
Area: 11,100 sq. mi. (28,748 sq km)
Language: Albanian, Greek
Money: Lek
Government: Republic

CHECK IT OUT

The Adriatic and Ionian Seas border
the western coast of Albania.

ALGERIA

Capital: Algiers
Population: 38,087,812
Area: 919,595 sq. mi.
(2,381,740 sq km)
Language: Arabic, Berber, French
Money: Dinar
Government: Republic

CHECK IT OUT

Algeria is the second-largest
country in Africa.

ANDORRA

Capital: Andorra la Vella
Population: 85,293
Area: 180 sq. mi. (468 sq km)
Language: Catalan, French,
Castillan, Portuguese
Money: Euro
Government: Parliamentary
democracy

CHECK IT OUT

Andorra is about half the size of
New York City. For 700 years, until
1993, this little country had two
rulers: France and Spain.

ANGOLA

Capital: Luanda
Population: 18,565,269
Area: 481,400 sq. mi. (1,246,700 sq km)
Language: Portuguese, Bantu,
others
Money: Kwanza
Government: Republic

CHECK IT OUT

Eighty-five percent of the
country's revenue (GDP) comes
from oil production.

ANTIGUA AND BARBUDA

Capital: St. John's
Population: 90,156
Area: 171 sq. mi. (443 sq km)
Language: English
Money: Dollar
Government: Parliamentary
democracy; independent
sovereign state within the
Commonwealth

CHECK IT OUT

Thousands of frigate birds live in
a sanctuary on Barbuda. A frigate
bird's wingspan can reach nearly
eight feet (2.4 m).

ARGENTINA

Capital: Buenos Aires
Population: 42,610,981
Area: 1,068,302 sq. mi.
(2,766,890 sq km)
Language: Spanish, Italian,
English, German, French
Money: Peso
Government: Republic

CHECK IT OUT

The Andes mountains run along
the western edge of Argentina,
on the border with Chile.

ARMENIA

Capital: Yerevan
Population: 2,974,184
Area: 11,484 sq. mi. (29,743 sq km)
Language: Armenian, Yezidi,
Russian
Money: Dram
Government: Republic

CHECK IT OUT

Armenia was the first nation to
formally adopt Christianity (in the
early fourth century).

AUSTRALIA

Capital: Canberra
Population: 22,262,501
Area: 2,967,909 sq. mi.
(7,686,850 sq km)
Language: English, Chinese,
Italian, aboriginal languages
Money: Dollar
Government: Constitutional
monarchy; democratic, federal-
state system recognizing British
monarchy as sovereign

CHECK IT OUT

The Great Barrier Reef, off the
coast of Australia, is larger than
the Great Wall of China.

AUSTRIA

Capital: Vienna
Population: 8,221,646
Area: 32,382 sq. mi. (83,870 sq km)
Language: German
Money: Euro
Government: Federal
parliamentary democracy

CHECK IT OUT

The Habsburg family ruled
Austria for nearly 750 years,
until the Treaty of St. Germain
in 1919 established the Republic
of Austria.

AZERBAIJAN

Capital: Baku
Population: 9,590,159
Area: 33,436 sq. mi. (86,600 sq km)
Language: Azerbaijani, Russian,
Armenian, others
Money: Manat
Government: Republic

CHECK IT OUT

The country's name is thought to
come from the ancient Persian
phrase that means "Land of Fire."

THE BAHAMAS

Capital: Nassau
Population: 319,031
Area: 5,382 sq. mi. (13,940 sq km)
Language: English, Creole
Money: Dollar
Government: Constitutional
parliamentary democracy

CHECK IT OUT

More than eight out of ten
Bahamians are of African
heritage.

BAHRAIN

Capital: Manama
Population: 1,281,332
Area: 257 sq. mi. (665 sq km)
Language: Arabic, English, Farsi, Urdu
Money: Dinar
Government: Constitutional monarchy

CHECK IT OUT

The land area of Bahrain is only three and a half times the size of Washington, DC.

BANGLADESH

Capital: Dhaka
Population: 163,654,860
Area: 55,599 sq. mi. (144,000 sq km)
Language: Bengali, Chakma, Bagh
Money: Taka
Government: Parliamentary democracy

CHECK IT OUT

The Bengal tiger is the national animal of Bangladesh.

BARBADOS

Capital: Bridgetown
Population: 288,725
Area: 166 sq. mi. (431 sq km)
Language: English
Money: Dollar
Government: Parliamentary democracy

CHECK IT OUT

The British settled Barbados in 1627. When they arrived, there was no one living there.

BELARUS

Capital: Minsk
Population: 9,625,888
Area: 80,155 sq. mi. (207,600 sq km)
Language: Belarusian, Russian
Money: Ruble
Government: Republic

CHECK IT OUT

The name of this Eastern European country means "White Russia."

BELGIUM

Capital:BrusselsPopulation:10,444,268Area:11,787 sq. mi. (30,528 sq km)
Language: Dutch, French, GermanMoney:EuroGovernment: Parliamentary democracy under a constitutional monarchyMany people call Belgium the chocolate capital of the world. Hundreds of thousands of tons of the sweet stuff are produced here yearly.

CHECK IT OUT

BELIZE

Capital: Belmopan
Population: 334,297
Area: 8,867 sq. mi. (22,966 sq km)
Language: English, Creole, Spanish, Mayan dialects
Money: Dollar
Government: Parliamentary democracy

CHECK IT OUT

The mahogany industry was central to Belize's economy hundreds of years ago. That's why a mahogany tree is pictured on the country's flag.

BENIN

Capital: Porto-Novo
Population: 9,877,292
Area: 43,483 sq. mi.
(112,620 sq km)
Language: French, Fon, Yoruba in the south; Nagot, Bariba, Dendi in the north
Money: CFA franc
Government: Republic under multiparty democratic rule

CHECK IT OUT

Benin is only 215 miles across (about 325 km) at its widest point. It's eight times smaller than Nigeria, its neighbor.

BHUTAN

Capital: Thimphu
Population: 725,296
Area: 18,147 sq. mi. (47,000 sq km)
Language: Dzongkha, Nepali, Tibetan
Money: Ngultrum
Government: Constitutional monarchy

CHECK IT OUT

The Great Himalaya Range, the highest mountain system in the world, runs through northern Bhutan.

BOLIVIA

Capital: La Paz
Population: 10,461,053
Area: 424,164 sq. mi. (1,098,580 sq km)
Language: Spanish, Quecha, Aymara, Guarani
Money: Boliviano
Government: Republic

CHECK IT OUT

Bolivia is named after independence fighter Simón Bolívar.

BOSNIA AND HERZEGOVINA

Capital: Sarajevo
Population: 3,875,723
Area: 19,772 sq. mi. (51,209 sq km)
Language: Bosnian, Serbian, Croatian
Money: Convertible marka
Government: Federal democratic republic

CHECK IT OUT

Sarajevo, the country's capital, hosted the 1984 Winter Olympics.

BOTSWANA

Capital: Gaborone
Population: 2,127,825
Area: 231,804 sq. mi. (600,370 sq km)
Language: English, Setswana, Kalanga
Money: Pula
Government: Parliamentary republic

CHECK IT OUT

Botswana has one of the healthiest economies in Africa. About 70—80 percent of its export revenues come from diamond mining.

BRAZIL

Capital: Brasilia
Population: 201,009,622
Area: 3,286,488 sq. mi. (8,511,965 sq km)
Language: Portuguese
Money: Real
Government: Federative republic

CHECK IT OUT

Brazil has the largest population in Latin America and the fifth-largest in the world.

BRUNEI

Capital: Bandar Seri Begawan
Population: 415,717
Area: 2,228 sq. mi. (5,770 sq km)
Language: Malay, English, Chinese
Money: Dollar
Government: Constitutional sultanate

CHECK IT OUT

For more than six centuries, the same royal family has ruled Brunei.

BULGARIA

Capital: Sofia
Population: 6,981,642
Area: 42,823 sq. mi. (110,910 sq km)
Language: Bulgarian, Turkish, Roma
Money: Lev
Government: Parliamentary democracy

CHECK IT OUT

One of Bulgaria's sweetest exports is rose oil, which is used throughout the world to make perfume.

BURKINA FASO

Capital: Ouagadougou
Population: 17,812,961
Area: 105,869 sq. mi. (274,200 sq km)
Language: French
Money: CFA franc
Government: Republic

CHECK IT OUT

Burkina Faso has western Africa's largest elephant population.

BURMA

Capital: Yangon (Rangoon)
Population: 55,167,330
Area: 261,970 sq. mi. (678,500 sq km)
Language: Burmese, many ethnic languages
Money: Kyat
Government: Military junta

CHECK IT OUT

The military junta ruling the nation changed Burma's name to Myanmar in 1989, but several countries, including the United States, refused to acknowledge the change. Others recognize Myanmar as the official name.

BURUNDI

Capital: Bujumbura
Population: 10,888,321
Area: 10,745 sq. mi. (27,830 sq km)
Language: Kirundi, French, Swahili
Money: Franc
Government: Republic

CHECK IT OUT

Burundi is on the shoreline of Lake Tanganyika, the second-deepest lake in the world.

CAMBODIA

Capital: Phnom Penh
Population: 15,205,539
Area: 69,900 sq. mi. (181,040 sq km)
Language: Khmer, French, English
Money: Riel
Government: Multiparty democracy under a constitutional monarchy

CHECK IT OUT

The Mekong River system, which runs through Cambodia, is the home of the giant catfish. These fish can reach 10 feet (3 m) in length and weigh up to 650 pounds (295 kg).

CAMEROON

Capital: Yaoundé
Population: 20,549,221
Area: 183,568 sq. mi. (475,440 sq km)
Language: French, English, 24 major African language groups
Money: CFA franc
Government: Republic

CHECK IT OUT

Mount Cameroon, the highest mountain in sub-Saharan west Africa, is an active volcano that last erupted in 2000.

Countries of the World

CANADA

Capital: Ottawa
Population: 34,568,211
Area: 3,855,103 sq. mi.
(9,984,670 sq km)
Language: English, French
Money: Dollar
Government: Confederation
with parliamentary democracy
and constitutional monarchy

CHECK IT OUT

In land area, Canada is the second-
largest country in the world. In
population, it ranks only 37.

CAPE VERDE

Capital: Praia
Population: 531,046
Area: 1,557 sq. mi. (4,033 sq km)
Language: Portuguese, Crioulo
Money: Escudo
Government: Republic

CHECK IT OUT

The group of islands that make
up Cape Verde was uninhabited
until the Portuguese discovered
it in 1460.

CENTRAL AFRICAN REPUBLIC

Capital: Bangui
Population: 5,166,510
Area: 240,535 sq. mi.
(622,984 sq km)
Language: Sangho, French,
tribal languages
Money: CFA franc
Government: Republic

CHECK IT OUT

There are more than 80 ethnic
groups in the Central African
Republic. Each group speaks its
own language.

CHAD

Capital: N'Djaména
Population: 11,193,452
Area: 495,755 sq. mi.
(1,284,000 sq km)
Language: French, Arabic,
more than 120 others
Money: CFA franc
Government: Republic

CHECK IT OUT

Chad is about three times the size
of California.

CHILE

Capital: Santiago
Population: 17,166,364
Area: 292,260 sq. mi.
(756,950 sq km)
Language: Spanish
Money: Peso
Government: Republic

CHECK IT OUT

The blue in Chile's flag stands
for the sky and the white for the
snow of the Andes mountains on
its eastern border.

CHINA

Capital: Beijing
Population: 1,349,585,838
Area: 3,705,407 sq. mi.
(9,596,960 sq km)
Language: Mandarin, Yue,
Wu, Minhel, Minnan, Xiang, Gan,
Hakka dialects, others
Money: Yuan
Government: Communist
Party—led state

CHECK IT OUT

The name *China* comes from the
Qin (or Ch'in) Dynasty, under which
China was unified in 221 BCE.

Countries of the World

95

COLOMBIA

Capital: Bogotá
Population: 45,745,783
Area: 439,736 sq. mi.
(1,138,910 sq km)
Language: Spanish
Money: Peso
Government: Republic

CHECK IT OUT

Historically Colombia has been the world's top producer of emeralds.

COMOROS

Capital: Moroni
Population: 838,152
Area: 838 sq. mi. (2,170 sq km)
Language: Arabic, French, Shikomoro
Money: Franc
Government: Republic

CHECK IT OUT

The three islands that make up Comoros are sometimes called the Perfume Islands. The country is the world's leading producer of essence of ylang-ylang, a flower oil used to make perfumes and soaps.

CONGO, Democratic Republic of the

Capital: Kinshasa
Population: 75,507,308
Area: 905,588 sq. mi.
(2,345,410 sq km)
Language: French, Lingala, Swahili, Kikongo, Tshiluba
Money: CFA franc
Government: Republic

CHECK IT OUT

This country's enormous land area is equal to the United States east of the Mississippi River, or all of western Europe.

CONGO, Republic of the

Capital: Brazzaville
Population: 4,492,689
Area: 132,047 sq. mi. (342,000 sq km)
Language: French, Lingala, Monokutuba, Kikongo
Money: CFA franc
Government: Republic

CHECK IT OUT

Oil is the country's largest revenue-generating industry.

COSTA RICA

Capital: San José
Population: 4,695,942
Area: 19,730 sq. mi. (51,100 sq km)
Language: Spanish, English
Money: Colón
Government: Democratic republic

CHECK IT OUT

For a bird's-eye view of the rain forest, tourists in Costa Rica swing through the canopy on pulleys attached to treetops.

CÔTE d'IVOIRE (Ivory Coast)

Capital: Yamoussoukro
Population: 22,400,835
Area: 124,503 sq. mi.
(322,460 sq km)
Language: French, Dioula, 59 other native dialects
Money: CFA franc
Government: Republic with multiparty presidential regime

CHECK IT OUT

Côte d'Ivoire is home to more than 60 ethnic groups.

CROATIA

Capital: Zagreb
Population: 4,475,611
Area: 21,831 sq. mi. (56,542 sq km)
Language: Croatian, Serbian
Money: Kuna
Government: Parliamentary democracy

CHECK IT OUT

Civil war ended in Croatia in 1998. Now tourists flock to its beautiful islands and national parks.

CUBA

Capital: Havana
Population: 11,061,886
Area: 42,803 sq. mi. (110,860 sq km)
Language: Spanish
Money: Peso
Government: Communist state

CHECK IT OUT

Cuba was controlled by the same leader, *Fidel Castro*, for nearly 50 years.

CYPRUS

Capital: Nicosia
Population: 1,155,403
Area: 3,571 sq. mi. (9,250 sq km)
Language: Greek, Turkish, English
Money: Euro
Government: Republic

CHECK IT OUT

Mythology says the goddess Aphrodite arose from the waves at a rock formation in Cyprus called *Petra tou Romiou*.

CZECH REPUBLIC

Capital: Prague
Population: 10,162,921
Area: 30,450 sq. mi. (78,866 sq km)
Language: Czech, Slovak
Money: Koruna
Government: Parliamentary democracy

CHECK IT OUT

In the country's capital is Prague Castle, the world's largest medieval castle.

DENMARK

Capital: Copenhagen
Population: 5,556,452
Area: 16,639 sq. mi. (43,094 sq km)
Language: Danish, Faroese, Greenlandic, English
Money: Krone
Government: Constitutional monarchy

CHECK IT OUT

LEGO blocks were invented in Denmark. The name comes from the Danish words *leg* and *godt*, which mean "play well."

DJIBOUTI

Capital: Djibouti
Population: 792,198
Area: 8,880 sq. mi. (23,000 sq km)
Language: French, Arabic, Afar, Somali
Money: Franc
Government: Republic

CHECK IT OUT

The Djibouti countryside features dramatic limestone chimneys created by deposits of calcium carbonate from hot springs.

DOMINICA

Capital: Roseau
Population: 73,286
Area: 291 sq. mi. (754 sq km)
Language: English, French patois
Money: Dollar
Government: Parliamentary democracy

CHECK IT OUT

Parts of Dominica can receive as much as 300 inches (762 cm) of rain every year.

DOMINICAN REPUBLIC

Capital: Santo Domingo
Population: 10,219,630
Area: 18,815 sq. mi. (48,730 sq km)
Language: Spanish
Money: Peso
Government: Democratic republic

CHECK IT OUT

The Dominican Republic is the second-largest country in the West Indies.

ECUADOR

Capital: Quito
Population: 15,439,429
Area: 109,483 sq. mi. (283,560 sq km)
Language: Spanish, Quechua, Jivaroan
Money: Dollar
Government: Republic

CHECK IT OUT

The Galápagos Islands, off Ecuador's coast, are home to the Galápagos tortoise. These ancient creatures can weigh up to 475 pounds (215 kg) and live more than 100 years.

EGYPT

Capital: Cairo
Population: 85,294,388
Area: 386,662 sq. mi. (1,001,450 sq km)
Language: Arabic, English, French
Money: Pound
Government: Republic

CHECK IT OUT

The Great Pyramid of Khufu (Cheops) is 480 feet (146 m) high—about the height of a 48-story building.

EL SALVADOR

Capital: San Salvador
Population: 6,108,590
Area: 8,124 sq. mi. (21,040 sq km)
Language: Spanish, Nahua
Money: Colón
Government: Republic

CHECK IT OUT

El Salvador is the smallest and most densely populated country in Central America.

EQUATORIAL GUINEA

Capital: Malabo
Population: 704,001
Area: 10,831 sq. mi. (28,051 sq km)
Language: Spanish, French, Fang, Bubi
Money: CFA franc
Government: Republic

CHECK IT OUT

Scientists come to Bioko Island, where this country's capital is located, to study unique species of plants and animals, including a rare monkey called a drill.

ERITREA

Capital: Asmara
Population: 6,233,682
Area: 46,842 sq. mi. (121,320 sq km)
Language: Afar, Arabic, Tigre,
Kunama
Money: Nakfa
Government: In transition

CHECK IT OUT

Many Eritreans wear a traditional
shawl known as a *gabbi*.

ESTONIA

Capital: Tallinn
Population: 1,266,375
Area: 17,462 sq. mi.
(45,226 sq km)
Language: Estonian, Russian,
Latvian
Money: Kroon
Government: Parliamentary
republic

CHECK IT OUT

Estonia is home to Old Town
Tallinn, one of Europe's best-
preserved medieval communities.
It has 26 watchtowers and
cobblestone streets.

ETHIOPIA

Capital: Addis Ababa
Population: 96,838,456
Area: 435,186 sq. mi.
(1,127,127 sq km)
Language: Amarigna, Oromigna,
Tigrigna, Somaligna, English
Money: Birr
Government: Federal republic

CHECK IT OUT

The Blue Nile river runs for more
than 500 miles (800 km) through
Ethiopia and carries the runoff
from the highlands to the desert.

FIJI

Capital: Suva
Population: 896,758
Area: 7,054 sq. mi. (18,270 sq km)
Language: English, Fijian,
Hindustani
Money: Dollar
Government: Republic

CHECK IT OUT

Fiji is composed of 333 different
islands in the South Pacific, but
most people live on the largest
one—Viti Levu.

FINLAND

Capital: Helsinki
Population: 5,266,114
Area: 130,559 sq. mi.
(338,145 sq km)
Language: Finnish, Swedish
Money: Euro
Government: Constitutional
republic

CHECK IT OUT

One-fourth of Finland is north of
the Arctic Circle, making winters
there long and very cold.

FRANCE

Capital: Paris
Population: 65,729,329
Area: 248,429 sq. mi.
(643,427 sq km)
Language: French
Money: Euro
Government: Republic

CHECK IT OUT

The TGV train, France's high-
speed rail service, runs at
speeds of up to 200 miles per
hour (322 kph).

GABON

Capital: Libreville
Population: 1,640,286
Area: 103,347 sq. mi.
(267,667 sq km)
Language: French, Fang, others
Money: CFA franc
Government: Republic

ⓘ CHECK IT OUT

The Kongou Falls, located in Gabon's Invindo National Park, is 2 miles (3.2 km) wide.

THE GAMBIA

Capital: Banjul
Population: 1,883,051
Area: 4,363 sq. mi. (11,300 sq km)
Language: English, Mandinka, Wolof, Fula, others
Money: Dalasi
Government: Republic

ⓘ CHECK IT OUT

The Gambia is the smallest country on the African continent.

GEORGIA

Capital: Tbilisi
Population: 4,555,911
Area: 26,911 sq. mi. (69,700 sq km)
Language: Georgian, Russian, Abkhaz
Money: Lari
Government: Republic

ⓘ CHECK IT OUT

Krubera Cave, in Georgia's Caucasus Mountains, is said to be the deepest cave in the world. It has been explored to depths of 7,185 feet (2,190 m).

GERMANY

Capital: Berlin
Population: 81,147,265
Area: 137,847 sq. mi.
(357,021 sq km)
Language: German
Money: Euro
Government: Federal republic

ⓘ CHECK IT OUT

The spires of the Cologne Cathedral are an amazing 515 feet (157 m) high—taller than a 50-story building.

GHANA

Capital: Accra
Population: 25,691,897
Area: 92,456 sq. mi. (239,460 sq km)
Language: English, Asante, Ewe, Fante
Money: Cedi
Government: Constitutional democracy

ⓘ CHECK IT OUT

Until 1957 Ghana was known as the Gold Coast because of the vast amounts of gold Portuguese explorers found there.

GREECE

Capital: Athens
Population: 10,772,967
Area: 50,942 sq. mi. (131,940 sq km)
Language: Greek, Turkish, English
Money: Euro
Government: Parliamentary republic

ⓘ CHECK IT OUT

The Parthenon, in Athens, is one of the oldest and most famous buildings in the world. The ancient temple was built to honor the Greek goddess Athena almost 2,500 years ago.

GRENADA

Capital: St. George's
Population: 109,590
Area: 133 sq. mi. (344 sq km)
Language: English, French patois
Money: Dollar
Government: Parliamentary democracy

! CHECK IT OUT

Grenada is known as the Spice of the Caribbean. The country produces one-third of the world's nutmeg.

GUATEMALA

Capital: Guatemala City
Population: 14,373,472
Area: 42,043 sq. mi. (108,890 sq km)
Language: Spanish, 23 Amerindian dialects
Money: Quetzal
Government: Constitutional democratic republic

! CHECK IT OUT

More than one-half of Guatemalans are descended from the Mayas. The Mayan Indian civilization developed a calendar with a 365-day year, among many other achievements.

GUINEA

Capital: Conakry
Population: 11,176,026
Area: 94,926 sq. mi. (245,857 sq km)
Language: French, Peul, Malinke, Soussou
Money: Franc
Government: Republic

! CHECK IT OUT

Despite its name, the guinea pig does not come from Guinea. It is native to South America. (And it's not a pig!)

GUINEA-BISSAU

Capital: Bissau
Population: 1,660,870
Area: 13,946 sq. mi. (36,120 sq km)
Language: Portuguese, Creole, French, others
Money: CFA franc
Government: Republic

! CHECK IT OUT

Guinea-Bissau's main export crop is cashew nuts.

GUYANA

Capital: Georgetown
Population: 739,903
Area: 83,000 sq. mi. (214,970 sq km)
Language: English, Guyanese, Creole
Money: Dollar
Government: Republic

! CHECK IT OUT

Guyana's Kaieteur Falls is five times as tall as Niagara Falls.

HAITI

Capital: Port-au-Prince
Population: 9,893,934
Area: 10,714 sq. mi. (27,750 sq km)
Language: French, Creole
Money: Gourde
Government: Republic

! CHECK IT OUT

On January 12, 2010, a devastating earthquake struck Haiti, killing or injuring hundreds of thousands in the Port-au-Prince area.

THE HOLY SEE
(VATICAN CITY)

Capital: Vatican City
Population: 836
Area: 0.17 sq. mi. (0.44 sq km)
Language: Italian, Latin, French, various others
Money: Euro
Government: Ecclesiastical

ⓘCHECK IT OUT

Vatican City, the seat of the Roman Catholic Church, is the world's smallest independent nation.

HONDURAS

Capital: Tegucigalpa
Population: 8,448,465
Area: 43,278 sq. mi. (112,090 sq km)
Language: Spanish, Amerindian dialects
Money: Lempira
Government: Democratic constitutional republic

ⓘCHECK IT OUT

The word *honduras* means "depths" in Spanish. Christopher Columbus named the area after the deep water off its coast when he landed there in 1502.

HUNGARY

Capital: Budapest
Population: 9,939,470
Area: 35,919 sq. mi. (93,030 sq km)
Language: Hungarian
Money: Forint
Government: Parliamentary democracy

ⓘCHECK IT OUT

The Danube River splits the capital city into two sides: Buda and Pest.

ICELAND

Capital: Reykjavik
Population: 315,281
Area: 39,769 sq. mi. (103,000 sq km)
Language: Icelandic
Money: Krona
Government: Constitutional republic

ⓘCHECK IT OUT

Iceland's glaciers, geysers, and warm, mineral-rich pools attract more than a quarter of a million tourists every year.

INDIA

Capital: New Delhi
Population: 1,220,800,359
Area: 1,269,346 sq. mi. (3,287,590 sq km)
Language: Hindi, English, 21 others
Money: Rupee
Government: Federal republic

ⓘCHECK IT OUT

India's Taj Mahal is one of the wonders of the world. It was built in the 1600s by Shah Jahan for his wife, Mumtaz Mahal.

INDONESIA

Capital: Jakarta
Population: 250,775,663
Area: 741,100 sq. mi. (1,919,440 sq km)
Language: Bahasa Indonesia, English, Dutch, Javanese
Money: Rupiah
Government: Republic

ⓘCHECK IT OUT

The largest volcanic eruption in history happened on the Indonesian island of Sumbawa in 1815. Scientists say that the eruption of Mount Tambora sent a massive cloud of ash 30 miles (43 km) into the atmosphere—much higher than a plane can fly—and killed 100,000 people.

IRAN

Capital: Tehran
Population: 79,853,900
Area: 636,296 sq. mi. (1,648,000 sq km)
Language: Persian, Turkic, Kurdish, Arabic, others
Money: Rial
Government: Islamic republic

ⓘCHECK IT OUT

For most of its history, Iran was called Persia.

IRAQ

Capital: Baghdad
Population: 31,858,481
Area: 168,754 sq. mi.
(437,072 sq km)
Language: Arabic, Kurdish,
Turkoman, Assyrian, Armenian
Money: Dinar
Government: Parliamentary
democracy

CHECK IT OUT

Iraq contains more oil than any
country in the world, except for
Saudi Arabia and Canada.

IRELAND

Capital: Dublin
Population: 4,775,982
Area: 27,135 sq. mi. (70,280 sq km)
Language: English, Gaelic
Money: Euro
Government: Parliamentary
republic

CHECK IT OUT

Ireland is known as the Emerald
Isle because of its beautiful green
fields and hillsides.

ISRAEL

Capital: Jerusalem
Population: 7,707,042
Area: 8,019 sq. mi. (20,770 sq km)
Language: Hebrew, Arabic,
English
Money: New shekel
Government: Republic

CHECK IT OUT

The Western Wall in Jerusalem
is also called the Wailing Wall. It
is one of Judaism's holiest places
and most sacred symbols.

ITALY

Capital: Rome
Population: 61,482,297
Area: 116,306 sq. mi.
(301,230 sq km)
Language: Italian, German,
French, Slovene
Money: Euro
Government: Republic

CHECK IT OUT

Engineers successfully stopped
Italy's famous Leaning Tower of
Pisa from collapsing through a
construction project in 2001.

JAMAICA

Capital: Kingston
Population: 2,909,714
Area: 4,244 sq. mi. (10,991 sq km)
Language: English, English patois
Money: Dollar
Government: Constitutional
monarchy with parliamentary
system

CHECK IT OUT

The pirate known as Blackbeard
(Edward Teach) is said to have
operated out of Jamaica in the
1700s. Some stories say that he
went into battle with lit matches
stuck in his hat to make enemies
think his head was smoking.

JAPAN

Capital: Tokyo
Population: 127,253,075
Area: 145,883 sq. mi.
(337,835 sq km)
Language: Japanese
Money: Yen
Government: Constitutional
monarchy with parliamentary
democracy

CHECK IT OUT

Japan has four major islands—
Honshu, Hokkaido, Kyushu, and
Shikoku—and thousands of
smaller ones.

JORDAN

Capital: Amman
Population: 6,482,081
Area: 35,637 sq. mi. (92,300 sq km)
Language: Arabic, English
Money: Dinar
Government: Constitutional monarchy

⟳ CHECK IT OUT

The points of the star on Jordan's flag stand for the first seven verses of the Koran, the holy book of Islam.

KAZAKHSTAN

Capital: Astana
Population: 17,736,896
Area: 1,049,155 sq. mi. (2,717,300 sq km)
Language: Kazakh, Russian, German
Money: Tenge
Government: Republic

⟳ CHECK IT OUT

The Caspian Sea, which borders Kazakhstan, is the largest enclosed body of water on Earth.

KENYA

Capital: Nairobi
Population: 44,037,656
Area: 224,962 sq. mi. (582,650 sq km)
Language: Kiswahili, English, numerous indigenous languages
Money: Shilling
Government: Republic

⟳ CHECK IT OUT

In Kenya's Lake Turkana area, scientists discovered a fossil known as Kenya Man, thought to be over three million years old.

KIRIBATI

Capital: Tawara
Population: 103,248
Area: 313 sq. mi. (811 sq km)
Language: English, I-Kiribati
Money: Dollar
Government: Republic

⟳ CHECK IT OUT

Kiribati consists of three groups of islands surrounded by coral reefs, roughly halfway between Australia and Hawaii.

KOREA, NORTH

Capital: Pyongyang
Population: 24,720,407
Area: 46,541 sq. mi. (120,540 sq km)
Language: Korean
Money: Won
Government: Communist state

⟳ CHECK IT OUT

North Korea has the fourth-largest army in the world.

KOREA, SOUTH

Capital: Seoul
Population: 48,955,203
Area: 38,023 sq. mi. (98,480 sq km)
Language: Korean, English
Money: Won
Government: Republic

⟳ CHECK IT OUT

South Korea has about twice as many people as North Korea, but much less land area. It's one of the mostly densely populated countries in the world.

KOSOVO

Capital: Pristina
Population: 1,847,708
Area: 4,203 sq. mi.
(10,887 sq km)
Language: Albanian, Serbian,
Bosnian, Turkish, Roma
Money: Euro
Government: Republic

CHECK IT OUT

Kosovo, a country in southeastern
Europe that is about the size
of Connecticut, declared its
independence from Serbia on
February 17, 2008.

KUWAIT

Capital: Kuwait City
Population: 2,695,316
Area: 6,880 sq. mi. (17,820 sq km)
Language: Arabic, English
Money: Dinar
Government: Constitutional
emirate

CHECK IT OUT

Summers in Kuwait are dry and
extremely hot, averaging
108—115°F (42—46°C).

KYRGYZSTAN

Capital: Bishkek
Population: 5,749,264
Area: 76,641 sq. mi.
(198,500 sq km)
Language: Kyrgyz, Russian, Uzbek
Money: Som
Government: Republic

CHECK IT OUT

Kyrgyzstan is one of 15
countries that became
independent with the collapse
of the Soviet Union in 1991.

LAOS

Capital: Vientiane
Population: 6,695,166
Area: 91,429 sq. mi.
(236,800 sq km)
Language: Lao, French,
English, other ethnic languages
Money: Kip
Government: Communist state

CHECK IT OUT

In 2008, cavers exploring the 6-
mile-long (almost 10 km) Xe Bang
Fai River cave in central Laos
found huge rooms and spiders
as big as dinner plates.

LATVIA

Capital: Riga
Population: 2,178,443
Area: 24,938 sq. mi.
(64,589 sq km)
Language: Latvian,
Lithuanian, Russian
Money: Lat
Government: Parliamentary
democracy

CHECK IT OUT

Latvia has a 100 percent
literacy rate.

LEBANON

Capital: Beirut
Population: 4,131,583
Area: 4,015 sq. mi.
(10,400 sq km)
Language: Arabic, English,
French, Armenian
Money: Pound
Government: Republic

CHECK IT OUT

Beirut is a lively pop music
center, with TV music
channels, yearly festivals,
and talent shows such
as *Star Academy* and
Superstar.

LESOTHO

Capital: Maseru
Population: 1,936,181
Area: 11,720 sq. mi.
(30,355 sq km)
Language: Sesotho,
English, Zulu, Xhosa
Money: Loti
Government:
Parliamentary constitutional
monarchy

CHECK IT OUT

To visualize Lesotho, think
of a doughnut hole—a small
circle of land surrounded
by the much larger nation of
South Africa.

LIBERIA

Capital: Monrovia
Population: 3,989,703
Area: 43,000 sq. mi. (111,370 sq km)
Language: English, about 20 ethnic languages
Money: Dollar
Government: Republic

CHECK IT OUT

Many Liberians are descendants of American slaves who were advised to live there in freedom by a U.S. antislavery group in the 1800s.

LIBYA

Capital: Tripoli
Population: 6,002,347
Area: 679,362 sq. mi. (1,759,540 sq km)
Language: Arabic, Italian, English
Money: Dinar
Government: In transition

CHECK IT OUT

Libya has a young population. About one-third of all Libyans are under 15.

LIECHTENSTEIN

Capital: Vaduz
Population: 37,009
Area: 62 sq. mi. (160 sq km)
Language: German, Alemannic dialect
Money: Swiss franc
Government: Constitutional monarchy

CHECK IT OUT

Tiny Liechtenstein shares some services with neighboring Switzerland. Its residents use Swiss money, and Switzerland runs Liechtenstein's telephone and postal systems.

LITHUANIA

Capital: Vilnius
Population: 3,515,858
Area: 25,212 sq. mi. (65,300 sq km)
Language: Lithuanian, Russian, Polish
Money: Litas
Government: Parliamentary democracy

CHECK IT OUT

Lithuania is the largest of the Baltic states, three countries on the eastern edge of the Baltic Sea. The others are Estonia and Latvia.

LUXEMBOURG

Capital: Luxembourg-Ville
Population: 514,862
Area: 998 sq. mi. (2,586 sq km)
Language: Luxembourgish, German, French
Money: Euro
Government: Constitutional monarchy

CHECK IT OUT

Luxembourg is an industrial country known particularly for two products: steel and computers.

MACEDONIA

Capital: Skopje
Population: 2,087,171
Area: 9,781 sq. mi. (25,333 sq km)
Language: Macedonian, Albanian, Turkish
Money: Denar
Government: Parliamentary democracy

CHECK IT OUT

About 80 percent of Macedonia consists of hills and mountains, but more than half the population lives in cities.

MADAGASCAR

Capital: Antananarivo
Population: 23,259,610
Area: 226,657 sq. mi.
(587,040 sq km)
Language: Malagasy, English,
French
Money: Ariary
Government: Republic

CHECK IT OUT

Madagascar is the world's fourth-largest island, after Greenland, New Guinea, and Borneo. It is home to a huge variety of unique plants and animals that evolved 165 million years ago.

MALAWI

Capital: Lilongwe
Population: 16,777,547
Area: 45,745 sq. mi. (118,480 sq km)
Language: Chichewa, Chinyan'ji,
Chiyao, Chitumbka
Money: Kwacha
Government: Multiparty
democracy

CHECK IT OUT

Lake Malawi is nearly 9,000 square miles (23,310 sq km). It takes up about a fifth of the country's total area.

MALAYSIA

Capital: Kuala Lumpur
Population: 29,628,392
Area: 127,317 sq. mi. (329,750 sq km)
Language: Bahasa Malaysia,
English, Chinese dialects, Panjabi,
Thai
Money: Ringgit
Government: Constitutional
monarchy

CHECK IT OUT

Malaysia's capital is the home of the 1,483-foot (452 m) Petronas Twin Towers. They were the tallest buildings in the world from 1996 to 2003.

MALDIVES

Capital: Male
Population: 393,988
Area: 116 sq. mi. (300 sq km)
Language: Maldivian Dhivehi,
English
Money: Rufiyaa
Government: Republic

CHECK IT OUT

About 1,000 of the 1,190 coral islands that make up Maldives, located south of India in the Indian Ocean, are uninhabited.

MALI

Capital: Bamako
Population: 14,917,533
Area: 478,767 sq. mi.
(1,240,000 sq km)
Language: French, Bambara,
numerous African languages
Money: CFA franc
Government: Republic

CHECK IT OUT

Most of Mali's people make their living farming or fishing around the Niger River.

MALTA

Capital: Valletta
Population: 411,277
Area: 122 sq. mi. (316 sq km)
Language: Maltese, English
Money: Euro
Government: Republic

CHECK IT OUT

This group of islands in the Mediterranean Sea south of Sicily has one of the world's healthiest populations. The average life expectancy is over 79 years.

MARSHALL ISLANDS

Capital: Majuro
Population: 69,747
Area: 70 sq. mi. (181 sq km)
Language: Marshallese, English
Money: U.S. dollar
Government: Constitutional government in free association with the United States

ⓘ CHECK IT OUT

The first hydrogen bomb was exploded in the Marshall Islands in 1952. Radiation levels in some areas are still high, but improving through environmental cleanup programs.

MAURITANIA

Capital: Nouakchott
Population: 3,437,610
Area: 397,955 sq. mi. (1,030,700 sq km)
Language: Arabic, Pulaar, Soninke, Wolof, French
Money: Ouguiya
Government: Military junta

ⓘ CHECK IT OUT

This western African nation has it together! It's a major producer of gum arabic, used to make glue.

MAURITIUS

Capital: Port Louis
Population: 1,322,238
Area: 788 sq. mi. (2,040 sq km)
Language: Creole, Bhojpuri, French
Money: Rupee
Government: Parliamentary democracy

ⓘ CHECK IT OUT

Mauritius has the second-highest per-person income in Africa. Most of the country's money comes from sugarcane.

MEXICO

Capital: Mexico City
Population: 116,220,947
Area: 761,606 sq. mi. (1,972,550 sq km)
Language: Spanish, various Mayan, Nahuati, other regional indigenous dialects
Money: Peso
Government: Federal republic

ⓘ CHECK IT OUT

Mexico has dozens of bullfighting rings, including one that holds 50,000 people—about the entire population of Biloxi, Mississippi.

MICRONESIA

Capital: Palikir
Population: 106,104
Area: 271 sq. mi. (702 sq km)
Language: English, Chuukese, Kosrean, Pohnpeian, Yapese
Money: U.S. dollar
Government: Constitutional government in free association with the United States

ⓘ CHECK IT OUT

Micronesia's first settlers have been traced back more than 4,000 years.

MOLDOVA

Capital: Chisinau
Population: 3,619,925
Area: 13,067 sq. mi. (333,843 sq km)
Language: Moldovan, Russian, Gagauz
Money: Leu
Government: Republic

ⓘ CHECK IT OUT

Moldova was the first former Soviet state to elect a Communist as president.

MONACO

Capital: Monaco
Population: 30,500
Area: 0.75 sq. mi. (1.95 sq km)
Language: French, English, Italian, Monegasque
Money: Euro
Government: Constitutional monarchy

CHECK IT OUT

Mini-sized Monaco covers about as much area as New York City's Central Park.

MONGOLIA

Capital: Ulan Bator
Population: 3,226,516
Area: 603,909 sq. mi. (1,564,116 sq km)
Language: Khalka Mongol, Turkic, Russian
Money: Togrog/Tughrik
Government: Mixed parliamentary/presidential

CHECK IT OUT

Mongolia's average population density is only 5 people per square mile (1.9 per sq km), although many people live in the cities.

MONTENEGRO

Capital: Podgorica
Population: 653,474
Area: 5,415 sq. mi. (14,026 sq km)
Language: Montenegrin, Serbian, Bosnian, Albanian, Croatian
Money: Euro
Government: Republic

CHECK IT OUT

Montenegro's name means "black mountain." The name comes from the dark forests on the mountains that once covered most of the country.

MOROCCO

Capital: Rabat
Population: 32,649,130
Area: 172,414 sq. mi. (446,550 sq km)
Language: Arabic, Berber dialects, French
Money: Dirham
Government: Constitutional monarchy

CHECK IT OUT

Morocco is a North African country about the size of California. Part of it is covered by the Sahara Desert, whose 3,500,000 square miles (9,064,958 sq km) make it the largest desert in the world.

MOZAMBIQUE

Capital: Maputo
Population: 24,096,669
Area: 309,496 sq. mi. (801,590 sq km)
Language: Portuguese, Emakhuwa, Xichangana, Elomwe, Cisena
Money: Metical
Government: Republic

CHECK IT OUT

Portuguese is the official language of Mozambique. However, most residents, who are of African descent, speak a form of Bantu.

NAMIBIA

Capital: Windhoek
Population: 2,182,852
Area: 318,696 sq. mi. (825,418 sq km)
Language: Afrikaans, German, English, other indigenous languages
Money: Dollar, South African rand
Government: Republic

CHECK IT OUT

Namibia's rich diamond deposits have made it one of the world's best sources of high-quality diamonds.

NAURU

Capital: Yaren
Population: 9,434
Area: 8 sq. mi. (21 sq km)
Language: Nauruan, English
Money: Australian dollar
Government: Republic

!CHECK IT OUT

Nauru joined the United Nations in 1999 as the world's smallest independent republic.

NEPAL

Capital: Kathmandu
Population: 30,430,267
Area: 56,827 sq. mi. (147,181 sq km)
Language: Nepali, Maithali, English
Money: Rupee
Government: Federal democratic republic

!CHECK IT OUT

Eight of the world's ten highest mountain peaks are in Nepal, including Mount Everest, the highest of them all—29,035 feet (8,850 m).

NETHERLANDS

Capital: Amsterdam
Population: 16,966,924
Area: 16,033 sq. mi. (41,526 sq km)
Language: Dutch, Frisian
Money: Euro
Government: Constitutional monarchy

!CHECK IT OUT

Most Netherlanders dress in modern clothing, but many farmers say wooden shoes, known as *klompen*, keep feet drier.

NEW ZEALAND

Capital: Wellington
Population: 4,365,113
Area: 103,738 sq. mi. (268,680 sq km)
Language: English, Maori, sign language
Money: Dollar
Government: Parliamentary democracy

!CHECK IT OUT

New Zealand was settled by the Polynesian Maori in 800 CE. Today Maori make up about 9.38 percent of the country's population.

NICARAGUA

Capital: Managua
Population: 5,788,531
Area: 49,998 sq. mi. (129,494 sq km)
Language: Spanish, English, indigenous languages on Atlantic coast
Money: Gold cordoba
Government: Republic

!CHECK IT OUT

Nicaragua got its name from Nicarao, a tribal chief who lived and reigned here in the 16th century.

NIGER

Capital: Niamey
Population: 16,899,327
Area: 489,191 sq. mi.
(1,267,000 sq km)
Language: French, Hausa,
Djerma
Money: CFA franc
Government: Republic

CHECK IT OUT

Niger is known as the Frying Pan of the World. It can get hot enough to make raindrops evaporate before they hit the ground.

NIGERIA

Capital: Abuja
Population: 161,236,294
Area: 356,669 sq. mi.
(923,768 sq km)
Language: English, Hausa,
Yoruba, Igbo, Fulani
Money: Naira
Government: Federal republic

CHECK IT OUT

Nigeria is the most heavily populated country in Africa. More than half the continent's people live there.

NORWAY

Capital: Oslo
Population: 4,722,701
Area: 125,021 sq. mi.
(323,802 sq km)
Language: Bokmal Norwegian,
Nynorsk Norwegian, Sami
Money: Krone
Government: Constitutional
monarchy

CHECK IT OUT

Moving glaciers during the Ice Age left Norway with a jagged coastline marked by long strips of water-filled fjords and thousands of islands.

OMAN

Capital: Muscat
Population: 3,154,134
Area: 82,031 sq. mi.
(212,460 sq km)
Language: Arabic, English,
Baluchi, Urdu, Indian dialects
Money: Rial
Government: Monarchy

CHECK IT OUT

Members of the Al Bu Said family have ruled Oman for more than 250 years.

PAKISTAN

Capital: Islamabad
Population: 193,238,868
Area: 310,403 sq. mi.
(803,940 sq km)
Language: English, Urdu,
Punjabi, Sindhi, Siraiki, Pashtu
Money: Rupee
Government: Federal republic

CHECK IT OUT

Pakistan is the sixth most heavily populated country in the world. The others, in order, are China, India, the United States, Indonesia, and Brazil.

PALAU

Capital: Melekeok
Population: 21,108
Area: 177 sq. mi. (458 sq km)
Language: English, Palauan,
various Asian languages
Money: U.S. dollar
Government: Constitutional
government in free association
with the United States

CHECK IT OUT

In March 2008, thousands of human bones, some of them ancient and very small, were found by scientists in Palau.

PANAMA

Capital: Panama City
Population: 3,559,408
Area: 30,193 sq. mi. (78,200 sq km)
Language: Spanish, English
Money: Balboa
Government: Constitutional democracy

CHECK IT OUT

Spain was the first country to think of cutting a canal across the Isthmus of Panama. The French started building the 51-mile-long (82 km) canal in 1881 and the United States finished it in 1914.

PAPUA NEW GUINEA

Capital: Port Moresby
Population: 6,431,902
Area: 178,704 sq. mi. (462,840 sq km)
Language: Melanesian Pidgin, English, 820 indigenous languages
Money: Kina
Government: Constitutional parliamentary democracy

CHECK IT OUT

Living in Papua New Guinea means coping with the constant threat of active volcanoes, frequent earthquakes, mud slides, and tsunamis.

PARAGUAY

Capital: Asuncíon
Population: 6,623,252
Area: 157,047 sq. mi. (406,750 sq km)
Language: Spanish, Guarani
Money: Guarani
Government: Constitutional republic

CHECK IT OUT

Paraguay's got the power! Hydroelectric dams, including the largest one in the world, keep the country well supplied with electricity.

PERU

Capital: Lima
Population: 29,849,303
Area: 496,226 sq. mi. (1,285,220 sq km)
Language: Spanish, Quechua, Aymara, numerous minor languages
Money: Nuevo sol
Government: Constitutional republic

CHECK IT OUT

The third-largest country in South America (after Brazil and Argentina), Peru is three times as big as California but has only two-thirds of that state's population.

Machu Picchu, Peru →

PHILIPPINES

Capital: Manila
Population: 105,720,644
Area: 115,831 sq. mi. (300,000 sq km)
Language: Filipino, English, 8 major dialects
Money: Peso
Government: Republic

CHECK IT OUT

Almost half of all working Filipinos earn their living by farming, although the farmland itself is owned by a wealthy few.

POLAND

Capital: Warsaw
Population: 38,383,809
Area: 120,726 sq. mi. (312,679 sq km)
Language: Polish
Money: Zloty
Government: Republic

CHECK IT OUT

Physicist Marie Curie and composer Frederic Chopin are just two of the many world-famous people who came from Poland.

PORTUGAL

Capital: Lisbon
Population: 10,799,270
Area: 35,672 sq. mi. (92,391 sq km)
Language: Portuguese, Mirandese
Money: Euro
Government: Republic, parliamentary democracy

CHECK IT OUT

The national music of Portugal is called *fado*. The songs are often sad but can also be funny.

QATAR

Capital: Doha
Population: 2,042,444
Area: 4,416 sq. mi. (11,437 sq km)
Language: Arabic, English
Money: Rial
Government: Emirate

CHECK IT OUT

Qatar is only about as big as Los Angeles County, California, but it holds more than 15 percent of the world's gas reserves.

ROMANIA

Capital: Bucharest
Population: 21,790,479
Area: 91,699 sq. mi. (237,500 sq km)
Language: Romanian, Hungarian, Romany (Gypsy)
Money: New leu
Government: Republic

CHECK IT OUT

Cruel 15th-century Romanian prince Vlad Tepes was the model for the horror novel *Dracula*. One of Vlad's homes, Bran Castle, is Romania's most popular tourist attraction.

RUSSIA

Capital: Moscow
Population: 142,500,482
Area: 6,592,772 sq. mi. (17,075,200 sq km)
Language: Russian, many minority languages
Money: Ruble
Government: Federation

CHECK IT OUT

Russia is the largest country in the world and contains the ninth-largest population. It was formerly the center of the Union of Soviet Socialist Republics (USSR), which broke up into 15 separate states in 1991.

RWANDA

Capital: Kigali
Population: 12,012,589
Area: 10,169 sq. mi. (26,338 sq km)
Language: Kinyarwanda, French, English, Swahili
Money: Franc
Government: Republic, presidential-multiparty system

CHECK IT OUT

Rwanda leads the world in terms of female representation in its parliamentary body. Roughly half of its legislators are women.

SAINT KITTS and NEVIS

Capital: Basseterre
Population: 51,134
Area: 101 sq. mi. (261 sq km)
Language: English
Money: Dollar
Government: Parliamentary democracy

CHECK IT OUT

These two Caribbean islands have been a single state since 1983.

SAINT LUCIA

Capital: Castries
Population: 162,781
Area: 238 sq. mi. (616 sq km)
Language: English, French patois
Money: Dollar
Government: Parliamentary democracy

CHECK IT OUT

This small Caribbean island changed hands between France and England 14 times before being given to the United Kingdom in 1814. It became independent in 1979.

SAINT VINCENT and the GRENADINES

Capital: Kingstown
Population: 103,220
Area: 150 sq. mi. (389 sq km)
Language: English, French patois
Money: Dollar
Government: Parliamentary democracy

CHECK IT OUT

These islands are the world's leading suppliers of arrowroot, which is used to thicken fruit pie fillings and sauces.

SAMOA

Capital: Apia
Population: 195,476
Area: 1,137 sq. mi. (2,944 sq km)
Language: Samoan, English
Money: Tala
Government: Parliamentary democracy

CHECK IT OUT

Author Robert Louis Stevenson (*Treasure Island*, *Kidnapped*) lived in Samoa from 1890 until he died in 1894. His Polynesian neighbors called him *Tusitala*, or "Storyteller."

SAN MARINO

Capital: San Marino
Population: 32,448
Area: 24 sq. mi. (61 sq km)
Language: Italian
Money: Euro
Government: Republic

CHECK IT OUT

San Marino, in central Italy, is the third-smallest state in Europe. Some historians say it was founded in 301 CE, making it the world's oldest republic.

SÃO TOMÉ and PRINCIPE

Capital: São Tomé
Population: 186,817
Area: 387 sq. mi. (1,001 sq km)
Language: Portuguese
Money: Dobra
Government: Republic

CHECK IT OUT

São Tomé and Principe are the two largest islands in an African island group in the Gulf of Guinea.

SAUDI ARABIA

Capital: Riyadh
Population: 26,939,583
Area: 830,000 sq. mi. (2,149,690 sq km)
Language: Arabic
Money: Riyal
Government: Monarchy

CHECK IT OUT

Saudi Arabia is known as the birthplace of Islam.

SENEGAL

Capital: Dakar
Population: 13,300,410
Area: 75,749 sq. mi. (196,190 sq km)
Language: French, Wolof, Pulaar, Jola, Mandinka
Money: CFA Franc
Government: Republic

CHECK IT OUT

Senegal's economy depends on peanuts. In recent years the country has produced more than 800,000 tons of them, 95 percent for oil.

SERBIA

Capital: Belgrade
Population: 7,243,007
Area: 29,913 sq. mi. (77,474 sq km)
Language: Serbian, Hungarian
Money: Dinar
Government: Republic

CHECK IT OUT

Favorite foods in Serbia are *cevacici*, a grilled meatball sandwich with raw onions, and *burek*, a pastry layered with cheese, meat, or jam.

SEYCHELLES

Capital: Victoria
Population: 90,846
Area: 176 sq. mi. (455 sq km)
Language: Creole, English
Money: Rupee
Government: Republic

CHECK IT OUT

From the early 1500s to the 1700s, Seychelles was a popular pirate hideout.

SIERRA LEONE

Capital: Freetown
Population: 5,612,685
Area: 27,699 sq. mi. (71,740 sq km)
Language: English, Mende and Temne vernaculars, Krio (English-based Creole)
Money: Leone
Government: Constitutional democracy

CHECK IT OUT

Sierra Leone is one of the wettest places in western Africa. Rainfall can reach 195 inches (495 cm) a year.

SINGAPORE

Capital: Singapore
Population: 5,460,302
Area: 269 sq. mi. (697 sq km)
Language: Mandarin, English, Malay, Hokkien, Cantonese, Teochew
Money: Dollar
Government: Republic

CHECK IT OUT

Singapore is a city-state—an independent state made up of a city and the areas around it. It is an important international business center with one of the busiest harbors in the world.

SLOVAKIA

Capital: Bratislava
Population: 5,488,339
Area: 18,859 sq. mi. (48,845 sq km)
Language: Slovak, Hungarian
Money: Koruna
Government: Parliamentary democracy

CHECK IT OUT

Following World War I, Slovaks and Czechs were joined into a single nation: Czechoslovakia. But in 1993 Czechoslovakia redivided into Slovakia and the Czech Republic.

SLOVENIA

Capital: Ljubljana
Population: 1,992,690
Area: 7,827 sq. mi. (20,273 sq km)
Language: Slovenian, Serbo-Croatian
Money: Euro
Government: Parliamentary democracy

CHECK IT OUT

Big puddles and small lakes can appear and disappear suddenly in Slovenia because of underground caves and channels.

SOLOMON ISLANDS

Capital: Honiara
Population: 597,248
Area: 10,985 sq. mi. (28,450 sq km)
Language: English, Melanesian pidgin, 120 indigenous languages
Money: Dollar
Government: Parliamentary democracy

CHECK IT OUT

On April 1, 2007, a massive underwater earthquake triggered a tsunami that caused widespread destruction in the Solomon Islands.

SOMALIA

Capital: Mogadishu
Population: 10,251,568
Area: 246,201 sq. mi. (637,657 sq km)
Language: English, Arabic, Italian
Money: Shilling
Government: In transition

CHECK IT OUT

Each point of the flag's white star stands for a region of Somalia.

SOUTH AFRICA

Capital: Pretoria (administrative), Cape Town (legislative), Bloemfontein (judicial)
Population: 48,601,098
Area: 471,011 sq. mi. (1,219,912 sq km)
Language: IsiZulu, IsiXhosa, Afrikaans, English, Sepedi, Setswana, Sesotho
Money: Rand
Government: Republic

CHECK IT OUT

South Africa is in a subtropical location—so how come penguins thrive there? The penguins' breeding grounds are cooled by Antarctic Ocean currents on the west coast.

SOUTH SUDAN

Capital: Juba
Population: 11,090,104
Area: 248,777 sq. mi. (644,329 sq km)
Language: English, Arabic, Dinka, Nuer, Bari, Zande, Shilluk
Money: South Sudanese pound
Government: Republic

CHECK IT OUT

South Sudan won its independence from Sudan on July 9, 2011. Its national anthem, "South Sudan Oyee! (Hooray!)," was written by a group of 49 students, poets, and teachers.

SPAIN

Capital: Madrid
Population: 47,370,542
Area: 194,897 sq. mi. (504,782 sq km)
Language: Castilian Spanish, Catalan, Galician, Basque
Money: Euro
Government: Parliamentary monarchy

CHECK IT OUT

Spain's capital city is in almost the exact center of the country.

SRI LANKA

Capital: Colombo
Population: 21,675,648
Area: 25,332 sq. mi. (65,610 sq km)
Language: Sinhala, Tamil, English
Money: Rupee
Government: Republic

CHECK IT OUT

Once named Ceylon, Sri Lanka was an important port in the ancient world. Arab traders called it Serendip, the origin of the word *serendipity*, which means "a pleasing chance discovery."

SUDAN

Capital: Khartoum
Population: 34,847,910
Area: 718,723 sq. mi. (1,861,484 sq km)
Language: Arabic, Nubian, Ta Bedawie, Nilotic, Nilo-Hamitic, Sudanic dialects, English
Money: Pound
Government: Power sharing, with military dominant (elections in April 2010)

CHECK IT OUT

Two branches of the Nile River, the White Nile and the Blue Nile, meet in Khartoum to form the main Nile River corridor.

SURINAME

Capital: Paramaribo
Population: 566,846
Area: 63,039 sq. mi. (163,270 sq km)
Language: Dutch, English, Sranang Tongo, Caribbean Hindustani, Javanese
Money: Dollar
Government: Constitutional democracy

CHECK IT OUT

Suriname is the smallest independent country in South America. It could fit into Brazil, its massive neighbor to the south, 52 times.

SWAZILAND

Capital: Mbabane
Population: 1,403,362
Area: 6,704 sq. mi. (17,363 sq km)
Language: English, siSwati
Money: Lilangeni
Government: Monarchy

CHECK IT OUT

Other parts of southern Africa suffer from drought, but four major rivers—the Komati, the Umbuluzi, the Ingwavuma, and the Great Usutu—keep Swaziland's water supply healthy.

SWEDEN

Capital: Stockholm
Population: 9,119,423
Area: 173,732 sq. mi. (449,964 sq km)
Language: Swedish, Finnish, Sami
Money: Krona
Government: Constitutional monarchy

CHECK IT OUT

Sweden has an army, navy, and air force, but its military can only be used in peacekeeping actions, not wars.

SWITZERLAND

Capital: Bern
Population: 7,670,478
Area: 15,942 sq. mi. (41,290 sq km)
Language: German, French, Italian, Romansch
Money: Franc
Government: Federal republic-like confederation

CHECK IT OUT

Switzerland's famous flag comes in two shapes. A square version is flown on land and a rectangular flag (like the one above) is flown at sea.

SYRIA

Capital: Damascus
Population: 22,457,336
Area: 71,498 sq. mi. (185,180 sq km)
Language: Arabic, Kurdish, Armenian, Aramaic, Circassian
Money: Pound
Government: Republic (under military regime)

CHECK IT OUT

In 2008, archaeologists excavating in the Syrian desert dug up a camel jawbone they said could be a million years old.

TAIWAN

Capital: Taipei
Population: 23,151,339
Area: 13,892 sq. mi. (35,980 sq km)
Language: Mandarin, Taiwanese, Hakka
Money: Dollar (yuan)
Government: Multiparty democracy

CHECK IT OUT

Taiwan's Palace Museum's collection of Chinese bronze, jade, calligraphy, painting, and porcelain is so big that only 1 percent of it is displayed at any one time.

TAJIKISTAN

Capital: Dushanbe
Population: 7,910,041
Area: 55,251 sq. mi. (143,100 sq km)
Language: Tajik, Russian
Money: Somoni
Government: Republic

CHECK IT OUT

When mountainous Tajikistan became independent after the breakup of the Soviet Union, it inherited a mountain called Communism Peak. The Tajiks quickly changed the name to Imeni Ismail Samani Peak.

TANZANIA

Capital: Dodoma
Population: 48,261,942
Area: 364,900 sq. mi. (945,087 sq km)
Language: Kiswahili, English, Arabic, many local languages
Money: Shilling
Government: Republic

CHECK IT OUT

Africa's highest mountain, 19,340-foot-high (5,895 m) Mount Kilimanjaro, is in Tanzania. Lions, elephants, giraffes, and other animals roam free, protected by the government, in Serengeti Park.

THAILAND

Capital: Bangkok
Population: 67,448,120
Area: 198,457 sq. mi. (514,000 sq km)
Language: Thai, English, other ethnic languages
Money: Baht
Government: Constitutional monarchy

CHECK IT OUT

Formerly Siam, this Southeast Asian country has contributed Thai food, kickboxing, and the musical *The King and I* to world culture—among many other things.

TIMOR-LESTE

Capital: Dili
Population: 1,224,818
Area: 5,794 sq. mi. (15,007 sq km)
Language: Tetum, Portuguese, Indonesian, English
Money: U.S. dollar
Government: Republic

CHECK IT OUT

Timor-Leste is a really young nation. It became independent amid protests in 1999, and in 2007 it held largely peaceful presidential and parliamentary elections for the first time.

TOGO

Capital: Lomé
Population: 7,154,237
Area: 21,925 sq. mi. (56,785 sq km)
Language: French, Ewe, Mina, Kabye, Dagomba
Money: CFA franc
Government: Republic (under transition to multiparty democratic rule)

CHECK IT OUT

Watch your step! Poisonous vipers—cobras, pythons, and green and black mambas—are abundant here. So are scorpions and spiders.

TONGA

Capital: Nuku'alofa
Population: 106,322
Area: 289 sq. mi. (748 sq km)
Language: Tongan, English
Money: Pa'anga
Government: Constitutional monarchy

CHECK IT OUT

Tonga, an archipelago of about 150 islands east of Australia, is the last remaining monarchy in the Pacific.

TRINIDAD and TOBAGO

Capital: Port of Spain
Population: 1,225,225
Area: 1,980 sq. mi. (5,128 sq km)
Language: English, Caribbean Hindustani, French, Spanish, Chinese
Money: Dollar
Government: Parliamentary democracy

CHECK IT OUT

Native animals include the quenck, a kind of wild hog, and the agouti, a rabbitlike rodent. Howler monkeys are also native, but increasing development has made them rare.

TUNISIA

Capital: Tunis
Population: 10,835,873
Area: 63,170 sq. mi. (163,610 sq km)
Language: Arabic, French
Money: Dinar
Government: Republic

CHECK IT OUT

Every Star Wars movie but one was filmed in Tunisia. So was *Indiana Jones: Raiders of the Lost Ark.*

TURKEY

Capital: Ankara
Population: 80,694,485
Area: 301,384 sq. mi. (780,580 sq km)
Language: Turkish, Kurdish, Dimli
Money: New lira
Government: Republican parliamentary democracy

CHECK IT OUT

Turkey gave the world the man who would become Santa Claus: St. Nicholas, a fourth-century bishop.

TURKMENISTAN

Capital: Ashgabat
Population: 5,113,040
Area: 188,456 sq. mi. (488,100 sq km)
Language: Turkmen, Russian, Uzbek
Money: Manat
Government: Republic under authoritarian presidential rule

CHECK IT OUT

Turkmenistan's stunning flag incorporates five traditional carpet designs. Each design is associated with a particular tribe.

TUVALU

Capital: Funafuti
Population: 10,698
Area: 10 sq. mi. (26 sq km)
Language: Tuvaluan, English, Samoan
Money: Australian dollar
Government: Constitutional monarchy with parliamentary democracy

CHECK IT OUT

Tuvalu is made up of nine coral atolls in the South Pacific. Eight are inhabited. The word *tuvalu* means "group of eight."

UGANDA

Capital: Kampala
Population: 37,181,372
Area: 91,136 sq. mi. (236,040 sq km)
Language: English, Ganda, Luganda
Money: Shilling
Government: Republic

CHECK IT OUT

Ugandans speak in more than 42 different dialects. In fact, no single language is understood by all Ugandans.

UKRAINE

Capital: Kyiv (Kiev)
Population: 44,573,205
Area: 233,090 sq. mi. (603,700 sq km)
Language: Ukrainian, Russian, Romanian, Polish, Hungarian
Money: Hryvnia
Government: Republic

CHECK IT OUT

Ukraine is the largest country completely landlocked within Europe.

UNITED ARAB EMIRATES

Capital: Abu Dhabi
Population: 5,473,972
Area: 32,278 sq. mi. (83,600 sq km)
Language: Arabic, Persian, English, Hindi, Urdu
Money: Dirham
Government: Federation of emirates

CHECK IT OUT

The United Arab Emirates consists of seven independent Arab states in southwestern Asia. City dwellers live in modern buildings. Country people live in huts, and most wear long robes. Nomadic tribes roam the desert regions with camels, goats, and sheep.

UNITED KINGDOM

Capital: London
Population: 63,395,574
Area: 94,526 sq. mi. (244,820 sq km)
Language: English, Welsh, Scottish form of Gaelic
Money: Pound
Government: Constitutional monarchy

CHECK IT OUT

Today the United Kingdom (UK) consists of England, Scotland, Wales, and Northern Ireland. At one time the British Empire extended to five other continents.

UNITED STATES

Capital: Washington, DC
Population: 316,668,567
Area: 3,794,083 sq. mi. (9,826,630 sq km)
Language: English, Spanish, Hawaiian, other minority languages
Money: Dollar
Government: Federal republic with strong democratic tradition

CHECK IT OUT

What is now the United States was the first European colony to become independent from its motherland (England).

URUGUAY

Capital: Montevideo
Population: 3,324,460
Area: 68,039 sq. mi. (176,220 sq km)
Language: Spanish, Portunol, Brazilero
Money: Peso
Government: Constitutional republic

CHECK IT OUT

Uruguay's name comes from a Guarani word meaning "river of painted birds."

UZBEKISTAN

Capital: Tashkent
Population: 28,661,637
Area: 172,742 sq. mi. (447,400 sq km)
Language: Uzbek, Russian, Tajik
Money: Som
Government: Republic with authoritarian presidential rule

CHECK IT OUT

The cities of Uzbekistan—Samarkand, Bukhara, and Khiva—were well-traveled centers on the Silk Road, an ancient trade route linking Asia to Europe.

VANUATU

Capital: Port-Vila
Population: 230,571
Area: 4,710 sq. mi. (12,200 sq km)
Language: Bislama, English, French, 100 local languages
Money: Vatu
Government: Parliamentary republic

CHECK IT OUT

Vanuatu is not just one island but more than 80 volcanic islands in a South Pacific archipelago.

VENEZUELA

Capital: Caracas
Population: 28,459,085
Area: 352,144 sq. mi. (912,050 sq km)
Language: Spanish, indigenous dialects
Money: Bolivar Fuerte
Government: Federal republic

CHECK IT OUT

Venezuela is home to the largest rodents in the world—the capybaras. They measure up to 4.3 feet (1.3 m) long and weigh up to 140 pounds (about 64 kg).

VIETNAM

Capital: Hanoi
Population: 92,477,857
Area: 127,244 sq. mi. (329,560 sq km)
Language: Vietnamese, English, French, Chinese, Khmer
Money: Dong
Government: Communist state

CHECK IT OUT

Vietnam is shaped like a long, skinny S. It measures 1,031 miles (1,650 km) from north to south, but at its narrowest point is only 31 miles (50 km) across.

YEMEN

Capital: Sanaa
Population: 25,408,288
Area: 203,850 sq. mi. (527,970 sq km)
Language: Arabic
Money: Rial
Government: Republic

CHECK IT OUT

According to legend, coffee was discovered by a goat herder who noticed his goats got livelier after eating berries from a certain plant. The plant was brought to Yemen, where it was developed into a drink.

ZAMBIA

Capital: Lusaka
Population: 14,746,280
Area: 290,586 sq. mi. (752,614 sq km)
Language: English, numerous vernaculars
Money: Kwacha
Government: Republic

CHECK IT OUT

One of the world's highest waterfalls, the Victoria Falls is created by the Zambezi River tumbling over cliffs between Zambia and Zimbabwe. The waterfall is twice as high as Niagara Falls.

ZIMBABWE

Capital: Harare
Population: 13,182,908
Area: 150,804 sq. mi. (390,580 sq km)
Language: English, Shona, Sindebele, minor tribal dialects
Money: Dollar
Government: Parliamentary democracy

CHECK IT OUT

Zimbabwe means "stone house." Ruins of the stone palaces of African kings can be seen in many parts of the country.

STAY TUNED Hawaii will always be a top spot for surfers, but it may lose its place as the newest state. Congress is considering a change in Puerto Rico's status from U.S. commonwealth to our 51st state. A majority of Puerto Ricans voted for statehood in November 2012. Read about Hawaii on p. 131 and Puerto Rico on p. 145.

States of the United States

Alaska

Juneau

Olympia
Washington

Salem

Oregon

Idaho
Boise

Montana
Helena

North Dakota
Bismarck

South Dakota
Pierre

Wyoming

Cheyenne

Nebraska

Lincolr

Sacramento Carson City
Nevada

Salt Lake City
Utah

Denver

Colorado

Kansas

To

California

Arizona
Phoenix

Santa Fe

New Mexico

Oklah
Oklahoma

Texas

Austin

Honolulu

Hawaii

U.S. States and Their Capital Cities

ota

aul

Wisconsin

Madison ⊙

Michigan

Lansing ⊙

a

oines

Illinois

Springfield ⊙

Indiana

Indianapolis ⊙

Ohio

Columbus ⊙

New Hampshire

Vermont

Montpelier ⊙

Maine

Augusta ⊙

Concord ⊙

Massachusetts
Boston ⊙

Albany ⊙

New York

Providence ⊙
Hartford ⊙ Rhode Island

Connecticut

Pennsylvania

Harrisburg ⊙

Trenton ⊙
New Jersey

Dover ⊙
Delaware

West
Virginia

Annapolis ⋆
Maryland

erson City

Missouri

Frankfort ⊙

Kentucky

Charleston ⊙

Richmond ⊙

Virginia

Washington, DC

rkansas

le Rock ⊙

Nashville ⊙

Tennessee

Raleigh ⊙

North Carolina

Mississippi

Jackson ⊙

Alabama

Montgomery ⊙

Georgia

Atlanta ⊙

Columbia
⊙
South
Carolina

ouisiana

Baton
Rouge ⊙

Tallahassee ⊙

Florida

125

State Quarters by Release Date (and Statehood Dates)

Release Date Statehood Date

Delaware
January 4, 1999
December 7, 1787

Pennsylvania
March 8, 1999
December 12, 1787

New Jersey
May 17, 1999
December 18, 1787

Georgia
July 19, 1999
January 2, 1788

Connecticut
October 12, 1999
January 9, 1788

Massachusetts
January 3, 2000
February 6, 1788

Maryland
March 13, 2000
April 28, 1788

South Carolina
May 22, 2000
May 23, 1788

New Hampshire
August 7, 2000
June 21, 1788

Virginia
October 16, 2000
June 25, 1788

New York
January 2, 2001
July 26, 1788

North Carolina
March 12, 2001
November 21, 1789

Rhode Island
May 21, 2001
May 29, 1790

Vermont
August 6, 2001
March 4, 1791

Kentucky
October 15, 2001
June 1, 1792

Tennessee
January 2, 2002
June 1, 1796

Ohio
March 11, 2002
March 1, 1803

Louisiana
May 20, 2002
April 30, 1812

Indiana
August 2, 2002
December 11, 1816

Mississippi
October 15, 2002
December 10, 1817

Illinois
January 2, 2003
December 3, 1818

Alabama
March 17, 2003
December 14, 1819

Maine
June 2, 2003
March 15, 1820

Missouri
August 4, 2003
August 10, 1821

Arkansas
October 20, 2003
June 15, 1836

States of the United States

■ Release Date   ■ Statehood Date

Michigan
January 26, 2004
January 26, 1837

Florida
March 29, 2004
March 3, 1845

Texas
June 1, 2004
December 29, 1845

Iowa
August 30, 2004
December 28, 1846

Wisconsin
October 25, 2004
May 29, 1848

California
January 31, 2005
September 9, 1850

Minnesota
April 4, 2005
May 11, 1858

Oregon
June 6, 2005
February 14, 1859

Kansas
August 29, 2005
January 29, 1861

West Virginia
October 14, 2005
June 20, 1863

Nevada
January 31, 2006
October 31, 1864

Nebraska
April 3, 2006
March 1, 1867

Colorado
June 14, 2006
August 1, 1876

North Dakota
August 28, 2006
November 2, 1889

South Dakota
November 6, 2006
November 2, 1889

Montana
January 29, 2007
November 8, 1889

Washington
April 2, 2007
November 11, 1889

Idaho
June 4, 2007
July 3, 1890

Wyoming
September 3, 2007
July 10, 1890

Utah
November 5, 2007
January 4, 1896

Oklahoma
January 28, 2008
November 16, 1907

New Mexico
April 7, 2008
January 6, 1912

Arizona
June 2, 2008
February 14, 1912

Alaska
August 25, 2008
January 3, 1959

Hawaii
November 3, 2008
August 21, 1959

127

ALABAMA

Capital: Montgomery
Postal Code: AL
Nickname: Heart of Dixie
Flower: Camellia
Bird: Yellowhammer
Area: 52,420 sq. mi. (135,768 sq km)
Population: 4,822,023

CHECK IT OUT

Huntsville, Alabama, is the site where the first rocket that took people to the moon was built.

ALASKA

Capital: Juneau
Postal Code: AK
Nickname: Last Frontier
Flower: Forget-me-not
Bird: Willow ptarmigan
Area: 664,988 sq. mi. (1,722,319 sq km)
Population: 731,449

CHECK IT OUT

Woolly mammoth remains have been found in Alaska's frozen ground.

ARIZONA

Capital: Phoenix
Postal Code: AZ
Nickname: Grand Canyon State
Flower: Saguaro cactus blossom
Bird: Cactus wren
Area: 113,990 sq. mi. (295,235 sq km)
Population: 6,553,255

CHECK IT OUT

There are more species of hummingbirds in Arizona than in any other state.

ARKANSAS

Capital: Little Rock
Postal Code: AR
Nickname: Land of Opportunity
Flower: Apple blossom
Bird: Mockingbird
Area: 53,178 sq. mi. (137,732 sq km)
Population: 2,949,131

CHECK IT OUT

Stuttgart, Arkansas, is home to the annual World's Championship Duck Calling Contest.

CALIFORNIA

Capital: Sacramento
Postal Code: CA
Nickname: Golden State
Flower: Golden poppy
Bird: California quail
Area: 163,694 sq. mi. (423,967 sq km)
Population: 38,041,430

CHECK IT OUT

The highest and lowest points in the continental United States are in California—Mount Whitney (14,494 ft./4,418 m) and Badwater in Death Valley (282 ft./86 m below sea level).

COLORADO

Capital: Denver
Postal Code: CO
Nickname: Centennial State
Flower: Rocky Mountain columbine
Bird: Lark bunting
Area: 104,094 sq. mi. (269,604 sq km)
Population: 5,187,582

CHECK IT OUT

The streets in Victor, Colorado, were actually paved in a low grade of gold back in 1890 to make use of the low-quality ore that couldn't be refined.

CONNECTICUT

Capital: Hartford
Postal Code: CT
Nickname: Constitution State
Flower: Mountain laurel
Bird: American robin
Area: 5,544 sq. mi. (14,358 sq km)
Population: 3,590,347

CHECK IT OUT

America's first newspaper, the *Hartford Courant*, was printed in 1764 in Connecticut.

DECEMBER 7, 1787

DELAWARE

Capital: Dover
Postal Code: DE
Nickname: First State
Flower: Peach blossom
Bird: Blue hen chicken
Area: 2,489 sq. mi. (6,445 sq km)
Population: 917,092

CHECK IT OUT

Delaware was the first state to ratify the U.S. Constitution.

FLORIDA

Capital: Tallahassee
Postal Code: FL
Nickname: Sunshine State
Flower: Orange blossom
Bird: Mockingbird
Area: 65,758 sq. mi. (170,312 sq km)
Population: 19,317,568

CHECK IT OUT

Florida's name comes from the Spanish word for "flowery." Ponce de Leon named it after the beautiful flowers he saw all around when he arrived there in 1513.

Florida wildflowers

States of the United States

GEORGIA

Capital: Atlanta
Postal Code: GA
Nickname: Empire State of the South
Flower: Cherokee rose
Bird: Brown thrasher
Area: 59,425 sq. mi. (153,911 sq km)
Population: 9,919,945

CHECK IT OUT

Georgia's top crops include peaches. The "World's Largest Peach Cobbler," which uses 75 gallons (285 L) of peaches and 150 pounds (68 kg) each of sugar and flour, is the star of the annual Georgia Peach Festival.

HAWAII

Capital: Honolulu
Postal Code: HI
Nickname: Aloha State
Flower: Yellow hibiscus
Bird: Nene, or Hawaiian goose
Area: 10,926 sq. mi. (28,300 sq km)
Population: 1,392,313

CHECK IT OUT

Hawaii is made up of 132 islands. The 8 main ones are Niihau, Kauai, Oahu, Maui, Molokai, Lanai, Kahoolawe, and the Big Island of Hawaii.

IDAHO

Capital: Boise
Postal Code: ID
Nickname: Gem State
Flower: Syringa
Bird: Mountain bluebird
Area: 83,568 sq. mi. (216,442 sq km)
Population: 1,595,728

CHECK IT OUT

The largest freshwater fish ever caught in America was a white sturgeon hauled out of Idaho's Snake River in 1898. It weighed 1,500 pounds (680 kg), about as much as a grown Holstein cow.

ILLINOIS

Capital: Springfield
Postal Code: IL
Nickname: Land of Lincoln
Flower: Native violet
Bird: Cardinal
Area: 57,916 sq. mi. (150,002 sq km)
Population: 12,875,255

CHECK IT OUT

The tallest building in the United States is the Willis (formerly Sears) Tower in Chicago, measuring 1,725 feet (526 m) from the ground to the tip of the antenna.

INDIANA

Capital: Indianapolis
Postal Code: IN
Nickname: Hoosier State
Flower: Peony
Bird: Cardinal (sometimes called northern cardinal)
Area: 36,417 sq. mi. (94,321 sq km)
Population: 6,537,334

CHECK IT OUT

Santa Claus, Indiana, receives over half a million letters at Christmastime.

IOWA

Capital: Des Moines
Postal Code: IA
Nickname: Hawkeye State
Flower: Wild prairie rose
Bird: Eastern goldfinch (also called American goldfinch)
Area: 56,273 sq. mi. (145,746 sq km)
Population: 3,074,186

CHECK IT OUT

Iowa is the only state name in America that begins with two vowels.

KANSAS

Capital: Topeka
Postal Code: KS
Nickname: Sunflower State
Flower: Native sunflower
Bird: Western meadowlark
Area: 82,278 sq. mi. (213,101 sq km)
Population: 2,885,905

CHECK IT OUT

In 1905, the element helium was discovered at the University of Kansas.

KENTUCKY

Capital: Frankfort
Postal Code: KY
Nickname: Bluegrass State
Flower: Goldenrod
Bird: Northern cardinal
Area: 40,411 sq. mi. (104,665 sq km)
Population: 4,380,415

CHECK IT OUT

The Kentucky Derby, held the first Saturday in May, is the oldest annual horse race in the United States.

LOUISIANA

Capital: Baton Rouge
Postal Code: LA
Nickname: Pelican State
Flower: Magnolia
Bird: Eastern brown pelican
Area: 51,988 sq. mi. (134,649 sq km)
Population: 4,601,893

CHECK IT OUT

Louisiana is the only state divided into parishes instead of counties.

MAINE

Capital: Augusta
Postal Code: ME
Nickname: Pine Tree State
Flower: White pine cone and tassel
Bird: Black-capped chickadee
Area: 35,384 sq. mi. (91,644 sq km)
Population: 1,329,192

CHECK IT OUT

Eastport, Maine, is the first town in America to see the sunrise because it is the town farthest east.

MARYLAND

Capital: Annapolis
Postal Code: MD
Nickname: Old Line State
Flower: Black-eyed Susan
Bird: Baltimore oriole
Area: 12,406 sq. mi. (32,131 sq km)
Population: 5,884,563

CHECK IT OUT

Maryland is famous for having the first dental school in the United States.

MASSACHUSETTS

Capital: Boston
Postal Code: MA
Nickname: Bay State
Flower: Mayflower
Bird: Black-capped chickadee
Area: 10,554 sq. mi. (27,336 sq km)
Population: 6,646,144

CHECK IT OUT

Volleyball was invented in 1895 in Holyoke, Massachusetts, by gym teacher William Morgan. The game was originally called mintonette. Basketball was invented in nearby Springfield.

MICHIGAN

Capital: Lansing
Postal Code: MI
Nickname: Wolverine State
Flower: Apple blossom
Bird: American robin
Area: 96,713 sq. mi. (250,486 sq km)
Population: 9,883,360

CHECK IT OUT

With over 11,000 inland lakes and over 36,000 miles (57,936 km) of rivers and streams, Michigan has the longest freshwater shoreline in the world.

MINNESOTA

Capital: St. Paul
Postal Code: MN
Nickname: Gopher State
Flower: Pink and white lady's slipper
Bird: Common loon
Area: 86,935 sq. mi. (225,163 sq km)
Population: 5,379,139

CHECK IT OUT

The Mall of America in Bloomington, Minnesota, is 9.5 million square feet (8,825,780 sq m)—about the size of 78 football fields!

MISSISSIPPI

Capital: Jackson
Postal Code: MS
Nickname: Magnolia State
Flower: Magnolia
Bird: Mockingbird
Area: 48,432 sq. mi. (125,438 sq km)
Population: 2,984,926

CHECK IT OUT

Edward Adolf Barq Sr. invented root beer in Biloxi, Mississippi, in 1898.

135

MISSOURI

Capital: Jefferson City
Postal Code: MO
Nickname: Show Me State
Flower: Hawthorn
Bird: Eastern bluebird
Area: 69,702 sq. mi. (180,529 sq km)
Population: 6,021,988

CHECK IT OUT

The St. Louis World's Fair in 1904 was so hot that Richard Blechyden decided to serve his tea over ice—and invented iced tea.

MONTANA

Capital: Helena
Postal Code: MT
Nickname: Treasure State
Flower: Bitterroot
Bird: Western meadowlark
Area: 147,039 sq. mi. (380,831 sq km)
Population: 1,005,141

CHECK IT OUT

The average square mile (1.6 sq km) of land in Montana contains 1.4 pronghorn antelope, 1.4 elk, and 3.3 deer. Montana has the largest number of mammal species in the United States.

NEBRASKA

Capital: Lincoln
Postal Code: NE
Nickname: Cornhusker State
Flower: Goldenrod
Bird: Western meadowlark
Area: 77,349 sq. mi. (200,334 sq km)
Population: 1,855,525

CHECK IT OUT

About 95 percent of Nebraska's area is taken up by farms and ranches—a higher percentage than any other state. The state's top crop is corn.

NEVADA

Capital: Carson City
Postal Code: NV
Nickname: Silver State
Flower: Sagebrush
Bird: Mountain bluebird
Area: 110,572 sq. mi. (286,382 sq km)
Population: 2,758,931

CHECK IT OUT

The Silver State produces more gold than any other state and is the third highest producer in the world after China and South Africa.

NEW HAMPSHIRE

Capital: Concord
Postal Code: NH
Nickname: Granite State
Flower: Purple lilac
Bird: Purple finch
Area: 9,348 sq. mi. (24,210 sq km)
Population: 1,320,718

CHECK IT OUT

The winds on top of New Hampshire's Mount Washington have been recorded at speeds over 231 miles (372 km an hour—the fastest winds on Earth!

NEW JERSEY

Capital: Trenton
Postal Code: NJ
Nickname: Garden State
Flower: Purple violet
Bird: Eastern goldfinch
Area: 8,723 sq. mi. (22,592 sq km)
Population: 8,864,590

CHECK IT OUT

The street names in the game Monopoly come from real street names in Atlantic City, New Jersey.

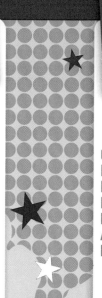

NEW MEXICO

Capital: Santa Fe
Postal Code: NM
Nickname: Land of Enchantment
Flower: Yucca flower
Bird: Roadrunner (also called greater roadrunner)
Area: 121,590 sq. mi. (314,919 sq km)
Population: 2,085,538

CHECK IT OUT

There are more than 110 caves in Carlsbad Caverns. One cave is 22 stories high and is home to tens of thousands of bats.

NEW YORK

Capital: Albany
Postal Code: NY
Nickname: Empire State
Flower: Rose
Bird: Eastern bluebird
Area: 54,555 sq. mi. (141,298 sq km)
Population: 19,570,261

CHECK IT OUT

More than 100 million people have visited the top of the Empire State Building in New York City. The building is 1,434 feet, (437 m) from the street to the top of the lightning rod.

NORTH CAROLINA

Capital: Raleigh
Postal Code: NC
Nickname: Tar Heel State
Flower: Dogwood
Bird: Cardinal
Area: 53,819 sq. mi. (139,391 sq km)
Population: 9,752,073

CHECK IT OUT

On March 7, 1914, in Fayetteville, North Carolina, George Herman "Babe" Ruth hit his first professional home run.

NORTH DAKOTA

Capital: Bismarck
Postal Code: ND
Nickname: Flickertail State
Flower: Wild prairie rose
Bird: Western meadowlark
Area: 70,698 sq. mi. (183,109 sq km)
Population: 699,628

🢂 CHECK IT OUT

Jamestown, North Dakota, is home to the World's Largest Buffalo monument. It stands 26 feet (7.9 m) high and 46 feet (14 m) long, and weighs 60 tons (54,441 kg).

OHIO

Capital: Columbus
Postal Code: OH
Nickname: Buckeye State
Flower: Scarlet carnation
Bird: Cardinal
Area: 44,825 sq. mi. (116,097 sq km)
Population: 11,544,225

🢂 CHECK IT OUT

The first traffic light in America began working on August 5, 1914, in Cleveland, Ohio.

OKLAHOMA

OKLAHOMA

Capital: Oklahoma City
Postal Code: OK
Nickname: Sooner State
Flower: Mistletoe
Bird: Scissor-tailed flycatcher
Area: 69,899 sq. mi. (181,038 sq km)
Population: 3,814,820

🢂 CHECK IT OUT

Not every state has a state amphibian, but Oklahoma does—the American bullfrog.

STATE OF OREGON

1859

OREGON

Capital: Salem
Postal Code: OR
Nickname: Beaver State
Flower: Oregon grape
Bird: Western meadowlark
Area: 98,379 sq. mi. (254,801 sq km)
Population: 3,899,353

☝CHECK IT OUT

Two pioneers founded Portland, Oregon. One was from Boston, Massachusetts, and the other was from Portland, Maine. They couldn't decide what to name the city, so they flipped a coin. Guess who won!

PENNSYLVANIA

Capital: Harrisburg
Postal Code: PA
Nickname: Keystone State
Flower: Mountain laurel
Bird: Ruffed grouse
Area: 46,055 sq. mi. (119,281 sq km)
Population: 12,763,536

☝CHECK IT OUT

In 1953, Dr. Jonas Salk created the polio vaccine at the University of Pittsburgh.

RHODE ISLAND

Capital: Providence
Postal Code: RI
Nickname: Ocean State
Flower: Violet
Bird: Rhode Island Red chicken
Area: 1,545 sq. mi. (4,001 sq km)
Population: 1,050,292

☝CHECK IT OUT

"I'm a Yankee Doodle Dandy" and "You're a Grand Old Flag" were written by George M. Cohan, who was born in Providence, Rhode Island, in 1878.

SOUTH CAROLINA

Capital: Columbia
Postal Code: SC
Nickname: Palmetto State
Flower: Yellow jessamine
Bird: Great Carolina wren
Area: 32,021 sq. mi. (82,934 sq km)
Population: 4,723,723

CHECK IT OUT

The first battle of the Civil War was fought at Fort Sumter, South Carolina.

SOUTH DAKOTA

Capital: Pierre
Postal Code: SD
Nickname: Mount Rushmore State
Flower: Pasqueflower
Bird: Ring-necked pheasant
Area: 77,116 sq. mi. (199,730 sq km)
Population: 833,354

CHECK IT OUT

The faces of George Washington, Thomas Jefferson, Theodore Roosevelt, and Abraham Lincoln are sculpted into Mount Rushmore, the world's greatest mountain carving. The carvings are taller than a four-story building.

TENNESSEE

Capital: Nashville
Postal Code: TN
Nickname: Volunteer State
Flower: Iris
Bird: Mockingbird
Area: 42,144 sq. mi. (109,154 sq km)
Population: 6,456,243

CHECK IT OUT

More than nine million people visit Smoky Mountain National Park in Tennessee every year, making it America's most visited national park. Over 30 species of salamanders and 1,500 black bears live there year-round.

TEXAS

Capital: Austin
Postal Code: TX
Nickname: Lone Star State
Flower: Bluebonnet
Bird: Mockingbird
Area: 268,597 sq. mi. (695,666 sq km)
Population: 26,059,203

!CHECK IT OUT

The name *Texas* is actually derived from a misunderstanding of *tejas*, a Caddo Indian word meaning "friend."

UTAH

Capital: Salt Lake City
Postal Code: UT
Nickname: Beehive State
Flower: Sego lily
Bird: California gull
Area: 84,897 sq. mi. (219,883 sq km)
Population: 2,855,287

!CHECK IT OUT

Utah's Great Salt Lake is several times saltier than seawater. It's so salty that you'd float on the surface of the water like a cork if you swam there!

VERMONT

Capital: Montpelier
Postal Code: VT
Nickname: Green Mountain State
Flower: Red clover
Bird: Hermit thrush
Area: 9,616 sq. mi. (24,906 sq km)
Population: 626,011

!CHECK IT OUT

Vermont is the only New England state that doesn't border the Atlantic Ocean.

VIRGINIA

Capital: Richmond
Postal Code: VA
Nickname: Old Dominion
Flower: American dogwood
Bird: Cardinal
Area: 42,775 sq. mi. (110,787 sq km)
Population: 8,185,867

CHECK IT OUT

More U.S. presidents come from Virginia than from any other state—George Washington, Thomas Jefferson, James Madison, James Monroe, William Henry Harrison, John Tyler, Zachary Taylor, and Woodrow Wilson.

WASHINGTON

Capital: Olympia
Postal Code: WA
Nickname: Evergreen State
Flower: Coast rhododendron
Bird: Willow goldfinch (also called American goldfinch)
Area: 71,298 sq. mi. (184,661 sq km)
Population: 6,897,012

CHECK IT OUT

Washington is a hotbed of volcanic activity. Mount Rainier erupted in 1969 and Mount St. Helens erupted in 1980.

WEST VIRGINIA

Capital: Charleston
Postal Code: WV
Nickname: Mountain State
Flower: Big rhododendron
Bird: Cardinal
Area: 24,230 sq. mi. (62,755 sq km)
Population: 1,855,413

CHECK IT OUT

Before the Civil War, West Virginia was part of Virginia. It became a separate state and remained part of the Union when Virginia decided to secede at the dawn of the war.

1848

WISCONSIN

Capital: Madison
Postal Code: WI
Nickname: Badger State
Flower: Wood violet
Bird: American robin
Area: 65,496 sq. mi. (169,636 sq km)
Population: 5,726,398

ⓘ CHECK IT OUT

Wisconsin produces 40 percent of all the cheese and 20 percent of all the butter melted, slathered, spread, and devoured in the United States. No wonder folks from Wisconsin are sometimes called "cheeseheads."

WYOMING

Capital: Cheyenne
Postal Code: WY
Nickname: Equality State
Flower: Indian paintbrush
Bird: Western meadowlark
Area: 97,812 sq. mi. (253,334 sq km)
Population: 576,412

ⓘ CHECK IT OUT

Devils Tower in northeastern Wyoming was the first national monument. It has been considered a sacred site by Northern Plains tribes for thousands of years.

States of the United States

144

Washington, DC
Our Nation's Capital

Every state has a capital, the city where all the state's official government business takes place. Our country's capital, Washington, DC, is the center for all national, or federal, business. But our nation's capital isn't located in a state. It's part of a federal district, the District of Columbia. Congress wanted the capital to be in a district, not a state, so as not to favor any one state above the others.

The city is named after our first president, George Washington, who chose its location in 1791. It became the capital in 1800. Before that the center of the federal government was Philadelphia, Pennsylvania.

The United States Capitol

WASHINGTON, DC

Flower: American Beauty rose
Area: 68 sq. mi. (177 sq km)
Population: 632,323
Government: Federal district under the authority of Congress; mayor and city council, elected to four-year terms, run the local government

❗CHECK IT OUT

The White House, at 1600 Pennsylvania Ave., is the official presidential residence. George Washington is the only U.S. president who never lived there.

PUERTO RICO

Besides the 50 states and the District of Columbia, the United States also includes a number of commonwealths and territories. A commonwealth has its own constitution and has more rights and independence than a territory, but neither one has all the rights of a state.

The largest commonwealth is Puerto Rico, which is made up of one large island and three smaller ones in the Caribbean Sea. Puerto Rico was given to the United States by Spain in 1898 and became a commonwealth in 1952.

PUERTO RICO

Capital: San Juan
Area: 5,325 sq. mi. (13,791 sq km)
Population: 3,667,084
Language: Spanish, English
Money: U.S. dollar
Goverment: U.S. territory with commonwealth status

❗CHECK IT OUT

Puerto Ricans are American citizens, but they cannot vote in U.S. presidential elections.

Other U.S. Commonwealths and Territories

The Northern Mariana Islands in the North Pacific Ocean are the only other U.S. commonwealth. U.S. territories are:

- American Samoa
- Guam
- The U.S. Virgin Islands

The United States Minor Outlying Islands:

- Midway Islands
- Johnston Atoll
- Navassa Island
- Baker, Howland, and Jarvis Islands
- Wake Island
- Kingman Reef
- Palmyra Atoll

PCGames

SAVE YOUR FAVORITE TOKEN OR IT'S LOCKED AWAY FOREVE

Vote now!

MONOPOLY

BREAKING NEWS

There's a new cat on board! Ten million Monopoly fans from 120 countries voted on Facebook to replace one of its pieces, the iron, with a cat. Monopoly was created more than 100 years ago and became really popular in the Great Depression of the 1930s, to help people forget their real-life money troubles.

Top 10 Best-Selling Video Games of 2012 (Any Platform)

1. Call of Duty: Black Ops II
2. Madden NFL 13
3. Halo 4
4. Assassins Creed III
5. Just Dance 4
6. NBA 2K13
7. Borderlands 2
8. Call of Duty: Modern Warfare 3
9. Lego Batman 2: DC Super Heroes
10. Fifa Soccer 13

Top 10 Best-Reviewed Video Games of 2012

Title	Platform
The Walking Dead: The Game	Xbox 360
Persona 4 Golden	PS Vita
Mass Effect 3	PS3
Mass Effect 3	Xbox 360
Journey	PS3
Xenoblade Chronicles	Wii
Dishonored	PC
Mark of the Ninja	PC
Borderlands 2	PS3
Far Cry 3	PS3

Top Ten Board Games of 2012

Video games are great, but sometimes it's fun to get unplugged. These board games were tops with teenagers and adults in 2012.

Cranium Wow Game

Loaded Questions

Apples to Apples Party Box

Deluxe Turntable Scrabble

Monopoly

Boxers or Briefs?

Deluxe Pit

TV Scene It? The DVD Game

Scene It? Music Edition

Catch Phrase!

Top 10 Games Played on Facebook
(April 6, 2013)

Candy Crush Saga
FarmVille 2
Texas HoldEm Poker
Pet Rescue Saga
Diamond Dash
Bubble Witch Saga
CoasterVille
Bubble Safari
Criminal Case
Words with Friends

Most-Downloaded Free iPad Game Apps of 2012

Angry Birds HD*

Angry Birds Rio HD*

Words with Friends HD

Fruit Ninja HD

Angry Birds Seasons HD*

Solitaire

*Also one of the 25 most downloaded apps of all time

Carrier 1:37 PM

Most-Downloaded Free iPhone Game Apps of 2012

Words with Friends Free

Angry Birds Free

Paper Toss

PAC-MAN Lite

Temple Run

Touch Hockey

Angry Birds Lite

Fruit Ninja Lite

A geyser is an underground spring heated by Earth's magma until it bursts out in a fountain of steam and hot water. Yellowstone National Park in Wyoming has about 500 geysers, more than anyplace else in the world. However, Iceland is so famous for its geysers, glaciers, and waterfalls that many thousands of tourists visit every year. That figure is expected to hit a million by 2015. The word "geyser" comes from an Icelandic word meaning "to gush."

Geography
World & U.S.

How to Read a Map

Directions

When you're reading a map, how do you figure out which way is which? On most—but not all—maps:

⬆ Up means north   ⬇ Down means south   ⬅ Left means west   ➡ Right means east

Some maps are turned or angled so that north is not straight up. Always look for a symbol called a compass rose to show you exactly where north is on the map you're reading.

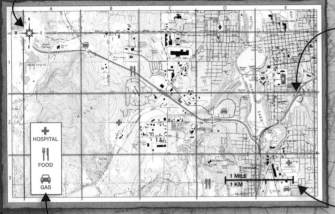

Location

Maps that show large areas such as countries and continents include lines of longitude and latitude. Maps of cities and streets are divided into blocks called grids. Grid maps have numbers on one side and letters on another. They also have an index that gives a number–letter combination for every place on the map.

Shapes and Symbols

Every picture, object, shape, and line on a map stands for something. A tiny red airplane stands for an airport. A thick line is one kind of road and a dotted line is another. A map's legend, or key, shows these symbols and explains what they stand for.

Distance

You can look at a map and think it's a hop, skip, and a jump from Maine to Maryland, but it's really a few million hops. The map scale shows you how many miles (or km) a certain length of map represents.

A Map Is a Map Is a Map . . .

All maps are not created equal. There are different maps for different purposes:

- A bathymetric map shows the depths and contours of the bottom of a body of water.
- A geological map shows earthquake faults, volcanoes, minerals, rock types, underground water, and landslide areas.
- A physical map shows mountains, lakes, and rivers.
- A planimetric map shows horizontal (not vertical, such as elevations) features.
- A political map shows boundaries of cities, states, countries, and provinces.
- A relief map uses different colors to show different elevations.
- A road map shows roads, highways, cities, and towns.
- A topographic map shows elevations.
- A weather map shows temperatures, fronts, rain, snow, sleet, storms, fog, and other weather conditions.

Geographical Terms

Term	Definition
Altitude	the distance above sea level
Archipelago	a group or chain of islands clustered together in an ocean or sea
Atlas	a book of maps
Atoll	an ocean island made out of an underwater ring of coral
Bay	a body of water protected and partly surrounded by land
Cartographer	a mapmaker
Compass rose	a four-pointed design on a map that shows north, south, east, and west
Continent	one of Earth's seven largest land masses
Degree	a unit of measurement used to calculate longitude and latitude
Delta	a flat, triangular piece of land that fans out at the mouth of a river
Elevation	the height of a point on the earth's surface above sea level
Equator	an imaginary circle around the earth halfway between the North Pole and the South Pole
Globe	a 3-D spherical map of the earth
GPS	short for Global Positioning System; finds longitude and latitude by bouncing information off satellites in space
Grid	a crisscross pattern of lines forming squares on a map
Hemisphere	one half of the world
Island	land that is surrounded by water on all sides
Isthmus	a narrow strip of land (with water on both sides) that connects two larger land areas
Latitude	distance north or south of the equator
Legend	a key to the symbols on a map
Longitude	distance east or west of the prime meridian
Map	a flat picture of a place drawn to scale
Meridian	an imaginary line running north and south and looping around the poles used to measure longitude
North Pole	the most northerly point on Earth
Ocean	the body of salt water surrounding the great land masses and divided by the land masses into several distinct portions
Parallel	an imaginary line parallel to the equator, used to measure latitude
Peninsula	a body of land surrounded by water on three sides
Scale	a tool on a map that helps calculate real distance
Sea level	the surface of the ocean
South Pole	the most southerly point on Earth
Strait	a narrow body of water that connects two larger bodies
Topography	the physical features of a place, such as mountains

Continental Drift

Maps are all well and good if things don't change. "Go east one mile and turn south and find Mt. Crumpet" works only if Mt. Crumpet doesn't decide to walk a few miles north. Sound ridiculous? Actually, the earth didn't always look like it does today. About 250 million years ago, all the continents were scrunched together in one lump called Pangaea.

Gradually the land drifted and changed into the seven continents we know today in a process called continental drift. And the land is still moving.

EUROPE and ASIA

NORTH AMERICA

SOUTH AMERICA

AFRICA

INDIA

ANTARCTICA

AUSTRALIA

Pangaea

Journey to the Center of the Earth

Earth isn't just one big blue ball with the same stuff all the way through. It's made up of layers.

The part we walk around on is the crust, or lithosphere. It's only about 60 miles (100 km) deep.

Beneath the lithosphere is the mantle. It's a layer about 1,800 miles (2,897 km) deep.

Beneath that is the core, which is made of two parts:

The outer core (1,375 miles, or 2,200 km, thick) is almost as big as the Moon and made up of soupy molten iron.

The inner core is about 781 miles (1,250 km) thick and about as hot as the surface of the Sun.

Earth's Layers

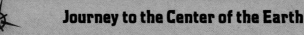

The Continents Today

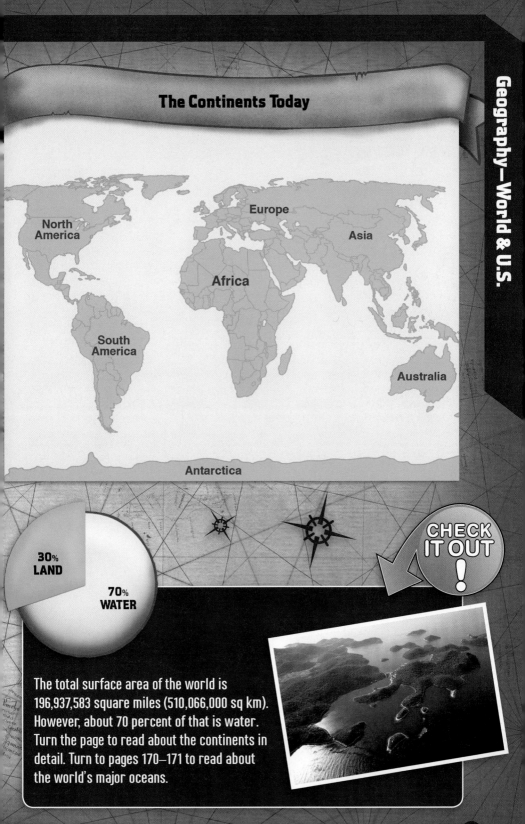

North America

Europe

Asia

Africa

South America

Australia

Antarctica

30% LAND

70% WATER

CHECK IT OUT !

The total surface area of the world is 196,937,583 square miles (510,066,000 sq km). However, about 70 percent of that is water. Turn the page to read about the continents in detail. Turn to pages 170–171 to read about the world's major oceans.

Arctic Ocean
LAND

Barents Sea

Kara Sea

Laptev Sea

East Siberian Sea

Istan

NEW SIBERIAN ISLANDS

SEVERNAYA ZEMLYA

NOVAYA ZEMLYA

Tiksi

Yakutsk

Arctic Circle

Noril'sk

SIBERIA

RUSSIA

VERKHOYANSK KHREBET

Chita

Nizhniy Novgorod

Kazan'

Perm'

Yekaterinburg

Chelyabinsk

Omsk

Krasnoyarsk

Novosibirsk

Irkutsk

Samara

Ufa

Astana

Qaraghandy (Karaganda)

KAZAKHSTAN

Ulaanbaatar

MONGOLIA

Sheny

GOBI DESERT

DA HINGGAN LING

Atryaū (Atryau)

Aral Sea

Lake Balkhash

Almaty

Ürümqi

Baotou

Beijing

Tbilisi

GEO.

ARM.

Yerevan

AZERBAIJAN

Baku

Tabriz

Caspian Sea

QIZIL QUM

UZBEKISTAN

TURKMENISTAN

Ashgabat

Tashkent

Bishkek

KYRGYZSTAN

Dushanbe

TAJIKISTAN

Kashi

TIEN SHAN

TAKLA MAKAN DESERT

Lanzhou

Tianjin

Taiyuan

Jinan

CHINA

Xi'an

Zhengzhou

Nanjin

KARAKUM

Tehran

Esfahān

Mashhad

ZAGROS MTS.

IRAN

Shīrāz

AFGHANISTAN

Kabul

Kandahār

Islamabad

Faisalābād

Quetta

Lahore

PAKISTAN

ALTUN MOUNTAINS

QING ZANG GAOYUAN

Mt. Everest (highest point in the world) (8850 m)

Lhasa

Chengdu

Chongqing

Changsha

Wuhan

Guiyang

Kunming

Guangzhou

Nanning

Ho

Macau

Bandar 'Abbās

Doha

QATAR

Abu Dhabi

U.A.E.

Muscat

SAUDI ARABIA

OMAN

Persian Gulf

Karāchi

Ludhiāna

New Delhi

Jaipur

Lucknow

Kānpur

NEPAL

Kathmandu

Patna

BHUTAN

Thimphu

BANGLADESH

Dhaka

Chittagong

Mandalay

Hanoi

Haiphong

Hainan Dao

LAOS

Vientiane

Da Nang

Ahmadābād

Indore

Surat

Nāgpur

INDIA

Kolkata

BURMA

Nay Pyi Taw

Rangoon

THAILAND

Bangkok

VIETNAM

SPRATLY ISLANDS

Mumbai

Pune

Hyderābād

DECCAN

WESTERN GHATS

EASTERN GHATS

Vishākhapatnam

Bay of Bengal

Arabian Sea

Bengaluru

Chennai

LAKSHADWEEP (INDIA)

Cochin

Jaffna

ANDAMAN ISLANDS (INDIA)

Andaman Sea

CAMBODIA

Phnom Penh

Ho Chi Minh City

Gulf of Thailand

Bandar Begav

BRUNE

Laccadive Sea

MALDIVES

Male

Colombo

SRI LANKA

NICOBAR ISLANDS (INDIA)

MALAYSIA

Kuala Lumpur

SINGAPORE

Singapore

Pontianak

MALAYS

Medan

Sumatra

Palembang

INDO

Jakarta

Semarang

Java

Bandung

Christmas Island (AUSTL.)

ASIA can be described best in one word: BIG. It's the biggest continent in size, covering about 30 percent of Earth's land area. It's biggest in population, with about 60 percent of all the people in the world living there. And in terms of contributions to the world, it's enormous. Asians founded the first cities; set up the first legal system; invented writing paper, printing, the magnetic compass, and gunpowder; and much more. All of the world's major religions began in Asia.

Asia rules in world-class geographical features, too. It has:
- The highest mountain range, the Himalayas, as well as the most mountains of any continent.
- The highest point on Earth, Mt. Everest, and the lowest, the Dead Sea.

Asia at a Glance

Area
17,226,200 sq. mi. (44,614,000 sq km)

Population
4,265,251,000

Number of countries
50

Largest country
China
3,705,407 sq. mi. (9,596,960 sq km)

Most populated urban area
Tokyo, Japan
37,217,400 people

Longest river
Yangtze, China
3,915 mi. (6,300 km)

Largest lake
Lake Baikal, Russia
12,200 sq. mi. (31,500 sq km)

Highest point
Mt. Everest, Nepal/China
29,035 ft. (8,850 m) above sea level

Lowest point
Dead Sea, Israel/Jordan
1,380 ft. (421 m) below sea level

CHECK IT OUT!

Asia has some of the world's largest international business centers, such as Tokyo, Japan; Singapore; and Hong Kong. Yet about half of all Asians are farmers.

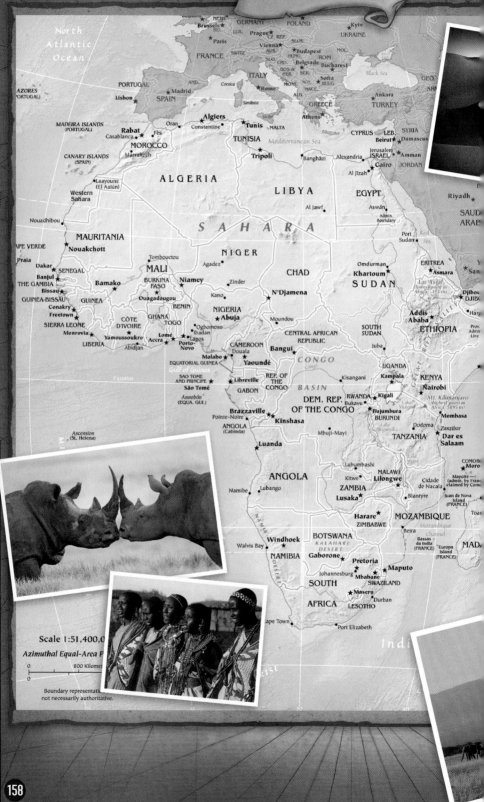

AFRICA is second to Asia in area and population, but it tops all continents in other categories:
- Biggest desert: The Sahara, covering about 3.5 million square miles (9 million sq km), or about one-third of the continent
- Longest freshwater lake: Lake Tanganyika, 420 miles (680 km)
- Most independent countries: 54

Africa is a land of treasures, from the lions, giraffes, rhinos, and other spectacular wildlife that inhabit its rain forests and grasslands to its rich supplies of gold and diamonds. However, most Africans remain poor because of drought, famine, disease, and other ongoing serious problems.

Africa at a Glance

Area
11,684,000 sq. mi. (30,262,000 sq km)

Population
1,099,181,000

Largest country
Algeria
919,595 sq. mi. (2,381,740 sq km)

Most populated urban area
Cairo, Egypt
11,169,000 people

Longest river
Nile
4,132 mi. (6,650 km)

Largest lake
Lake Victoria, Tanzania/Uganda/Kenya
26,828 sq. mi. (69,484 sq km)

Highest point
Mount Kilimanjaro, Tanzania
19,340 ft. (5,895 m) above sea level

Lowest point
Lake Assal, Djibouti
509 ft. (155 m) below sea level

CHECK IT OUT!

From fossils found in Africa, scientists say that the earliest human beings lived here about 2 million years ago.

NORTH AMERICA

RUSSIA

Cherskiy
Pevek
East Siberian Sea
Providehiya
Anadyr'
Chukchi Sea
Bering Strait
Bering Sea
Nome
Bethel

Arctic Ocean

Alert

Greenl
(DENMA

Ellesmere Island
Qaanaaq (Thule)

QUEEN ELIZABETH ISLANDS

Baffin Bay

Barrow

Prudhoe Bay

Resolute

Pond Inlet

Banks Island

Beaufort Sea

Victoria Island

Gjoa Haven

Baffin Island

UNITED STATES

Mt. McKinley (highest point in North America, 6194 m)

Inuvik

Cambridge Bay

Iqaluit

Fairbanks

ALASKA

Anchorage
Valdez
Gulf of Alaska
ALEUTIAN

Dawson

Great Bear Lake

Rankin Inlet

CANADA

Whitehorse

Great Slave Lake

Arviat

Hudson Bay

Juneau

Fort Nelson

Lake Athabasca

Churchill

Chisasibi

C (S

ROCKY MOUNTAINS

Prince George

Fort McMurray

Edmonton

Saskatoon

Lake Winnipeg

Moosonee

North

Vancouver

Calgary

Regina

Sudbury   Otta
Thunder Bay

Victoria

Seattle

Winnipeg

Lake Superior

M
Lak
Hur

Pacific

Portland

CASCADES

Boise

Fargo

Lake Michigan

Toronto
Hamilton
London   Detroit
Cleveland
Pittsburgh
Columbus
Cincinnati

Ocean

Minneapolis

Milwaukee

Chicago

SIERRA NEVADA

Great Salt Lake

Salt Lake City

Omaha

Indianapolis

Saint Louis

Louisville

Sacramento
San Francisco
San Jose
Fresno

Death Valley (lowest point in North America, -86 m)

Denver

Kansas City

UNITED

Nashville

Memphis

Atlan

Las Vegas

STATES

Los Angeles
San Diego
Tijuana
Mexicali

Albuquerque

Phoenix

Oklahoma City

Birminghar

Tucson

Dallas

Jackson

El Paso

Ciudad Juárez

Austin

Houston

New Orleans

Hermosillo

Chihuahua

San Antonio

Guadeloupe

Gulf of Mexico

Torreón

Monterrey

Matamoros

La Paz

Culiacán

SIERRA MADRE

MEXICO

San Luis Potosi

Tampico

Mérida

Scale: 1:36,000,000

Aguascalientes
León
Guadalajara
Morelia
Toluca

Querétaro

Mexico

Veracruz

Bahía de Campeche

BEL
Belm

Lambert Conformal Conic Projection, standard parallels 25°N and 77°N

ISLAS REVILLAGIGEDO (MEXICO)

Puebla

Oaxaca

MIDDLE AMERICA TRENCH

HO
Te

SIERRA MADRE DEL SUR

Acapulco

Guatemala

| 0 | 300 | 600 Kilometers |
| 0 | 300 | 600 Miles |

GUATEMALA

San Salvador
EL SALVADOR

NORTH AMERICA

NORTH AMERICA, the third-largest continent in area and the fourth-largest in population, is all about variety. The continent has an enormous mix of climates and habitats, from the frozen Arctic to warm, humid Central American rain forests, which support an amazing number of plants and animals. North American human inhabitants live in a variety of environments, too, from rural farms to such bustling, densely populated urban centers as Mexico City. Many—but not all—North Americans enjoy a high standard of living compared to inhabitants of the rest of the world.

Of all the continents, North America has:
- The world's largest island: Greenland,* 836,330 square miles (2,166,086, sq km)
- The world's largest freshwater lake: Lake Superior
- The longest coastline: 190,000 miles (300,000 km), or more than 60,000 times the distance across the Atlantic Ocean

*Except for Australia, which is classified as a continent as well as an island

North America at a Glance

Area
9,352,000 sq. mi. (24,220,000 sq km)

Population
551,676,000

Number of countries
23

Largest country
Canada
3,855,101 sq. mi. (9,984,670 sq km)

Most populated urban area
Mexico City, Mexico
20,445,800 people

Longest river
Mississippi-Missouri, United States
3,710 mi. (5,971 km) long

Largest lake
Lake Superior, United States/Canada
31,700 sq. mi. (82,100 sq km)

Highest point
Mt. McKinley, Alaska
20,320 ft. (6,194 m) above sea level

Lowest point
Death Valley, California
282 ft. (86 m) below sea level

CHECK IT OUT!

Nearly half of all Canadians and about a third of Americans come from English, Irish, Scottish, or Welsh ancestors. However, North America's first settlers were from Asia. Scientists say that these Native Americans, now sometimes called Indians, walked across the Bering Strait, which was dry land between 15,000 and 35,000 years ago. Before they came, there were no people on the continent.

Tegucigalpa
Providencia (COLOMBIA)
Aruba (NETH.)
Antilles (NETH.)
ST. VINCENT AND THE GRENADINES
BARBADOS
GRENADA
NICARAGUA
Managua
Isla de San Andrés (COLOMBIA)
Barranquilla
Maracaibo
Caracas
Port-of-Spain
TRINIDAD AND TOBAGO
San José
Panama
Cartagena
Barquisimeto
Valencia
Barcelona
COSTA RICA
PANAMA
Cúcuta
San Cristobal
Ciudad Guayana
Georgetown
Paramaribo
Cayenne
Medellín
Bucaramanga
VENEZUELA
GUYANA
SURINAME
French Guiana (FRANCE)
Pereira
Ibague
Bogotá
Rio Orinoco
GUIANA HIGHLAND
Isla de Malpelo (COLOMBIA)
Cali
COLOMBIA
Boa Vista
Macapá
Quito
Equator
ECUADOR
Guayaquil
A M A Z O N
Rio Negro
Manaus
Santarém
Belém
Cuenca
Iquitos
Rio Amazon
Rio Xingu
Piura
B A S I N
Rio Madeira
Chiclayo
Pucallpa
Rio Branco
Pôrto Velho
Rio Tapajós
Rio Tocantins
Trujillo
Huánuco
PERU
Huancayo
Cusco
Trinidad
MATO GROSSO PLATEAU
Cuiabá
BRAZIL
BRAZIL
Brasília
Lima
Ica
B R A Z I L
Arequipa
La Paz
BOLIVIA
Golânia
HIGHL
Arica
Cochabamba
Santa Cruz
Uberlândia
Sucre
Potosí
Iquique
ATACAMA DESERT
Campo Grande
Rio Paraná
Londrina
Campinas
Antofagasta
Salta
PARAGUAY
São Paulo
Santos
Ambrosio (CHILE)
San Miguel de Tucumán
Asunción
Ciudad del Este
Curitiba
Joinvile
Resistencia
Florianópolis
CHILE
Cerro Aconcagua (highest point in South America, 6962 m)
Córdoba
Santa Fe
Porto Alegre
Valparaíso
Mendoza
Rosario
Salto
URUGUAY
Santiago
PAMPAS
Buenos Aires
La Plata
Montevideo
Concepcion
ARGENTINA
Bahía Blanca
Temuco
San Carlos de Bariloche
Puerto Montt
ANDES
PATAGONIA
Comodoro Rivadavia
Laguna del Carbón (lowest point in South America and the Western Hemisphere, -105 m)
Río Gallegos
Stanley
Falkland Islands (Islas Malvinas) (administered by U.K., claimed by ARGENTINA)
Punta Arenas
Strait of Magellan
Ushuaia
Cape Horn

South Pacific Ocean

PERU-CHILE TRENCH

NAZCA RIDGE

COCOS RIDGE

Scale 1:35,000,000
Azimuthal Equal-Area Projection

0   500 Kilometers
0   500 Miles

Boundary representation is not necessarily authoritative.

162

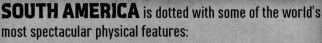

SOUTH AMERICA is dotted with some of the world's most spectacular physical features:

- The longest mountain range, the Andes, stretching 4,500 miles (7,200 km) from Chile in the south, to Venezuela and Panama in the north.
- The largest rain forest, the Amazon, covering about 2 million square miles (5.2 million sq km), or two-fifths of the continent.
- The highest waterfall, Angel Falls in Venezuela, plunging 3,212 feet (979 m).

South America is the fourth-largest continent, but only Australia and Antarctica have fewer people. About 80 percent of the people live in urban areas such as São Paulo, Brazil. South America's economy is growing fast, led by Brazil, Argentina, Colombia, and Chile.

South America at a Glance

Area
6,887,000 sq. mi. (17,836,000 sq km)

Population
402,047,000

Number of countries
12

Largest country
Brazil
3,287,613 sq. mi. (8,514,877 sq km)

Most populated urban area
São Paulo, Brazil
19,924,458 people

Longest river
Amazon, Brazil
4,000 mi. (6,437 km)

Largest lake
Lake Maracaibo, Venezuela
5,217 sq. mi. (13,512 sq km)

Highest point
Aconcagua, Argentina
22,835 ft. (6,960 m) above sea level

Lowest point
Valdes Peninsula, Argentina
131 ft. (40 m) below sea level

CHECK IT OUT!

The Amazon rain forest is home to an estimated one in ten plant and animal species on Earth.

Jan Mayen
(NORWAY)

Greenland
Sea

Nordkapp

Hammerfest

Denmark
Strait

Norwegian Sea

Tromsø

Kiruna

Reykjavik
ICELAND

Arctic Circle

NORWAY

Luleå

Oulu

Trondheim

SWEDEN

Umeå

FINLA

Faroe Islands
(DENMARK)

Tórshavn

Tampere

Gulf
of
Bothnia

Turku

Helsinki

Gävle

SHETLAND
ISLANDS

Bergen

ÅLAND
ISLANDS

Ta

EST

ORKNEY
ISLANDS

Oslo

Stockholm

HEBRIDES

Stavanger

Göteborg

Gotland

Riga

Aberdeen

Baltic Sea

Öland

LITHU-

Glasgow
Edinburgh

North
Sea

DENMARK

Malmö

Bornholm

Vil

Belfast

UNITED

Isle
of
Man
(U.K.)

Irish
Sea

Leeds

Copenhagen

Kaliningrad
RUSSIA

Dublin

Liverpool
Manchester

Gdańsk

IRELAND

KINGDOM

Birmingham

Hamburg

Bremen

Berlin

Poznań

Warsaw

POLAND

Cardiff

Amsterdam

NETH.

Rotterdam

Essen

Leipzig

Łódź

Celtic
Sea

London

Brussels

Lille

BEL.

Cologne

Bonn

GERMANY

Wrocław

Prague

CZECH REPUBLIC

Kraków

English Channel

Guernsey (U.K.)
Jersey (U.K.)

Frankfurt

Brno

SLOVAKIA

Paris

LUX.

Luxembourg

Strasbourg

Stuttgart

Munich

Bratislava

Vienna

Budapes

Nantes

LIECH.

Loire

Zürich
Vaduz

Bern
SWITZ.

AUSTRIA

HUNGARY

Bay of
Biscay

Geneva

FRANCE

MASSIF
CENTRAL

Lyon

Milan

Venice

SLOVENIA

Ljubljana

Zagreb

Turin

Danube

Bordeaux

Genoa

Ligurian
Sea

SAN
MARINO

BOSNIA AND
HERZEGOVINA

CROATIA

Belg

A Coruña

Bilbao

Toulouse

MONACO

Florence

Sarajevo

MONT.

Porto

Zaragoza

**Andorra
la Vella**

ANDORRA

Marseille

Corsica

ITALY

Adriatic
Sea

Podgorica

Tirana

PYRENEES

Barcelona

VATICAN
CITY

Rome

AL

PORTUGAL

Madrid

Balearic
Sea

Sardinia

Naples

Tyrrhenian
Sea

Lisbon

SPAIN

Valencia

Ionian
Sea

Sevilla

BALEARIC
ISLANDS

Cagliari

Palermo

Gibraltar
(U.K.)

Málaga

Mediterranean Sea

Sicily

Ceuta
(SPAIN)

Alborán
Sea

Melilla
(SPAIN)

Oran

Algiers

Tunis

Valletta

MALTA

Scale 1:

Lambert Conform
standard paral

Rabat

Casablanca

ALGERIA

TUNISIA

MOROCCO

EUROPE is a small continent divided into many individual countries, with at least 50 different languages and up to 100 different dialects spoken. With the third-largest population and the second-smallest area of any continent, Europe is densely populated. Still, there's plenty of natural beauty in its rivers, lakes, canals, and towering mountain ranges such as the Urals and the Alps. Straddling the border between Europe and Asia is the largest inland body of water in the world, the saltwater Caspian Sea, which covers 149,200 square miles (386,400 sq km). European contributions in art, music, philosophy, and culture formed the basis for Western civilization.

Europe at a Glance

Area
4,033,000 sq. mi. (10,445,000 sq km)
Population
740,794,000
Number of countries
49
Largest country (entirely in Europe)
Ukraine
233,090 sq. mi. (603,628 sq km)
Most populated urban area
Moscow, Russia
11,620,600 people
Longest river
Volga, Russia
2,194 mi. (3,531 km) long
Largest lake
Lake Ladoga, Russia
6,835 sq. mi. (17,702 sq km)
Highest point
Mt. Elbrus, Russia
18,510 ft. (5,642 m) above sea level
Lowest point
Shore of the Caspian Sea
92 ft. (28 m) below sea level

CHECK IT OUT!

Europe has some of the world's longest railroad tunnels, including the Channel Tunnel, or Chunnel, which runs 31.1 miles (50 km) under the English Channel and connects the United Kingdom and France.

South Atlantic
Ocean

area of
enlargement

Queen Maud Land

Enderby
Land

Halley

Weddell Sea

Mac. Robertson
Land

Palmer
Land

Ronne
Ice Shelf

80

Bellingshausen
Sea

Ellsworth

Vinson Massif
(highest point in Antarctica, 4897 m)

South Pole
2800 m.

Peter I Island

Land

▽ Bentley Subglacial Trench
(lowest point in Antarctica, -2540 m)

Marie Byrd
Land

Ross
Ice Shelf

Amundsen
Sea

80

Ross Sea

average minimum
extent of sea ice

Victoria Land

Wilk

70

Scott
Island

Antarctic Circle

BALLENY
ISLANDS

South
Pacific
Ocean

70

ANTARCTICA is the southernmost continent and the coldest place on Earth. It's almost entirely covered with ice that in some places is ten times as high as Chicago's Willis Tower, the tallest building in the United States. Gusts of wind up to 120 miles per hour (190 kph) make it feel even colder.

Antarctica is so cold, windy, and dry that humans never settled there. There are no countries, cities, or towns. However, researchers and scientists from different countries come to study earthquakes, the environment, weather, and more at scientific stations established by 19 countries. Some of these nations have claimed parts of Antarctica as their national territory, although other countries do not recognize the claims.

Few land animals can survive the continent's harsh conditions. The biggest one is a wingless insect called a midge, which is only one-half inch long. However, a great variety of whales, seals, penguins, and fish live in and near the surrounding ocean.

Antarctica at a Glance

Area
About 5,400,000 sq. mi. (14,000,000 sq km)

Population
No native people, but researchers come for various periods

Number of countries claiming territory
7

Number of research stations
60

Longest river
Onyx River 19 mi. (31 km) long

Highest point
Vinson Massif
16,050 ft. (4,892 m) above sea level

Lowest point
Bentley Subglacial Trench
8,383 ft. (2,555 m) below sea level

CHECK IT OUT !

The ice sheets covering Antarctica form the largest body of fresh water or ice in the world—7.25 million cubic miles (30 million cubic km), or about 70 percent of the world's fresh water.

Oceania
(Including Australia)

Equator

Samarinda · Palu
Balikpapan
Banjarmasin
Makassar
Celebes
Kendari
Molucca Sea
Ternate
Sorong
Biak
Jayapura
Wewak
New Ireland
Buru
Ceram
Ambon
PAPUA NEW GUINEA
Madang
Boug
Jaya Sea
Surabaya
INDONESIA
Banda Sea
New Guinea
Mount Hagen
Lae
New Britain
Java
Bali
Denpasar
Sumbawa
Lombok
Flores
Kupang
Dili
TIMOR-LESTE
Awara
Solomon Sea
Sumba
Timor
Timor Sea
Port Moresby
Gu
Arafura Sea
Ashmore and
Cartier Island
(AUSTRALIA)
Darwin
Torres Strait
Indian Ocean
Gulf of Carpentaria
Cor
Isl
C
KING LEOPOLD RANGE
MACDONNELL RANGE
Cairns
Townsville
-20-
Port Hedland
HAMMERSLEY RANGE
GREAT SANDY DESERT
Mount Isa
Mackay
GREAT DIVIDING RANGE
Alice Springs
Rockhampton
Gladstone
GIBSON DESERT
AUSTRALIA
SIMPSON DESERT
Toowoomba
Brisbane
Geraldton
GREAT VICTORIA DESERT
Lake Eyre
(lowest point in Australia, -15 m)
Gold Coast
Kalgoorlie
DARLING RANGE
FLINDERS RANGE
Broken Hill
Perth
Rockingham
Bunbury
Whyalla
Newcastle
Sydney
Wollongong
Esperance
Adelaide
Canberra
Mount Kosciuszko
(highest point in Australia, 2229 m)
Tas
Se
Great Australian
Bight
Geelong
Melbourne
-40-
Bass Strait

Pacific Islands

Johnston Atoll
(U.S.)

North Pacific Ocean

CLARION FRACTURE

Enewetak
MARSHALL ISLANDS
Kingman Reef
(U.S.)
CLIPPERTON FRACTURE ZONE
Pohnpei
Palikir
Kwajalein
Majuro
Palmyra Atoll
(U.S.)
Kiritimati
(Christmas Island)
(KIRIBATI)
KIRIBATI
(GILBERT ISLANDS)
Howland Island
(U.S.)
Equator
Tarawa
Baker Island
(U.S.)
Jarvis Island
(U.S.)
LINE ISLANDS
ÎLES MARQUISES
Yaren District ★
NAURU
Banaba
RAWAKI
(PHOENIX ISLANDS)
Bougainville
SOLOMON ISLANDS
KIRIBATI
KIRIBATI
Honiara
SANTA CRUZ ISLANDS
TUVALU
Funafuti
Tokelau
(N.Z.)
Guadalcanal
Rotuma
Swains Island
Cook Islands
(N.Z.)
SOCIETY ISLANDS
ARCHIPEL DES TUAMOTU
Coral Sea
Wallis and Futuna
(FRANCE)
Mata-Utu
SAMOA
Apia
Pago Pago
American Samoa
(U.S.)
Papeete
Tahiti
VANUATU
FIJI
Vanua Levu
TONGA
New Caledonia
(FRANCE)
Port-Vila
Suva
Viti Levu
Alofi
Niue
(N.Z.)
Avarua
French Polynesia
(FRANCE)
Mururoa
Noumea
Ceva-i-Ra
Nuku'Alofa
Adamston
Minerva Reefs
Tropic of Capricorn
ÎLES TUBUAI
ston
Kingston
Norfolk Island
(AUSTRALIA)
KERMADEC ISLANDS
(N.Z.)
sbane

OCEANIA is a large geographical area that includes Australia, New Zealand, Papua New Guinea, 11 other independent countries, and thousands of smaller islands. Australia is the world's smallest continent and the only continent that is also a country. Because Australia is surrounded by water, it is also technically an island.

Most of Australia is low and flat, with deserts covering about one-third of the continent. The world's largest coral reef, the Great Barrier Reef, is in the Coral Sea off the coast of Queensland in northeast Australia. Huge cattle and sheep ranches make Australia a leading producer of beef, mutton, and wool. Still, 90 percent of Australians live in cities and towns.

Oceania at a Glance

Area
3,300,000 sq. mi. (8,600,000 sq km)

Population
36,271,000

Number of countries
14

Most populated urban area
Sydney, Australia
4,543,205 people

Longest river
Murray-Darling, Australia
2,094 mi. (3,376 km) long

Largest lake
Lake Eyre, Australia
3,708 sq. mi. (9,399 sq km)

Highest point
Mount Wilhelm, Papua New Guinea
14,793 ft. (4,509 m)

Lowest point
Lake Eyre
-52 ft. (-16 m)

CHECK IT OUT !

All of Australia is located below the equator. This is why the continent is called "the land Down Under."

The Continents and Major Oceans

HOW MANY oceans are there? Actually, there's only one. Although the seven continents split the ocean into five major parts, the ocean is one huge connected body of water. This *world ocean* has an average depth of 13,000 feet (4,000 m), with parts plunging almost three times that deep. On the ocean floor is a landscape of valleys and ridges that is constantly changing, as magma from underwater volcanoes seeps out and forms new land.

The ocean provides food, energy, medicines, minerals, and most of the precipitation that falls to the earth. It regulates the world's climate by storing and releasing heat from the Sun. Without the ocean, there could be no life on our planet.

North America

Atlantic Ocean

South America

Pacific Ocean

Area
About 66 million sq. mi.
(171 million sq km)

Greatest depth
35,840 ft. (10,924 m), in the Challenger Deep

Surface temperature
Highest: 82°F (28° C), near the equator in August
Lowest: 30°F (–1° C), in the polar region in winter

Area
About 34 million sq. mi.
(88 million sq km)

Greatest depth
28,232 ft. (8,605 m) in the Puerto Rico Trench

Surface temperature
Highest: About 86°F (30° C), near the equator in summer
Lowest: 28°F (–2° C), at and near the boundary with the Southern Ocean in winter

Area
About 3,680,000 sq. mi. (9,530,000 sq km)

Greatest depth
18,399 ft. (5,608 m), in Molloy Hole, northwest of Svalbard

Surface temperature
Highest: 29°F (-1.5°C), in July
Lowest: 28°F (-2°C), in January

Arctic Ocean

Asia

Europe

Area
About 26.6 million sq. mi.
(69 million sq km)

Greatest depth
23,812 ft. (7,258 m), in the Java Trench

Surface temperature
Highest: 90°F (32° C), in the Persian Gulf and Red Sea during July
Lowest: Below 30°F (-1° C), near the Southern Ocean during July

Africa

Indian Ocean

Australia

Southern Ocean

Antarctica

Area
About 8.5 million sq. mi. (22 million sq km)

Greatest depth
23,737 ft. (7,235 m), at the southern end of the South Sandwich Trench

Surface temperature
Highest: 30 to 43°F (-1 to 6°C), near 60° south latitude in February
Lowest: 28 to 30°F (-2 to-1°C), near Antarctica in August

171

World's **5** Deepest Oceans and Seas

(Ranked by average depth)

Pacific Ocean
14,040 ft. (4,279 m)

Indian Ocean
12,800 ft. (3,900 m)

Atlantic Ocean
11,810 ft. (3,600 m)

Caribbean Sea
8,448 ft. (2,575 m)

Sea of Japan
5,468 ft. (1,666 m)

World's **5** Largest Lakes

Caspian Sea
Azerbaijan/Iran/Kazakhstan/
Russia/Turkmenistan
146,101 sq. mi.
(378,401 sq km)

Lake Superior
Canada/United States
31,699 sq. mi.
(378,401 sq km)

Lake Victoria
Kenya/Tanzania/Uganda
26,828 sq. mi.
(69,485 sq km)

Lake Huron
Canada/United States
23,004 sq. mi.
(59,580 sq km)

Lake Michigan
United States
22,278 sq. mi.
(57,700 sq km)

World's **5** Highest Waterfalls

Angel
Venezuela
Tributary of Caroni River
3,212 ft. (979 m)

Tugela
South Africa
Tugela River
3,110 ft. (948 m)

Tres Hermanas
Peru
Cutivireni River
3,000 ft. (914 m)

Olo'upena
United States
2,953 ft. (900 m)

Yumbilla
Peru
2,938 ft. (896 m)

World's **5** Longest River Systems

Nile
Tanzania/Uganda/Sudan/Egypt
4,145 mi.
(6,670 km)

Amazon
Peru/Brazil
4,007 mi.
(6,448 km)

Yangtze-Kiang
China
3,915 mi.
(6,300 km)

Mississippi-Missouri-Red
United States
3,710 mi.
(5,971 km)

Yenisey-Angara-Selenga
Mongolia/Russia
2,500 mi.
(4,000 km)

World's **5** Highest Mountains

(Height of principal peak; lower peaks of same mountain excluded)

Mt. Everest
Nepal/Tibet
29,035 ft. (8,850 m)

K2
Kashmir/China
28,250 ft. (8,611 m)

Kanchenjunga
Nepal/Sikkim
28,208 ft. (8,598 m)

Lhotse
Tibet
27,923 ft. (8,511 m)

Makalu
Nepal/Tibet
27,824 ft. (8,480 m)

173

Redwood Forest
Location: California

Grand Canyon
Location: Arizona

Yellowstone
Location: Wyoming

Bryce Canyon
Location: Utah

Crater Lake
Location: Oregon

Geography—World & U.S.

10 Largest States in Total Area

1. Alaska	663,267 sq. mi. (1,717,854 sq km)
2. Texas	268,581 sq. mi. (695,622 sq km)
3. California	163,696 sq. mi. (423,971 sq km)
4. Montana	147,042 sq. mi. (380,837 sq km)
5. New Mexico	121,589 sq. mi. (314,914 sq km)
6. Arizona	113,998 sq. mi. (295,253 sq km)
7. Nevada	110,561 sq. mi. (286,352 sq km)
8. Colorado	104,094 sq. mi. (269,602 sq km)
9. Oregon	98,381 sq. mi. (254,806 sq km)
10. Wyoming	97,814 sq. mi. (253,337 sq km)

10 Smallest States in Total Area

1. Rhode Island	1,545 sq. mi. (4,002 sq km)
2. Delaware	2,489 sq. mi. (6,446 sq km)
3. Connecticut	5,543 sq. mi. (14,356 sq km)
4. New Jersey	8,721 sq. mi. (22,587 sq km)
5. New Hampshire	9,350 sq. mi. (24,216 sq km)
6. Vermont	9,614 sq. mi. (24,900 sq km)
7. Massachusetts	10,555 sq. mi. (27,337 sq km)
8. Hawaii	10,931 sq. mi. (28,311 sq km)
9. Maryland	12,407 sq. mi. (32,134 sq km)
10. West Virginia	24,230 sq. mi. (62,755 sq km)

5 Highest U.S. Mountains

Mt. McKinley
Alaska
20,320 ft. (6,194 m)

Mt. St. Elias
Alaska–Yukon
18,008 ft. (5,489 m)

Mt. Foraker
Alaska
17,400 ft. (5,304 m)

Mt. Bona
Alaska
16,550 ft. (5,044 m)

Mt. Blackburn
Alaska
16,390 ft. (4,996 m)

10 Longest U.S. Rivers

Mississippi
2,348 mi. (3,779 km)

Missouri
2,315 mi. (3,726 km)

Yukon
1,979 mi. (3,186 km)

Rio Grande
1,900 mi. (3,058 km)

Arkansas
1,459 mi. (2,348 km)

Red
1,290 mi. (2,076 km)

Columbia
1,243 mi. (2,000 km)

Snake
1,038 mi. (1,670 km)

Ohio
981 mi. (1,579 km)

St. Lawrence
800 mi. (1,287 km)

10 Largest U.S. National Historical Parks

(By total acreage and hectares)

Chaco Culture
New Mexico
33,960 acres (13,743 h)

Cumberland Gap
Kentucky/Tennessee/Virginia
22,365 acres (9,050 h)

Jean Lafitte
Louisiana
20,001 acres (8,094 h)

Chesapeake & Ohio Canal
Maryland/West Virginia/
Washington, DC
19,615 acres (7,938 h)

Klondike Gold Rush
Alaska/Washington
12,996 acres (5,259 h)

Colonial
Virginia
8,676 acres (3,511 h)

Pecos
New Mexico
6,669 acres (2,699 h)

Nez Perce
Idaho/Montana/
Oregon/Washington
4,570 acres (1,849 h)

Harpers Ferry
West Virginia/Maryland/Virginia
3,647 acres (1,476 h)

Cedar Creek & Belle Grove
Virginia
3,712 acres (1,502 h)

The Great Lakes—Facts and Figures

Lake Superior
Area	31,700 sq. mi. (82,103 sq km)
Borders	Minnesota, Wisconsin, Michigan (United States); Ontario (Canada)
Major Ports	Duluth, Superior, Sault Ste. Marie (United States); Sault Ste. Marie, Thunder Bay (Canada)

Lake Huron
Area	23,000 sq. mi. (59,570 sq km)
Borders	Michigan (United States); Ontario (Canada)
Major Ports	Port Huron (United States); Sarnia (Canada)

Lake Michigan
Area	22,300 sq. mi. (57,570 sq km)
Borders	Illinois, Indiana, Michigan, Wisconsin (United States)
Major Ports	Milwaukee, Racine, Kenosha, Chicago, Gary, Muskegon (United States)

Lake Erie
Area	9,940 sq. mi. (25,745 sq km)
Borders	Michigan, New York, Ohio, Pennsylvania (United States); Ontario (Canada)
Major Ports	Toledo, Sandusky, Lorain, Cleveland, Erie, Buffalo (United States)

Lake Ontario
Area	7,340 sq. mi. (19,011 sq km)
Borders	New York (United States); Ontario (Canada)
Major Ports	Rochester, Oswego (United States); Toronto, Hamilton (Canada)

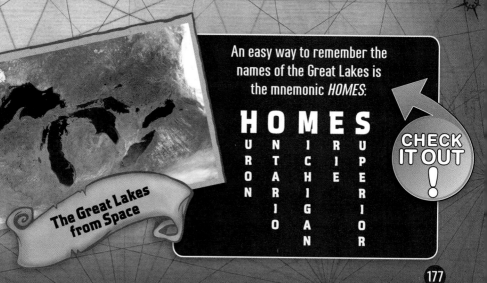

The Great Lakes from Space

An easy way to remember the names of the Great Lakes is the mnemonic *HOMES*:

H URON
O NTARIO
M ICHIGAN
E RIE
S UPERIOR

CHECK IT OUT!

National Parks by State

Alaska
Denali
Gates of the Arctic
Glacier Bay
Katmai
Kenai Fjords
Kobuk Valley
Lake Clark
Wrangell-St. Elias

Arizona
Grand Canyon
Petrified Forest
Saguaro

Arkansas
Hot Springs

California
Channel Islands
Death Valley
Joshua Tree
Kings Canyon
Lassen Volcanic
Redwood
Sequoia
Yosemite

Colorado
Black Canyon of the Gunnison
Great Sand Dunes
Mesa Verde
Rocky Mountain

Florida
Biscayne
Dry Tortugas
Everglades

Hawaii
Haleakala
Hawaii Volcanoes

Idaho
Yellowstone

Kentucky
Mammoth Cave

Maine
Acadia

Michigan
Isle Royale

Minnesota
Voyageurs

Montana
Glacier
Yellowstone

Nevada
Death Valley
Great Basin

New Mexico
Carlsbad Caverns

North Carolina
Great Smoky Mountains

North Dakota
Theodore Roosevelt

Ohio
Cuyahoga Valley

Oregon
Crater Lake

South Carolina
Congaree

South Dakota
Badlands
Wind Cave

Tennessee
Great Smoky Mountains

Texas
Big Bend
Guadalupe Mountains

Utah
Arches
Bryce Canyon
Capitol Reef
Canyonlands
Zion

Virginia
Shenandoah

Washington
Mount Rainier
North Cascades
Olympic

Wyoming
Grand Teton
Yellowstone

10 Most Visited U.S. National Parks

Park (Location)	Visitors in 2012
Great Smoky Mountains (Tennessee/North Carolina)	9,685,829
Grand Canyon (Arizona)	4,421,352
Yosemite (California)	3,853,404
Yellowstone (Wyoming)	3,447,729
Rocky Mountain (Colorado)	3,229,617
Zion (Utah)	2,973,607
Olymipc (Washington)	2,824,908
Grand Teton (Wyoming)	2,705,256
Acadia (Maine)	2,431,052
Cuyahoga Valley (Ohio)	2,299,722

U.S. National Memorials

Memorial	State	Description
Arkansas Post	Arkansas	First permanent French settlement in the lower Mississippi River valley
Arlington House (Robert E. Lee Memorial)	Virginia	Lee's home overlooking the Potomac
Chamizal	Texas	Commemorates 1963 settlement of 99-year border dispute with Mexico
Coronado	Arizona	Commemorates first European exploration of the Southwest
De Soto	Florida	Commemorates 16th-century Spanish explorations
Father Marquette	Michigan	Commemorates Father Jacques Marquette, a French Jesuit missionary who helped establish Michigan's first European settlement at Sault Ste. Marie in 1668
Federal Hall	New York	First seat of U.S. government under the Constitution
Flight 93	Pennsylvania	Commemorates the passengers and crew of Flight 93, who lost their lives to bring down a plane headed to attack the nation's capital on September 11, 2001
Fort Caroline	Florida	On St. Johns River; overlooks site of a French Huguenot colony
Fort Clatsop	Oregon	Lewis and Clark encampment, 1805–1806
Franklin Delano Roosevelt	DC	Statues of President Roosevelt and First Lady Eleanor Roosevelt, as well as waterfalls and gardens; dedicated May 2, 1997
General Grant	New York	Grant's Tomb
Hamilton Grange	New York	Home of Alexander Hamilton
Jefferson National Expansion Monument	Missouri	Commemorates westward expansion
Johnstown Flood	Pennsylvania	Commemorates tragic flood of 1889
Korean War Veterans	DC	Dedicated in 1995; honors those who served in the Korean War
Lincoln Boyhood	Indiana	Site of Lincoln cabin, boyhood home, and grave of Lincoln's mother
Lincoln Memorial	DC	Marble statue of the 16th U.S. president
Lyndon B. Johnson Grove on the Potomac	DC	Honors the 36th president; overlooks the Potomac River vista of the capital
Martin Luther King Jr. Memorial	DC	Dedicated October 16, 2011; honors the civil rights leader with a sculpture, the "Stone of Hope"
Mount Rushmore	South Dakota	World-famous sculpture of four presidents
Oklahoma City	Oklahoma	Commemorates the April 19, 1995, bombing of the Alfred P. Murrah Federal Building
Perry's Victory and International Peace Memorial	Ohio	The world's largest Doric column, constructed 1912–1915, promotes pursuit of international peace through arbitration and disarmament
Roger Williams	Rhode Island	Memorial to founder of Rhode Island
Thaddeus Kosciuszko	Pennsylvania	Memorial to Polish hero of the American Revolution
Theodore Roosevelt Island	DC	Statue of the 26th president in wooded island sanctuary
Thomas Jefferson Memorial	DC	Statue of the 3rd president in a circular, colonnaded structure
USS Arizona	Hawaii	Memorializes American losses at Pearl Harbor
Vietnam Veterans	DC	Black granite wall inscribed with names of those missing or killed in action in the Vietnam War
Washington Monument	DC	Obelisk honoring the 1st U.S. president
World War II	DC	Oval plaza with central pool commemorating those who fought and died in World War II
Wright Brothers	North Carolina	Site of first powered flight

U.S. National Battlefields

Stones River, Tennessee
Scene of battle that began Union offensive to trisect Confederacy

Fort Donelson, Tennessee
Site of first major Union victory

Antietam, Maryland
Battle here ended first Confederate invasion of North, Sept. 17, 1862

Big Hole, Montana
Site of major battle between Nez Perce and U.S. Army

Petersburg, Virginia
Scene of 10-month Union campaigns, 1864–1865

Fort Necessity, Pennsylvania
Some of the first battles of French and Indian War

Wilson's Creek, Missouri
Scene of Civil War battle for control of Missouri

Tupelo, Mississippi
Site of crucial Civil War battle over Sherman's supply line

Cowpens, South Carolina
American Revolution battlefield

Monocacy, Maryland
Civil War battle in defense of Washington, DC, fought here July 9,

Moores Creek, North Carolina
1776 battle between Patriots and Loyalists commemorated here

Stats on the Statue of Liberty

The Statue of Liberty was designed by French sculptor Frederic Auguste Bartholdi and arrived in 214 packing cases from Rouen, France, in June 1885. The completed statue was dedicated on October 28, 1886, by President Grover Cleveland. It was designated a National Monument in 1924 and is one of America's most famous symbols of freedom.

Part of Statue	Measurement
Height from heel to torch	151 ft. 1 in. (45.3 m)
Height from base of pedestal to torch	305 ft. 1 in. (91.5 m)
Length of hand	16 ft. 5 in. (5 m)
Length of index finger	8 ft. 0 in. (2.4 m)
Circumference at second finger joint	3 ft. 6 in. (1 m)
Size of fingernail	13 x 10 in. (33 x 25 cm)
Height of head from chin to cranium	17 ft. 3 in. (5 m)
Thickness of head from ear to ear	10 ft. 0 in. (3 m)
Distance across eye	2 ft. 6 in. (0.76 m)
Length of nose	4 ft. 6 in. (1.4 m)
Length of right arm	42 ft. 0 in. (12.8 m)
Thickness of right arm at thickest point	12 ft. 0 in. (3.7 m)
Thickness of waist	35 ft. 0 in. (10.7 m)
Width of mouth	3 ft. 0 in. (1 m)
Length of tablet	23 ft. 7 in. (7.2 m)
Width of tablet	13 ft. 7 in. (4.1 m)
Thickness of tablet	2 ft. 0 in. (0.6 m)

Geography—World & U.S.

Select National Sites of Washington, DC

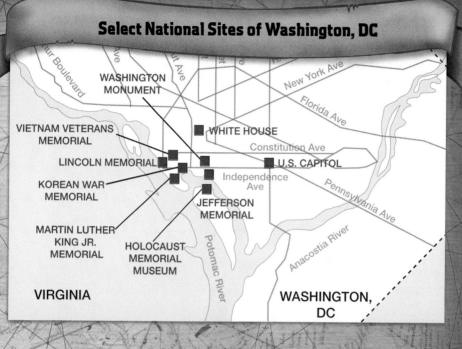

WASHINGTON MONUMENT

VIETNAM VETERANS MEMORIAL

LINCOLN MEMORIAL

KOREAN WAR MEMORIAL

MARTIN LUTHER KING JR. MEMORIAL

HOLOCAUST MEMORIAL MUSEUM

JEFFERSON MEMORIAL

WHITE HOUSE

New York Ave

Florida Ave

Constitution Ave

U.S. CAPITOL

Independence Ave

Pennsylvania Ave

Anacostia River

Potomac River

VIRGINIA

WASHINGTON, DC

U.S. Capitol
The Capitol is open to the public for guided tours 8:50 AM to 3:20 PM, Monday through Saturday. Tickets are available at tour kiosks at the east and west fronts of the Capitol. Phone: (202) 226-8000

Holocaust Memorial Museum
The museum is open daily, beginning at 10:00 AM, except Yom Kippur and December 25. 100 Raoul Wallenburg Pl., SW (formerly 15th St., SW) near Independence Ave. Phone: (202) 488-0400

Jefferson Memorial
The memorial, which is located on the south edge of the Tidal Basin, is open 8 AM to 11:45 PM every day except Christmas Day. An elevator and curb ramps for the disabled are in service. Phone: (202) 426-6841

Korean War Memorial
The $18 million military memorial, which was funded by private donations, is open 24 hours a day. Phone: (202) 426-6841

Lincoln Memorial
The memorial, which is located in West Potomac Park, is open 8 AM to 11:45 PM every day except Christmas Day. An elevator and curb ramps for the disabled are in service. Phone: (202) 426-6841

Martin Luther King Jr. Memorial
This memorial features a sculpture of the late civil rights leader that seems to be rising from a mountain of granite and a wall inscribed with some of his famous quotes. It is open 24 hours a day throughout the year. Phone: (202) 426-6841

Vietnam Veterans Memorial
The memorial is open 24 hours a day. Phone: (202) 426-6841

Washington Monument
The memorial is open 9:00 AM–4:45 PM daily, except July 4 and December 25. Tickets are required for entry and can be either reserved ahead of time or picked up same day. Earthquake damage forced the monument to close, but it is scheduled to reopen in 2014. Phone: (202) 426-6841

The White House
Free reserved tickets for guided tours can be obtained up to six months in advance. Contact your senators or representatives for tickets. Phone: (202) 456-7041

Health & Wellness

Sports are fun to play and exciting to watch, but without the right training and the right equipment, players can get hurt—sometimes badly. The National Football League (NFL) is studying new helmets that will keep their players safer from head injuries called concussions, which are also increasing in high-school sports.

> **Wear a Helmet When You ...**

> Bike   > Skateboard
> Skate   > Ski
> Play football, lacrosse, soccer, or hockey

Systems of the Human Body

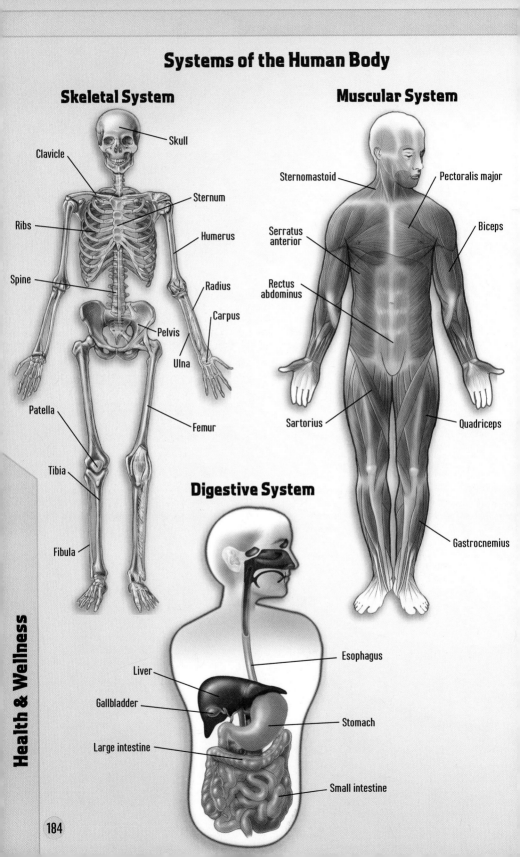

Skeletal System

- Skull
- Clavicle
- Sternum
- Ribs
- Humerus
- Spine
- Radius
- Carpus
- Pelvis
- Ulna
- Patella
- Femur
- Tibia
- Fibula

Muscular System

- Sternomastoid
- Pectoralis major
- Serratus anterior
- Biceps
- Rectus abdominus
- Sartorius
- Quadriceps
- Gastrocnemius

Digestive System

- Esophagus
- Liver
- Gallbladder
- Stomach
- Large intestine
- Small intestine

Health & Wellness

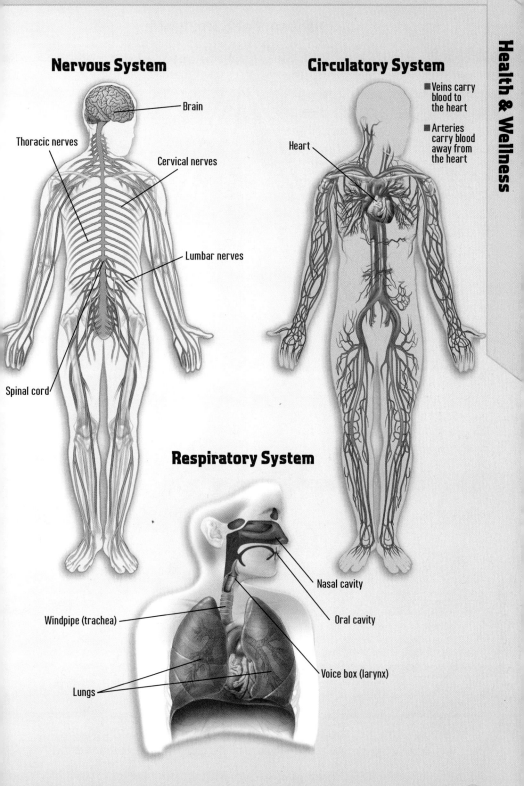

Nervous System

Brain

Thoracic nerves

Cervical nerves

Lumbar nerves

Spinal cord

Circulatory System

- Veins carry blood to the heart
- Arteries carry blood away from the heart

Heart

Respiratory System

Nasal cavity

Oral cavity

Windpipe (trachea)

Voice box (larynx)

Lungs

The New Food Pyramid

In 2005, the U.S. Department of Agriculture (USDA) created a new food pyramid. The colored parts of the pyramid stand for different food groups. The width of each part shows what portion of your daily diet should be from that food group.

The amounts shown below are based on what a 12-year-old boy of average height and weight who is moderately active should eat every day. To figure out your own personal food pyramid plan, go to **www.mypyramid.gov**.

The most popular fruit in the world is one you may think is a vegetable—the tomato. Scientifically speaking, a tomato is considered a fruit because it comes from a flowering plant that contains seeds. Sixty million tons of tomatoes are produced every year.

CHECK IT OUT!

Grains	Vegetables	Fruits	Milk	Meat & Beans
Seven ounces of bread, cereal, crackers, rice, or pasta every day. At least half should be whole grains.	Three cups every day, fresh or frozen. Dark green, orange, light green—mix it up!	Two cups of nature's sweet treats a day. Go easy on the fruit juice.	Three cups a day. Choose nonfat or lowfat milk products.	Six ounces of lean protein a day: meat, fish, or poultry, or nuts, seeds, beans, and peas.

Oils Oils aren't a food group, but you need some for good health. Nuts and fish are good sources. Be sure to limit sugars and solid fats such as butter. Read the labels—you might be surprised!

Kids' Top 5 Favorite Activities

According to a study by the Outdoor Foundation, these are the favorite activities of kids between the ages of 6 and 17:

1. Running/ Jogging   2. Biking   3. Skateboarding   4. Fishing   5. Camping

While millions of kids love outdoor activities, millions of others don't get enough exercise. What are they doing instead? According to Let'sMove.gov, the kid's health program started by First Lady Michelle Obama, young people spend an average of 7.5 hours a day watching TV or movies, using computers, playing video games, and talking or texting on cell phones. To control weight and limit risk of certain diseases, experts recommend at least 60 minutes of exercise every day. Find an activity you love and start moving in a healthy direction!

Your Amazing Body, by the Numbers

Your heart pumps blood along 60,000 miles (97,000 km) of veins and arteries. It beats 100,000 times a day—that's 40 million times a year and more than 3 billion times in an average lifetime.

Your brain weighs only about 3 pounds (1.4 kg), but it has about 100 billion nerve cells. Nerves help you think, move, dream, feel happy or sad, and regulate unconscious activities such as digesting food and breathing.

Your digestive system consists of about 30 feet (9 m) of tubes that carry food along a journey from top to bottom, squeezing out nutrients to keep you healthy and processing waste materials.

Your skin is your body's largest organ, weighing about 8 pounds (3.6 kg) and measuring about 22 square feet (2 sq m). Be good to your skin by keeping it clean and well protected from the Sun.

Inventors & Inventions

SAVE THE DATE Every January 17, celebrate Benjamin Franklin's birthday and National Kid Inventors' Day (K.I.D.)-No kidding—Franklin invented the first swim flippers when he was 11.

> **Invented by Kids**

> trampoline
> snowmobile
> popsicle

Show the world your own great idea! Check out these competitions for young inventors at the National Museum of Education, www.nmoe.org/students/siba.htm.

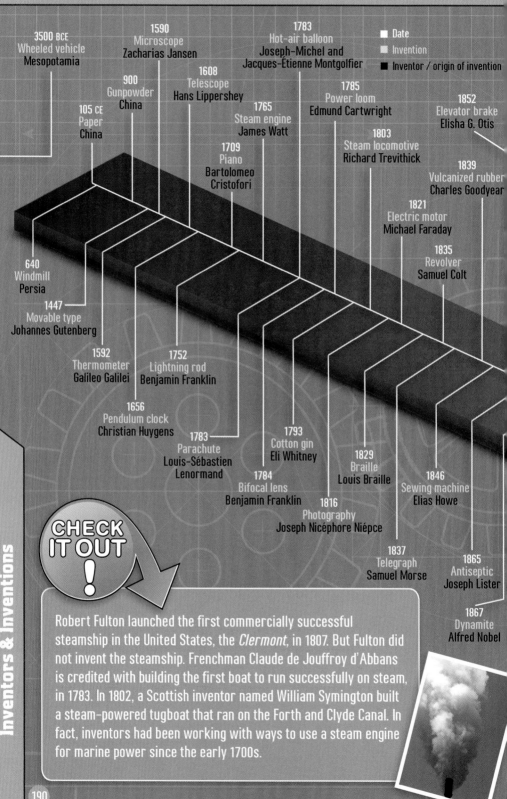

3500 BCE
Wheeled vehicle
Mesopotamia

1590
Microscope
Zacharias Jansen

1608
Telescope
Hans Lippershey

1783
Hot-air balloon
Joseph-Michel and
Jacques-Etienne Montgolfier

900
Gunpowder
China

1765
Steam engine
James Watt

1785
Power loom
Edmund Cartwright

1852
Elevator brake
Elisha G. Otis

105 CE
Paper
China

1709
Piano
Bartolomeo
Cristofori

1803
Steam locomotive
Richard Trevithick

1839
Vulcanized rubber
Charles Goodyear

1821
Electric motor
Michael Faraday

1835
Revolver
Samuel Colt

640
Windmill
Persia

1447
Movable type
Johannes Gutenberg

1592
Thermometer
Galileo Galilei

1752
Lightning rod
Benjamin Franklin

1656
Pendulum clock
Christian Huygens

1783
Parachute
Louis-Sébastien
Lenormand

1793
Cotton gin
Eli Whitney

1829
Braille
Louis Braille

1846
Sewing machine
Elias Howe

1784
Bifocal lens
Benjamin Franklin

1816
Photography
Joseph Nicéphore Niépce

1837
Telegraph
Samuel Morse

1865
Antiseptic
Joseph Lister

1867
Dynamite
Alfred Nobel

■ Date
■ Invention
■ Inventor / origin of invention

CHECK IT OUT !

Robert Fulton launched the first commercially successful steamship in the United States, the *Clermont*, in 1807. But Fulton did not invent the steamship. Frenchman Claude de Jouffroy d'Abbans is credited with building the first boat to run successfully on steam, in 1783. In 1802, a Scottish inventor named William Symington built a steam-powered tugboat that ran on the Forth and Clyde Canal. In fact, inventors had been working with ways to use a steam engine for marine power since the early 1700s.

Important Inventions and Their Inventors

These are just a few of the inventions that have shaped our world and changed our lives. The inventors listed are either those who received patents for the invention or the ones widely credited with introducing the version of the invention we use today. But in many cases, other inventors contributed to the invention by doing experiments or making earlier versions. Do some additional research for the whole story behind these inventions and others.

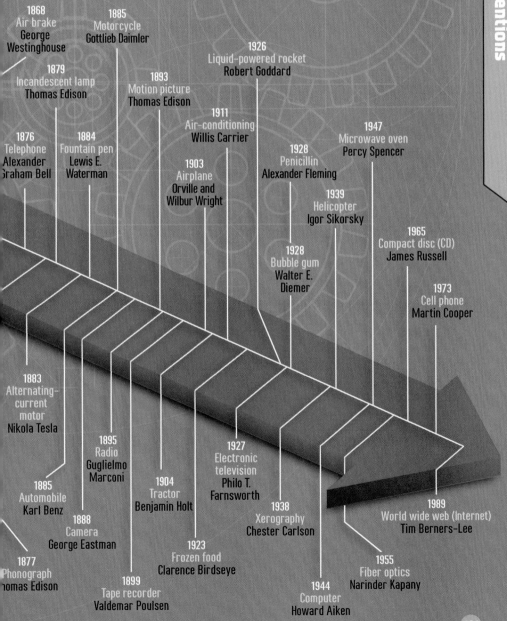

1868
Air brake
George
Westinghouse

1885
Motorcycle
Gottlieb Daimler

1926
Liquid-powered rocket
Robert Goddard

1879
Incandescent lamp
Thomas Edison

1893
Motion picture
Thomas Edison

1911
Air-conditioning
Willis Carrier

1947
Microwave oven
Percy Spencer

1876
Telephone
Alexander
Graham Bell

1884
Fountain pen
Lewis E.
Waterman

1928
Penicillin
Alexander Fleming

1903
Airplane
Orville and
Wilbur Wright

1939
Helicopter
Igor Sikorsky

1965
Compact disc (CD)
James Russell

1928
Bubble gum
Walter E.
Diemer

1973
Cell phone
Martin Cooper

1883
Alternating-
current
motor
Nikola Tesla

1895
Radio
Guglielmo
Marconi

1927
Electronic
television
Philo T.
Farnsworth

1885
Automobile
Karl Benz

1904
Tractor
Benjamin Holt

1938
Xerography
Chester Carlson

1989
World wide web (Internet)
Tim Berners-Lee

1888
Camera
George Eastman

1923
Frozen food
Clarence Birdseye

1955
Fiber optics
Narinder Kapany

1877
Phonograph
Thomas Edison

1899
Tape recorder
Valdemar Poulsen

1944
Computer
Howard Aiken

RECORD HOLDER

There are almost 7,000 languages in the world, and more than 820 of them of them are spoken in tiny Papua New Guinea. The country's remote location helps maintain the languages, but on average, globally, one language is lost forever every two weeks. The United Nations has launched a program to try and keep language alive.

> Where Are the Most Languages Spoken?

Continent/ Region	Percentage of World Languages
Asia	32.4
Africa	30.2
Oceania	18.5
North and South America	14.9
Europe	4.0

Languages

Common Words and Phrases in Select Languages

MANDARIN CHINESE

Hello	Ni hao (nee how)
Good-bye	Zài jiàn (zay GEE-en)
Yes	Shide (SURE-due)
No	Bu shi (BOO sure
Please	Qing (ching
Thank you	Xièxiè (shieh-shieh
You're welcome	Búkèqi (boo-keh-chee
Excuse me	Duìbúqi (doo-ee-boo-che

SPANISH

Hello	Hola (OH-lah)
Good-bye	Adiós (ah-dee-OHSS)
Good morning	Buenas días (BWAY-nahs DEE-ahs)
Good afternoon	Buenas tardes (BWAY-nahs TAHR-dehs)
Good evening	Buenas noches (BWAY-nahs NOH-chehs)
Yes	Sí (SEE)
No	No (NOH)
Please	Por favor (por fa-VOHR)
Thank you	Gracias (GRAH-see-ahs)
You're welcome	De nada (DE nada)
What's going on?	¿Qué pasa? (kay PAH-sah)
How are you?	¿Cómo está usted? (COH-mo es-TAH oo-STEHD)

GERMAN

Hello	Guten Tag (GOO-tin TAHK)
Good-bye	Auf Wiedersehen (ahf VEE-dehr-zeh-hehn)
Good morning	Guten Morgen (GOO-tin MOR-gun)
Yes	Ja (yah)
No	Nein (nine)
Please	Bitte (BIT-uh)
Thank you	Danke (DAHN-keh)
You're welcome	Bitte schön (BIT-uh shane)

Privet!

góðan dag

Languages

194

ITALIAN

Hi, 'bye (informal)	Ciao (chow)
Good-bye	Arrivederci (ah-ree-vay-DEHR-chee)
Good morning, good afternoon, or a general hello	Buon giorno (bwohn JOOR-noh)
Yes	Sì (SEE)
No	No (NOH)
Please	Per favore (purr fa-VO-ray)
Thank you	Grazie (GRAH-tsee-ay)
You're welcome	Prego (PRAY-go)
How are you?	Come sta? (KOH-may STAH)
Fine, very well	Molto bene (MOHL-toh BAY-nay)
Excuse me	Scusi (SKOO-zee)

EGYPTIAN ARABIC

Good morning	Sabah el khair (sa-BAH el KHAIR)
Good-bye	Ma salama (MA sa-LA-ma)
Yes	Aiwa (aye-wa)
No	La (la)
Please	Min fadlak (min FAD-lak)
Thank you	Shukran (SHU-kran)
No problem	Ma fee mushkila (ma FEE mush-KI-la)
How are you?	Izzayak? (iz-ZAY-ak)
What is your name?	Ismak ay? (IS-mak AY)

JAPANESE

Hi	Konnichiwa (koh-nee-chee-wah)
Good-bye	Ja mata (jahh mah-tah)
Yes	Hai (hah-ee)
No	Iie (EE-eh)
Good morning	Ohayō gozaimasu (oh-hah-yohh goh-zah-ee-mahs)
Excuse me	Sumimasen (soo-mee-mah-sehn)
Pleased to meet you	Yoroshiku (yoh-roh-shee-koo)
One	Ichi (ee-chee)
Thank you	Dōmo arigatō (dohh-moh ah-ri-gah-toh)

FRENCH

Hello	Bonjour (bohn-zhoor)
Good-bye	Au revoir (oh reh-vwah)
Yes	Oui (wee)
No	Non (no)
Excuse me	Pardonnez-moi (par-dough-nay mwah)
Please	S'il vous plaît (see voo play)
Thank you	Merci (mare-SEE)
How are you?	Comment allez-vous? (co-mahn-tah-lay voo

KOREAN

Hello	Anyŏng haseyo (ahn-n'yohng hah-say-yoh)
Good-bye	Anyŏng-hi kyeseyo (ahn-n'yohng-he kuh-say-yoh)
Please	Jwe-song-ha-ji-mahn (chey-song-hah-gee-mon)
Thank you	Kamsahamnida (kahm-sah-hahm-need-dah)
Excuse me	Miam hamnida (Me-ahn hahm-nee-dah)
One	Hana (hah-nah)
Ten	Yeol (yuhl)

xin chào

Hi

NIGERIAN
(four of the major Nigerian language groups)

English	Fulani	Hausa	Ibo	Yoruba
I'm fine	Jam tan (JAM-taan)	Kalau (KA-lay-U)	Adimnma (ah-DEE-mm-NMAA)	A dupe (ah-DEW-pa
one	gogo (GO-quo)	daya (DA-ya)	otu (o-TOO)	eni (EE-nee)
two	didi (DEE-dee)	biyu (BEE-you)	abua (ah-BOO-ah)	eji (EE-gee)
three	tati (TA-tea)	uku (OO-coo)	ato (ah-TOE)	eta (EE-ta)
nine	jeenayi (gee-NA-yee)	tara (TAA-ra)	iteghete (IT-egg-HE-tee)	esan (EE-san)
ten	sappo (SAP-poe)	goma (GO-ma)	iri (EE-ree)	ewa (EE-wa)

Languages

196

Which Languages Are Spoken Most?

The following languages have the most speakers in the world. The languages combine individual varieties and dialects that may have different names. The numbers include only first-language (mother-tongue) speakers.

Language	Estimated Number of Speakers (in millions)
Chinese	1,213
Spanish	329
English	328
Arabic	221
Hindi	182
Bengali	181
Portuguese	178
Russian	144
Japanese	122
German	90
Javanese	85
Lahnda	78
Telugu	70
Vietnamese	69
French	68
Marathi	68
Korean	66
Tamil	66
Italian	62
Urdu	61

dzień dobry

talofa

hej

alô

CHECK IT OUT !

Portugal isn't the only place where people speak Portuguese. About 150 million people speak it in Brazil, where it is the official language.

Math

A pentagon is a polygon with five sides. (What's a polygon? See page 204.) The Pentagon, in Washington, DC, is shaped like a—pentagon! It is also the biggest office building in the world. Despite its enormous size, the building's geometric layout lets people walk from one point to any other point in seven minutes.

> **Pentagon Math**

> Corridors .... 17.5 miles
> Stairways 131
> Restrooms 284
> Water fountains 691
> Light fixtures 16,250
> Occupants daily 25,000
> Telephone cables ..... 100,000 miles

MULTIPLICATION TABLE

	1	2	3	4	5	6	7	8	9	10	11	12
1	1	2	3	4	5	6	7	8	9	10	11	12
2	2	4	6	8	10	12	14	16	18	20	22	24
3	3	6	9	12	15	18	21	24	27	30	33	36
4	4	8	12	16	20	24	28	32	36	40	44	48
5	5	10	15	20	25	30	35	40	45	50	55	60
6	6	12	18	24	30	36	42	48	54	60	66	72
7	7	14	21	28	35	42	49	56	63	70	77	84
8	8	16	24	32	40	48	56	64	72	80	88	96
9	9	18	27	36	45	54	63	72	81	90	99	108
10	10	20	30	40	50	60	70	80	90	100	110	120
11	11	22	33	44	55	66	77	88	99	110	121	132
12	12	24	36	48	60	72	84	96	108	120	132	144

Math

Squares and Square Roots

Multiplying a number by itself is also called squaring it (or raising it to its second power). For example, 3 squared (3^2) is 9. By the same token, the square root of 9 is 3. The symbol for square root is called a radical sign ($\sqrt{}$).

Examples of squaring
2 squared: $2^2 = 2 \times 2 = 4$
3 squared: $3^2 = 3 \times 3 = 9$
4 squared: $4^2 = 4 \times 4 = 16$

Examples of Square Roots
Square root of 16: $\sqrt{16} = 4$
Square root of 9: $\sqrt{9} = 3$
Square root of 4: $\sqrt{4} = 2$

SQUARE ROOTS TO 40

$\sqrt{1} = 1$	$\sqrt{36} = 6$	$\sqrt{121} = 11$	$\sqrt{256} = 16$	$\sqrt{441} = 21$	$\sqrt{676} = 26$	$\sqrt{961} = 31$	$\sqrt{1,296} = 36$
$\sqrt{4} = 2$	$\sqrt{49} = 7$	$\sqrt{144} = 12$	$\sqrt{289} = 17$	$\sqrt{484} = 22$	$\sqrt{729} = 27$	$\sqrt{1,024} = 32$	$\sqrt{1,369} = 37$
$\sqrt{9} = 3$	$\sqrt{64} = 8$	$\sqrt{169} = 13$	$\sqrt{324} = 18$	$\sqrt{529} = 23$	$\sqrt{784} = 28$	$\sqrt{1,089} = 33$	$\sqrt{1,444} = 38$
$\sqrt{16} = 4$	$\sqrt{81} = 9$	$\sqrt{196} = 14$	$\sqrt{361} = 19$	$\sqrt{576} = 24$	$\sqrt{841} = 29$	$\sqrt{1,156} = 34$	$\sqrt{1,521} = 39$
$\sqrt{25} = 5$	$\sqrt{100} = 10$	$\sqrt{225} = 15$	$\sqrt{400} = 20$	$\sqrt{625} = 25$	$\sqrt{900} = 30$	$\sqrt{1,225} = 35$	$\sqrt{1,600} = 40$

Some Mathematical Formulas

To find the CIRCUMFERENCE of a:
- Circle—Multiply the diameter by π

To find the AREA of a:
- Circle—Multiply the square of the radius by π
- Rectangle—Multiply the base by the height
- Sphere (surface)—Multiply the square of the radius by π and multiply by 4
- Square—Square the length of one side
- Trapezoid—Add the two parallel sides, multiply by the height, and divide by 2
- Triangle—Multiply the base by the height and divide by 2

π (pi)
= 3.1416
(See page 204.)

To find the VOLUME of a:
- Cone—Multiply the square of the radius of the base by π, multiply by the height, and divide by 3
- Cube—Cube (raise to the third power) the length of one edge
- Cylinder—Multiply the square of the radius of the base by π and multiply by the height
- Pyramid—Multiply the area of the base by the height and divide by 3
- Rectangular prism—Multiply the length by the width by the height
- Sphere—Multiply the cube of the radius by π, multiply by 4, and divide by 3

LARGE NUMBERS AND HOW MANY ZEROS THEY CONTAIN

million	6	1,000,000
billion	9	1,000,000,000
trillion	12	1,000,000,000,000
quadrillion	15	1,000,000,000,000,000
quintillion	18	1,000,000,000,000,000,000

sextillion	21	1,000,000,000,000,000,000,000
septillion	24	1,000,000,000,000,000,000,000,000
octillion	27	1,000,000,000,000,000,000,000,000,000
nonillion	30	1,000,000,000,000,000,000,000,000,000,000
decillion	33	1,000,000,000,000,000,000,000,000,000,000,000

NUMBERS GLOSSARY

COUNTING NUMBERS
Counting numbers, or natural numbers, begin with the number 1 and continue into infinity.

WHOLE NUMBERS
Whole numbers are the same as counting numbers, except that the set of whole numbers begins with 0.

INTEGERS
Integers include 0, all counting numbers (called positive whole numbers), and all whole numbers less than 0 (called negative whole numbers).

RATIONAL NUMBERS
Rational numbers include any number that can be written in the form of a fraction (or a ratio), as long as the denominator (the bottom number of the fraction) is not equal to 0. All counting numbers and whole numbers are also rational numbers because all counting numbers and whole numbers can be written as fractions with a denominator equal to 1.

PRIME NUMBERS
Prime numbers are counting numbers that can be divided by only two numbers: 1 and themselves.

Prime numbers between 1 and 1,000
2, 3, 5, 7, 11, 13, 17, 19, 23, 29, 31, 37, 41, 43, 47, 53, 59, 61, 67, 71, 73, 79, 83, 89, 97, 101, 103, 107, 109, 113, 127, 131, 137, 139, 149, 151, 157, 163, 167, 173, 179, 181, 191, 193, 197, 199, 211, 223, 227, 229, 233, 239, 241, 251, 257, 263, 269, 271, 277, 281, 283, 293, 307, 311, 313, 317, 331, 337, 347, 349, 353, 359, 367, 373, 379, 383, 389, 397, 401, 409, 419, 421, 431, 433, 439, 443, 449, 457, 461, 463, 467, 479, 487, 491, 499, 503, 509, 521, 523, 541, 547, 557, 563, 569, 571, 577, 587, 593, 599, 601, 607, 613, 617, 619, 631, 641, 643, 647, 653, 659, 661, 673, 677, 683, 691, 701, 709, 719, 727, 733, 739, 743, 751, 757, 761, 769, 773, 787, 797, 809, 811, 821, 823, 827, 829, 839, 853, 857, 859, 863, 877, 881, 883, 887, 907, 911, 919, 929, 937, 941, 947, 953, 967, 971, 977, 983, 991, 997

COMPOSITE NUMBERS
Composite numbers are all counting numbers that are not prime numbers. In other words, composite numbers are numbers that have more than two factors. The number 1, because it has only one factor (itself), is not a composite number.

Composite numbers between 1 and 100
4, 6, 8, 9, 10, 12, 14, 15, 16, 18, 20, 21, 22, 24, 25, 26, 27, 28, 30, 32, 33, 34, 35, 36, 38, 39, 40, 42, 44, 45, 46, 48, 49, 50, 51, 52, 54, 55, 56, 57, 58, 60, 62, 63, 64, 65, 66, 68, 69, 70, 72, 74, 75, 76, 77, 78, 80, 81, 82, 84, 85, 86, 87, 88, 90, 91, 92, 93, 94, 95, 96, 98, 99, 100

Roman Numerals

I	1	XI	11	CD	400
II	2	XIX	19	D	500
III	3	XX	20	CM	900
IV	4	XXX	30	M	1,000
V	5	XL	40	$\overline{V}$	5,000
VI	6	L	50	$\overline{X}$	10,000
VII	7	LX	60	$\overline{L}$	50,000
VIII	8	XC	90	$\overline{C}$	100,000
IX	9	C	100	$\overline{D}$	500,000
X	10	CC	200	$\overline{M}$	1,000,000

Fractions, Decimals, and Percents

To find the equivalent of a fraction in decimal form, divide the numerator (top number) by the denominator (bottom number). To change from a decimal to a percent, multiply by 100. To change from a percent to a decimal, divide by 100.

Fraction	Decimal	Percent
1/16 (= 2/32)	0.0625	6.25
1/8 (= 2/16)	0.125	12.5
3/16 (= 6/32)	0.1875	18.75
1/4 (= 2/8; = 4/16)	0.25	25.0
5/16 (= 10/32)	0.3125	31.25
1/3 (= 2/6; = 4/12)	0.333	33.3
3/8 (= 6/16)	0.375	37.5
7/16 (= 14/32)	0.4375	43.75
1/2 (= 2/4; = 4/8; = 8/16)	0.5	50.0
9/16 (= 18/32)	0.5625	56.25
5/8 (= 10/16)	0.625	62.5
2/3 (= 4/6; = 8/12)	0.666	66.6
11/16 (= 22/32)	0.6875	68.75
3/4 (= 6/8; = 12/16)	0.75	75.0
13/16 (= 26/32)	0.8125	81.25
7/8 (= 14/16)	0.875	87.5
15/16 (= 30/32)	0.9375	93.75
1 (= 2/2; = 4/4; = 8/8; = 16/16)	1.0	100.0

Geometry Glossary

Acute angle	Any angle that measures less than 90°
Angle	Two rays that have the same endpoint form an angle
Area	The amount of surface inside a closed figure
Chord	A line segment whose endpoints are on a circle
Circumference	The distance around a circle
Congruent figures	Geometric figures that are the same size and shape
Degree (angle)	A unit for measuring angles
Diameter	A chord that passes through the center of a circle
Endpoint	The end of a line segment
Line of symmetry	A line that divides a figure into two identical parts if the figure is folded along the line
Obtuse angle	Any angle that measures greater than 90°
Perimeter	The distance around the outside of a plane figure
Pi (π)	The ratio of the circumference of a circle to its diameter; when rounded to the nearest hundredth, pi equals 3.14
Polygon	A simple closed figure whose sides are straight lines
Protractor	An instrument used to measure angles
Quadrilateral	A polygon with four sides
Radius	A straight line that connects the center of a circle to any point on the circumference of the circle
Ray	A straight line with one endpoint
Rectangle	A four-sided figure with four right angles
Right angle	An angle that measures 90°
Square	A rectangle with congruent sides and 90° angles in all four corners
Surface area	The total outside area of an object
Symmetrical	A figure that, when folded along a line of symmetry, has two halves that superimpose exactly on each other
Triangle	A three-sided figure
Vertex	The common endpoint of two or more rays that form angles
Vertices	The plural of vertex

Math

All About Polygons

Polygons are two-dimensional, or flat, shapes formed from three or more line segments.

Examples

Triangles

Triangles are polygons that have three sides and three vertices; the common endpoints of two or more rays form angles.

- **Right triangles** are formed when two of three line segments meet in a 90° angle. In a right triangle, the longest side has a special name: the hypotenuse.

HYPOTENUSE

- **Isosceles triangles** have two sides of equal length.

- **Scalene triangles** have no sides of equal length.

- **Equilateral triangles** have three sides of equal length.

Quadrilaterals

Quadrilaterals are polygons that have four sides and four vertices.

- **Trapezoids** are quadrilaterals that have one pair of parallel sides.

- **Parallelograms** are quadrilaterals that have parallel line segments in both pairs of opposite sides.

- **Rectangles** are parallelograms formed by line segments that meet at right angles. A rectangle always has four right angles.

- **Squares** are rectangles that have sides of equal length and four right angles.

- **Rhombuses** are parallelograms that have sides of equal length but don't meet at right angles.

Circles

A circle is a set of points within a plane. Each point on the circle is at an equal distance from a common point inside the circle called the center.

The distance from the center of the circle to any point on the circle is called the radius (r = radius).

A line segment drawn through the center of the circle to points on either side of the circle is called the diameter (d = diameter). The circle is bisected, or cut in two equal parts, along the diameter line. Diameter is equal to two times the radius (2r = diameter).

The distance around the circle is called the circumference (πd or π2r = circumference).

Women make up more than 15 percent of the 1.4 million active U.S. troops. More than 280,000 women have served in Iraq, Afghanistan, and other war zones. However, women have been kept out of the middle of the fighting. In January 2013, the Department of Defense lifted its ban on women in combat roles.

Military

Top 10 Best-Armed Nations

The world's strongest militaries are built with manpower, financial resources, training, and equipment.

Country	Active Troops	Annual Defense Budget ($ in billions, rounded)	Tanks	Ships	Combat Aircraft
China	2,285,000	$76.4	7,400+	149	1,305
United States	1,589,000	$693.6	5,855	174	1,110
India	1,325,000	$30.9	3.233+	35	762
North Korea	1,190,000	Not available	3,500+	75	489+
Russia	956,000	$41.9	2,800+	20	1,142
South Korea	655,000	$25.1	2,414	43	462
Pakistan	642,000	$5.6	2,411+	18	393
Iran	523,000	$10.6	1,663+	23	297+
Turkey	511,000	$17.4	4,503	32	338+
Vietnam	482,000	$2.6	1,315	4	231

Bring in the 'Bots

In today's military, high-tech devices help keep humans out of harm's way.

Explosive Ordinance Disposal (EOD) is a military unit that consists of robots designed to handle chemical, biological, radiological, nuclear, and explosive threats.

Precision Urban Hopper is a GPS-guided robot that can hop more than 25 feet (7.6 m) in the air, allowing it to jump over fences and barricades. It's designed especially to be used in cities.

MQ-1 Predator is a plane that can be piloted remotely for surveillance and attack.

Branches of the U.S. Military

Army
The oldest and largest branch of the United States military serves to defend and protect the nation at home and abroad. The most elite units, Army Rangers and Special Forces, train in advanced combat methods.

Navy
Members are especially skilled to handle any operations on and under the sea and in the air. Navy Divers and SEALs undergo specialized training for the most complex warfare operations.

Marines
The smallest branch of the nation's military is known for being the first on the ground in combat. Marines live by a strict code of honor, courage, and commitment.

Air Force
The technologically advanced members of the Air Force specialize in air and space operations to protect American interests.

Coast Guard
During peacetime, this branch protects national waterways, providing law enforcement, environmental cleanup, as well as search and rescue operations. During wartime, Coast Guard members serve with the Navy.

Beyond the Call of Duty

Military medals, or decorations, are awarded for bravery in and out of combat, loss of life or injury in combat, and other reasons. Most medals can be awarded to a member of any branch of the armed forces. The top 12 awards are listed in order, beginning with the highest.

Military Medals
1. Medal of Honor
2. Army Distinguished Service Cross, Navy Cross, Air Force Cross
3. Distinguished Service Medal
4. Silver Star
5. Defense Superior Service Medal
6. Legion of Merit
7. Distinguished Flying Cross
8. Soldier's Medal, Navy and Marine Corps Medal, Airman's Medal, Coast Guard Medal
9. Gold Lifesaving Medal
10. Bronze Star
11. Purple Heart
12. Defense Meritorious Service Medal

CHECK IT OUT!

Liquid Body Armor is made of Kevlar soaked with Shear Thickening Fluid (STF), silica particles mixed with polyethylene glycol. The material's liquid form makes it lightweight and flexible, but it hardens in milliseconds if struck by a bullet or shrapnel.

Movies & TV

STAY TUNED

Star Wars has been one of the most popular movie series ever, earning about $27 billion in ticket sales, videos, computer games, books, and merchandise. The last *Star Wars* movie came out in 2005, and now the Force will be with us again. A new movie is scheduled for 2015, and there will probably be at least two more after that.

Movies

10 Top-Grossing Movies of 2012

Movie	Box-Office Receipts
1. *The Avengers*	$1.5 billion
2. *Skyfall*	$1.1 billion
3. *The Dark Knight Rises*	$1.08 billion
4. *The Hobbit: An Unexpected Journey*	$1.01 billion
5. *Ice Age: Continental Drift*	$877.2 million
6. *The Twilight Saga: Breaking Dawn—Part 2*	$829.2 million
7. *The Amazing Spider-Man*	$752.2 million
8. *Madagascar 3: Europe's Most Wanted*	$742.1 million
9. *The Hunger Games*	$686.5 million
10. *Men in Black 3*	$624 million

Daniel Day-Lew

2013 Oscar Winners

Best Picture: *Argo*

Best Director: Ang Lee, *Life of Pi*

Best Actor: Daniel Day-Lewis, *Lincoln*

Best Actress: Jennifer Lawrence, *Silver Linings Playbook*

Best Supporting Actor: Christoph Waltz, *Django Unchained*

Best Supporting Actress: Anne Hathaway, *Les Misérables*

Best Animated Film: *Brave*

Best Foreign Film: *Amour*

Best Original Screenplay: *Django Unchained*, Quentin Tarantino

Best Adapted Screenplay: *Argo*, Chris Terrio

2013 Golden Globe Winners

Best Picture, Drama: *Argo*
Best Actor, Drama: Daniel Day-Lewis, *Lincoln*
Best Actress, Drama: Jessica Chastain, *Zero Dark Thirty*
Best Picture, Comedy or Musical: *Les Misérables*
Best Actor, Comedy or Musical: Hugh Jackman, *Les Misérables*
Best Actress, Comedy or Musical: Jennifer Lawrence, *Silver Linings Playbook*
Best Director: Ben Affleck, *Argo*
Best Supporting Actor: Christoph Waltz, *Django Unchained*
Best Supporting Actress: Anne Hathaway, *Les Misérables*
Best Animated Film: *Brave*
Best Foreign Film: *Amour*
Best Screenplay: *Django Unchained*, Quentin Tarantino

2013 Nickelodeon Kids' Choice Awards Movie Winners

Favorite Movie: *The Hunger Games*
Favorite Movie Actor: Johnny Depp
Favorite Movie Actress: Kristen Stewart
Favorite Animated Movie: *Wreck-It Ralph*
Favorite Voice from an Animated Movie:
Adam Sandler, *Hotel Transylvania*

Johnny Depp

2012 Teen Choice Awards Movie Winners

Action: *Abduction*
Actor, Action: Taylor Lautner, *Abduction*
Actress, Action: Zoe Saldana, *Colombiana*
Comedy: *21 Jump Street*
Actor, Comedy: Channing Tatum, *21 Jump Street*
Actress, Comedy: Emma Stone, *Crazy, Stupid, Love*
Drama: *The Lucky One*
Actor, Drama: Zac Efron, *The Lucky One*
Actress, Drama: Emma Stone, *The Help*
Romance: *The Twilight Saga: Breaking Dawn—Part 1*
Sci-Fi/Fantasy: *The Hunger Games*
Actor, Sci-Fi/Fantasy: Josh Hutcherson, *The Hunger Games*
Actress, Sci-Fi Fantasy: Jennifer Lawrence, *The Hunger Games*
Scene Stealer, Male: Liam Hemsworth, *The Hunger Games*
Breakout Female: Rihanna, *Battleship*
Villain: Alexander Ludwig, *The Hunger Games*

Emma Stone

Most-Watched Regularly Scheduled TV Shows of 2012

NBC Sunday Night Football
American Idol
Dancing with the Stars
NCIS
The Voice
NFL Regular Season
Vegas

Mark Harmon

2012 Emmy Award Winners

Outstanding Series, Drama: *Homeland*
Outstanding Series, Comedy: *Modern Family*
Outstanding Reality Program, Competition: *The Amazing Race*
Outstanding Actor, Drama: Damian Lewis, *Homeland*
Outstanding Actress, Drama: Claire Danes, *Homeland*
Outstanding Actor, Comedy: Jon Cryer, *Two and a Half Men*
Outstanding Actress, Comedy: Julia Louis-Dreyfus, *Veep*
Outstanding Supporting Actor, Drama: Aaron Paul, *Breaking Bad*
Outstanding Supporting Actress, Drama: Maggie Smith, *Downton Abbey*
Outstanding Supporting Actor, Comedy: Eric Stonestreet, *Modern Family*
Outstanding Supporting Actress, Comedy: Julie Bowen, *Modern Family*

2013 Nickelodeon Kids' Choice Awards TV Winners

Favorite TV Show: *Victorious*
Favorite Reality Show: *Wipeout*
Favorite TV Actor: Ross Lynch
Favorite TV Actress: Selena Gomez
Favorite Cartoon: *SpongeBob SquarePants*

Ross Lynch

Movies & TV

214

2012 Teen Choice Awards
TV Winners

Animated Show: *The Simpsons*
Action: *CSI: Miami*
Actor, Action: Adam Rodriguez, *CSI: Miami*
Actress, Action: Linda Hunt, *NCIS: Los Angeles*
Comedy: *Glee*
Actor, Comedy: Chris Colfer, *Glee*
Actress, Comedy: Lea Michele, *Glee*
Drama: *Pretty Little Liars*
Actor, Drama: Ian Harding, *Pretty Little Liars*
Actress, Drama: Lucy Hale, *Pretty Little Liars*
Fantasy/Sci-Fi: *The Vampire Diaries*
Actor, Fantasy/Sci-Fi: Ian Somerhalder, *The Vampire Diaries*
Actress, Fantasy/Sci-Fi: Nina Dobrev, *The Vampire Diaries*
Reality: *Punk'd*
Female, Reality/Variety: The Kardashians, *Keeping up with the Kardashians*
Male, Reality/Variety: Paul "Pauly D" DelVecchio, *Jersey Shore* and *The Pauly D Project*
Reality Competition: *The X Factor*
Breakout Star, Female: Hannah Simone, *New Girl*
Breakout Star, Male: Beau Mirchoff, *Awkward*
Personality Male: Simon Cowell, *The X Factor*
Personality Female: Jennifer Lopez, *American Idol*
Villain: Janel Parrish, *Pretty Little Liars*

Selena Gomez

CHECK IT OUT !

Multitalented Selena Gomez is a singer, TV and movie star, has her own fashion line and fragrance, and was the youngest-ever ambassador appointed for UNICEF.

They didn't win the second season of Simon Cowell's *The X Factor*, but "girl group" Fifth Harmony is becoming a pop music sensation anyway. The five teens have performed with Demi Lovato, and in January 2013 they signed with Cowell's record label. What's next? Maybe they'll follow the lead of another famous *The X Factor* loser, One Direction, and go on to win a Grammy.

Top 10 Albums of 2012

Album	Artist
21	Adele
Red	Taylor Swift
Up All Night	One Direction
Babel	Mumford & Sons
Take Me Home	One Direction
Believe	Justin Bieber
Blown Away	Carrie Underwood
Tailgates & Tanlines	Luke Bryan
Tuskegee	Lionel Richie
Night Train	Jason Aldean

Top 10 Digitally Downloaded Songs of 2012

Song	Artist
"Somebody That I Used to Know"	Gotye featuring Kimbra
"Call Me Maybe"	Carly Rae Jepsen
"We Are Young"	fun. featuring Janelle Monáe
"Payphone"	Maroon 5
"Starships"	Nicky Minaj
"What Makes You Beautiful"	One Direction
"Some Nights"	fun.
"Stronger"	Kelly Clarkson
"Gangnam Style"	Psy
"One More Night"	Maroon 5

Music

2013 Grammy Award Winners

Record of the Year: "Somebody That I Used to Know," Gotye Featuring Kimbra

Album of the Year: *Babel*, Mumford & Sons

Song of the Year: "We Are Young," Jack Antonoff, Jeff Bhasker, Andrew Dost & Nate Ruess, songwriters (fun. featuring Janelle Monáe)

Best New Artist: fun.

Best Rap Album: *Take Care*, Drake

Best Rap Song: "N****s in Paris," Shawn Carter, Mike Dean, Chauncey Hollis & Kanye West, songwriters (W. A. Donaldson, songwriter) (Jay-Z & Kanye West)

Best R & B Album: *Black Radio*, Robert Glasper Experiment

Best R & B Song: "Adorn," Miguel Pimentel, songwriter Miguel Pimentel

Best Rock Album: *El Camino*, The Black Keys

Best Rock Song: "Lonely Boy," Dan Auerbach, Brian Burton & Patrick Carney, songwriters (The Black Keys)

Best Alternative Music Album: *Making Mirrors*, Gotye

Best Pop Vocal Album: *Stronger*, Kelly Clarkson

Best Country Song: "Blown Away," Josh Kear & Chris Tompkins, songwriters (Carrie Underwood)

2012 Teen Choice Awards

Rock Song: "Paradise," Coldplay

Rock Group: fun.

R & B/Hip-Hop Track: "Starships," Nicki Minaj

R & B/Hip-Hop Artist: Nicki Minaj

Love Song: "What Makes You Beautiful," One Direction

Breakout Artist: Carly Rae Jepsen

Female Artist: Taylor Swift

Male Artist: Justin Bieber

Group: Selena Gomez & The Scene

Single, Female: "Eyes Open," Taylor Swift

Single, Male: "Boyfriend," Justin Bieber

2013 Nickelodeon Kids' Choice Awards

Favorite Music Group: One Direction

Favorite Song: "What Makes You Beautiful"

Favorite Male Singer: Justin Bieber

Favorite Female Singer: Katy Perry

All plants remove carbon dioxide from the air through photosynthesis. Now a NASA study shows that certain houseplants can scrub out other indoor pollutants, such as benzene and formaldehyde. NASA hopes to use plants on future orbiting space stations to help keep life-support systems contaminant-free.

Plants

> **Green Cleaners**

> Bamboo palm
> Chinese evergreen
> English ivy
> Gerbera daisy

> Peace lily
> Chrysanthemum
> Spider plant
> Philodendron

Biological Classification of Plants

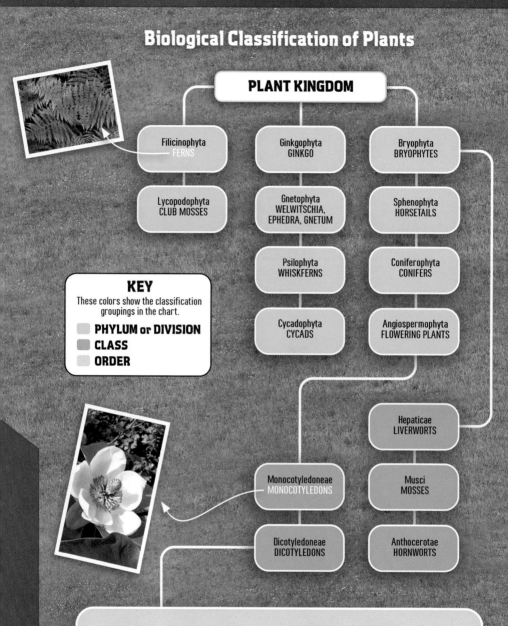

PLANT KINGDOM

| Filicinophyta FERNS |
| Lycopodophyta CLUB MOSSES |

| Ginkgophyta GINKGO |
| Gnetophyta WELWITSCHIA, EPHEDRA, GNETUM |
| Psilophyta WHISKFERNS |
| Cycadophyta CYCADS |

| Bryophyta BRYOPHYTES |
| Sphenophyta HORSETAILS |
| Coniferophyta CONIFERS |
| Angiospermophyta FLOWERING PLANTS |

| Hepaticae LIVERWORTS |
| Musci MOSSES |
| Anthocerotae HORNWORTS |

| Monocotyledoneae MONOCOTYLEDONS |
| Dicotyledoneae DICOTYLEDONS |

KEY
These colors show the classification groupings in the chart.

- **PHYLUM or DIVISION**
- **CLASS**
- **ORDER**

Liliaceae	LILY, TULIP
Orchidaceae	ORCHIDS
Poaceae	WHEAT, BAMBOO
Iridaceae	IRIS, GLADIOLUS
Arecaceae	COCONUT PALM, DATE PALM
Bromeliaceae	BROMELIAD, PINEAPPLE
Cyperaceae	SEDGES
Juncaceae	RUSHES
Musaceae	BANANA
Amaryllidaceae	DAFFODIL, AMARYLLIS
Ranunculaceae	BUTTERCUP, DELPHINIUM
Brassicaceae	CABBAGE, TURNIP
Roasceae	APPLE, ROSE
Fabaceae	BEAN, PEANUT
Magnoliaceae	MAGNOLIA, TULIP TREE
Apiaceae	CARROT, PARSLEY
Solonaceae	POTATO, TOMATO
Lamiaceae	MINT, LAVENDER
Asteraceae	SUNFLOWER, DANDELION
Salicaceae	WILLOW, POPLAR
Cucurbitaceae	MELON, CUCUMBER
Malvaceae	HIBISCUS, HOLLYHOCK
Cactaceae	CACTUS

Plants

Where Do Plants Grow?

Plants grow everywhere in the world, except where there is permanent ice. However, different types of plants grow best in different regions. A region's plant life depends on the climate, the amount of water and sun, the type of soil, and other features. For instance, plants in the tundra grow close to the ground, away from the region's icy winds. Desert plants have thick skins to hold in every drop of water. This map shows five major regions where certain kinds of plants grow best, and the areas where the climate is too harsh for any plant life at all.

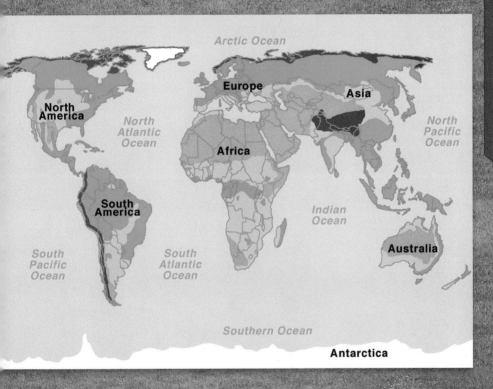

Region	Types of Plants
Aquatic	Cattails, seaweed
Grassland	Short and tall grasses
Forest	Trees, shrubs, ferns, wildflowers
Tundra	Small shrubs, mosses
Desert	Many kinds of cacti
Permanent ice	No plant life

BREAKING NEWS

Grand Central Station in New York City is celebrating its 100th birthday all throughout 2013 and into 2014. Every day, up to 750,000 commuters and visitors stream through its halls, increasing to 1,000,000 during the holidays. More than 20 million people live in and around New York, making it the most populated urban area in the United States.

Population

Population by Continent

Country	Population
Asia	4,265,251,000
Africa	1,099,181,000
Europe	740,794,000
North America	551,676,000
South America	402,047,000
Oceania	36,271,000

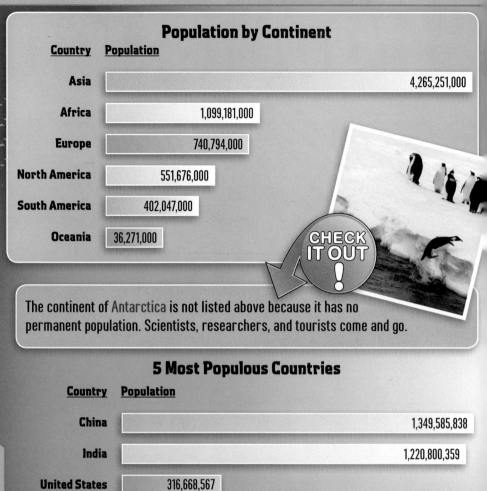

CHECK IT OUT!

The continent of Antarctica is not listed above because it has no permanent population. Scientists, researchers, and tourists come and go.

5 Most Populous Countries

Country	Population
China	1,349,585,838
India	1,220,800,359
United States	316,668,567
Indonesia	251,160,124
Brazil	201,009,622

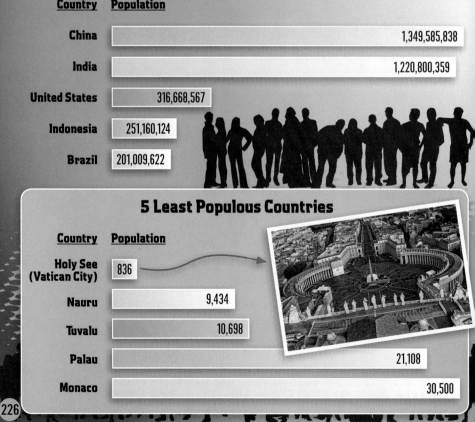

5 Least Populous Countries

Country	Population
Holy See (Vatican City)	836
Nauru	9,434
Tuvalu	10,698
Palau	21,108
Monaco	30,500

Population

5 Most Densely Populated Countries

Country	Persons per sq. mi. (persons per sq km)
Monaco	40,667 (15,641)
Singapore	20,298.5 (7,834)
Holy See (Vatican City)	4,917.6 (1,900)
Bahrain	4,985.7 (1,926.8)
Maldives	3,396.4 (1,313.3)

5 Most Sparsely Populated Countries

Country	Persons per sq. mi. (persons per sq km)
Mongolia	5.3 (2.1)
Namibia	6.8 (2.6)
Australia	7.5 (2.9)
Iceland	7.9 (3.1)
Libya	8.8 (3.4)

5 Largest World Cities

City	Population (includes surrounding densely populated areas)
Tokyo, Japan	37,217,400
New Delhi, India	22,653,600
Mexico City, Mexico	20,445,800
New York, NY, United States	20,351,700
Shanghai, China	20,207,600

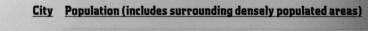

CHECK IT OUT !

You can figure out population density by dividing the population by the land area. Land areas for all countries can be found on pages 90–121. Land areas for each state of the United States, Puerto Rico, and Washington, DC, can be found on pages 128–145.

227

10 Most Populous States

State	Population
California	38,041,430
Texas	26,059,203
New York	19,570,261
Florida	19,317,568
Illinois	12,875,255
Pennsylvania	12,763,536
Ohio	11,544,225
Georgia	9,919,945
Michigan	9,883,360
North Carolina	9,752,073

10 Least Populous States

State	Population
Wyoming	576,412
Vermont	626,011
North Dakota	699,628
Alaska	731,449
South Dakota	833,354
Delaware	917,092
Montana	1,005,141
Rhode Island	1,050,292
New Hampshire	1,320,718
Maine	1,329,192

U.S. Population Growth 1790–2012

Population

Year	Population (in millions)
1790	3.9
1830	12.9
1870	38.6
1890	62.9
1910	92.2
1930	123.2
1950	151.3
1970	203.2
1990	248.7
2000	281.4
2010	308.7
2012	319.3

10 Most Populous U.S. Cities

City	Population
New York, NY	8,244,910
Los Angeles, CA	3,819,702
Chicago, IL	2,707,120
Houston, TX	2,145,146
Philadelphia, PA	1,536,471
Phoenix, AZ	1,469,471
San Antonio, TX	1,359,758
San Diego, CA	1,326,179
Dallas, TX	1,223,229
San Jose, CA	967,487

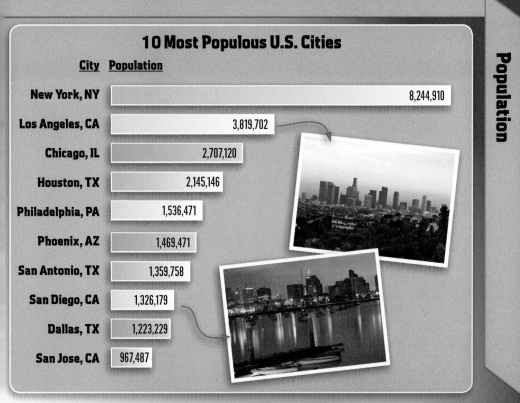

10 Fastest-Growing U.S. Cities

City	Percent Increase from 2000 to 2012
Raleigh, NC	47.8
Austin, TX	44.9
Las Vegas, NV	43.6
Orlando, FL	34.2
Charlotte, NC	32.8
Riverside-San Bernardino, CA	32.7
Phoenix, AZ	32.1
Houston, TX	31.0
San Antonio, TX	29.9
Dallas-Fort Worth, TX	27.9

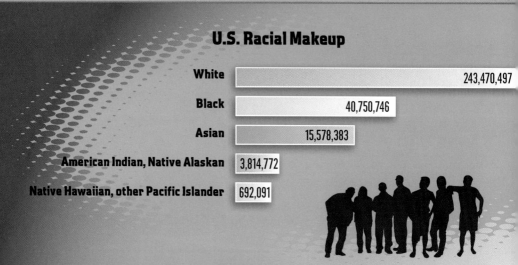

U.S. Racial Makeup

Race	Population
White	243,470,497
Black	40,750,746
Asian	15,578,383
American Indian, Native Alaskan	3,814,772
Native Hawaiian, other Pacific Islander	692,091

Hispanic is an ethnic background, not a race. Hispanic people can be of any race. As of July 2011, there were more than 52 million Hispanics in the United States. California leads the way in Hispanic population with more than 14 million.

States with the Highest Population by Race

White
California	27,883,136
Texas	20,769,382
Florida	14,959,040

Black
New York	3,400,374
Florida	3,242,840
Texas	3,138,725

Asian
California	5,142,382
New York	1,517,556
Texas	1,039,470

American Indian, Native Alaskan
California	636,860
Arizona	339,580
Oklahoma	338,069

Native Hawaiian, other Pacific Islander
California	185,415
Hawaii	138,310
Washington	44,424

Population

Our Foreign-Born Residents

According to the U.S. Census Bureau, about 40 million U.S. residents were born in a different country. That's about 13 percent of the population.

Where Do They Come from?

Continent or Region	Percentage of foreign-born
Latin America and the Caribbean	53
Asia	28
Europe	12
Africa	4
Northern America	2
Oceania	Less than 1

10 Top Countries of Origin

Country	Percentage of foreign-born
Mexico	28.9
China	5.5
India	4.6
Philippines	4.5
El Salvador	3.1
Vietnam	3.1
Cuba	2.7
North and South Korea	2.7
Dominican Republic	2.2
Guatemala	2.1

Where Do They Live?

Foreign-born residents live in every state, but more than half live in California, New York, Texas, and Florida.

10 States with Highest Foreign-Born Percentage

State	Percentage
California	27.2
New York	21.8
New Jersey	20.6
Florida	19.2
Texas	16.2
Massachusetts	14.7
Arizona	13.9
Illinois	13.7
Washington	12.8
Virginia	11.0

Foreign-Born Percentage in 10 Most Populous U.S. Cities

City	Percentage
Los Angeles	39.4
San Jose	38.6
New York City	36.8
Houston	28.4
San Diego	25.6
Dallas	24.6
Phoenix	21.5
Chicago	21.0
San Antonio	13.7
Philadelphia	11.6

CHECK IT OUT! More than one in four California residents and more than one in five residents of New York and New Jersey were born in another country. In Miami, FL, 56.4 percent of residents are foreign-born, the highest percentage of any major U.S. city.

Religion

Taktsang, meaning "Tiger's Nest," is a Buddhist monastery in Bhutan perched on a mountainside in the Himalayas. The monastery takes its name from the Bengal tigers that make their home in the area, along with snow leopards. Read about Buddhism and the rest of the world's top five religions on p. 234.

Major Religions of the World

Buddhism

Buddhism began about 525 BCE, reportedly in India. This religion is based on the teachings of Gautama Siddhartha, the Buddha, who achieved enlightenment through intense meditation. The Buddha taught that though life is full of pain, you can break the cycle and achieve peace by being mindful, meditating, and doing good deeds. There are Buddhists all over the world, but mostly in Asia. The Buddha's teachings can be read in spiritual texts, or scriptures, called sutras.

Christianity

Christianity is the world's biggest religion, with over 2 billion worshippers in the world. It is based on the teachings of Jesus Christ, who lived between 8 BCE and 29 CE. The Old and New Testaments of the Bible are the key scriptures. Christians believe that Jesus Christ is the son of God, who died on the cross to save humankind and later rose from the dead.

Hinduism

To Hindus, there is one overarching divine principle, with a variety of gods such as Vishnu, Shiva, and Shakti representing different parts of it. Hindus believe that by being mindful and doing good deeds you can break meaningless cycles and improve the purity of your actions, known as your karma. Hinduism was founded about 1500 BCE. The main scriptures are called Vedas.

Religion

Islam

Islam was founded in 610 CE by Muhammad. People who practice Islam are called Muslims. They believe in one god, Allah, who gave the spiritual writings of the Qu'ran (also known as the Koran) to Muhammad so he could teach truth and justice to all people. There are two major Muslim groups, the Shiites and the Sunni.

Judaism

Judaism was founded about 2000 BCE. The prophet Abraham is recognized as the founder. Jews believe in one god. They believe God created the universe, and they believe in being faithful to God and in following God's laws as outlined in key scriptures such as the Torah and the Hebrew Bible. There are people practicing Judaism all over the world. Many of them are in Israel and the United States.

5 Largest World Religions

Religion	Members
Christianity	2,298,093,000
Islam	1,560,391,300
Hinduism	959,941,000
Chinese folk religions	468,451,000
Buddhism	467,546,000

CHECK IT OUT!

In February 2013, Pope Benedict XVI, 85-year-old spiritual leader of the Roman Catholic Church, announced that he was resigning for health- and age-related reasons. He is the first pope to step down in about 600 years. His successor, Cardinal Jorge Bergoglio of Argentina, was named on March 13, 2013. There are almost 1.2 billion Roman Catholics in the world.

Science

BREAKING RECORDS

On October 14, 2013, skydiver Felix Baumgartner became the first human to break the sound barrier outside an aircraft. Wearing a high-tech spacesuit, he jumped from more than 24 miles (39 km) above Earth to land safely in eastern New Mexico.

High-Flying Numbers

> Speed ....843.6 mph (1357.6 kph)
> Length of trip...........9 minutes
> YouTube viewers.....More than 8 million live streams

The 5 Kingdoms of Life

To understand living things, life scientists divide them into groups that share certain features. This process is called classification. A classification system created in 1735 by Carolus Linnaeus divides life-forms into five kingdoms: animals, plants, fungi, protista, and monera. Here are some (not all) of the types of life-forms within each kingdom.

ANIMAL KINGDOM	Vertebrates (such as mammals, birds, and reptiles), sponges, worms, insects and arthropods, crustaceans, and jellyfish
PLANT KINGDOM	Ferns, mosses, ginkgos, horsetails, conifers, flowering plants, liverworts, and bladderworts
FUNGI KINGDOM	Molds, mildews, blights, smuts, rusts, mushrooms, puffballs, stinkhorns, lichens, dung fungi, yeasts, morels, and truffles
PROTISTA KINGDOM	Yellow-green algae, golden algae, protozoa, green algae, brown algae, and red algae
MONERA KINGDOM	Bacteria and blue-green algae

The kingdoms are subdivided into smaller and more specific groups.

	Category	Example: Human Being
Most general	**Kingdom**	Animal
	Phylum	Chordate
	Subphylum	Vertebrate (animals with backbones)
	Superclass	Vertebrate with jaws
	Class	Mammal
	Subclass	Advanced mammal
	Infraclass	Placental mammal
	Order	Primate
	Family	Hominid
Most specific	**Genus**	*Homo*
	Species	*Homo sapiens*

The Domain System

In 1990, biologist Carl R. Woese and other scientists proposed a slightly different classification system. They suggested dividing living things into three domains, based on their cell structure. Domain Eukaryota includes multi-celled organisms: animals, plants, fungi, and protista. Domains Archaea and Bacteria are made up of microscopic one-celled organisms. The huge majority of all living things belong to these two domains. Scientists believe that Archaea are among the oldest forms of life on Earth.

Some Major Discoveries in Life Science

Year	Discovery
400 BCE	Aristotle classifies 500 species of animals into 8 classes.
1628 CE	William Harvey discovers how blood circulates in the human body.
1683	Anton van Leeuwenhoek observes bacteria.
1735	Carolus Linnaeus introduces the classification system.
1859	Charles Darwin publishes *On the Origin of Species*, which explains his theories of evolution.
1860	Gregor Mendel discovers the laws of heredity through experiments with peas and fruit flies.
1861	Louis Pasteur, the "father of bacteriology," comes up with a theory that certain diseases are caused by bacteria.
1953	James D. Watson and Francis H. Crick develop the double helix model of DNA, which explains how traits are inherited. Jonas Salk invents the polio vaccine.
1996	Dolly the sheep is cloned in Scotland.
2009	Doctors successfully treat blindness, brain disorders, and immune system deficiencies by inserting genes into patients' cells and tissues. However, the procedure remains controversial because of dangerous side effects.
2011	Early tests of a vaccine for malaria give scientists hope the disease can someday be wiped out. Malaria is carried by certain types of mosquitoes and is a leading cause of death for children in many countries.
2012	Scientists create artificial compounds called XNAs that can copy and store information and evolve, like DNA.

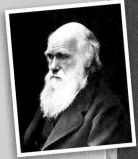

CHECK IT OUT!

In 1952, nearly 60,000 cases of polio, with 3,000 deaths, were reported in the United States. Because of the Salk vaccine, the disease was virtually wiped out in this country by 1979. However, polio is still circulating in three countries today—Afghanistan, Pakistan, and Nigeria—and it could spread. Until it's eliminated worldwide, it's important that kids continue to get vaccinated.

The Rock Cycle

Rocks don't grow like plants and animals, but they change from one form to another in a never-ending process called the **rock cycle**. Geologists, or scientists who study rocks, divide them into three groups.

Igneous

Igneous rock makes up about 95 percent of the upper part of Earth's crust. There are two kinds:

Intrusive igneous rock forms when melted rock, or magma, cools beneath Earth's surface. Granite is a common type of intrusive igneous rock. Intrusive igneous rocks are constantly being pushed up to the surface by natural forces.

Extrusive igneous rock forms when the melted rock erupts as lava and cools on Earth's surface. Basalt is a common type of extrusive igneous rock.

Granite

Basalt

Sedimentary

Igneous rocks on Earth's surface can be broken down into tiny pieces and moved around by wind, rain, and ocean waves. These little pieces, called sediments, pile up in water and are squeezed into layers with other sediments such as bits and pieces of plants or dead animals. Limestone is a common type of sedimentary rock.

Limestone

Metamorphic

Pressure and heat can flatten and fold igneous or sedimentary rock into a whole new shape, color, and mineral structure. Marble is a metamorphic rock that often comes from limestone.

Marble

CHE IT O !

Plymouth Rock in Plymouth, Massachusetts, is made of granite scientists think was formed more than 600 million years ago. The famous landmark is much smaller today than it was in 1620, when the Pilgrims arrived from England. It has been worn down by erosion and chipped away by souvenir-hunting tourists.

What's the Difference Between Rocks and Minerals?

The difference is simple: Rocks are made of minerals, but minerals are not made of rocks. Minerals are chemical compounds found on, in, and below Earth's crust. There are about 4,000 known minerals on Earth.

Quartz is one of the most common minerals, making up about 12 percent of Earth's crust. Some quartz is so clear you can see straight through it. Other types are pink, green, yellow, or purple. The color varies depending on how the quartz was formed. But quartz does more than look pretty. Under certain conditions, quartz can generate electricity to power clocks, computers, TVs, heaters, and other devices.

A Scratch Test for Minerals

The Mohs Scale, invented by German mineralogist Frederich Mohs, ranks ten minerals on hardness based on their resistance to scratches. Minerals with higher numbers can scratch minerals with lower numbers.

Mineral	Rank
Talc	1
Gypsum	2
Calcite	3
Fluorite	4
Apatite	5
Orthoclase feldspar	6
Quartz	7
Topaz	8
Corundum	9
Diamond	10

Hard to Say

Here's how certain items would rank in hardness on the Mohs scale.

Fingernails	2.5
Gold, silver	2.5–3
Copper penny	3
Iron	4–5
Knife blade	5.5
Glass	6–7
Hardened steel file	7+

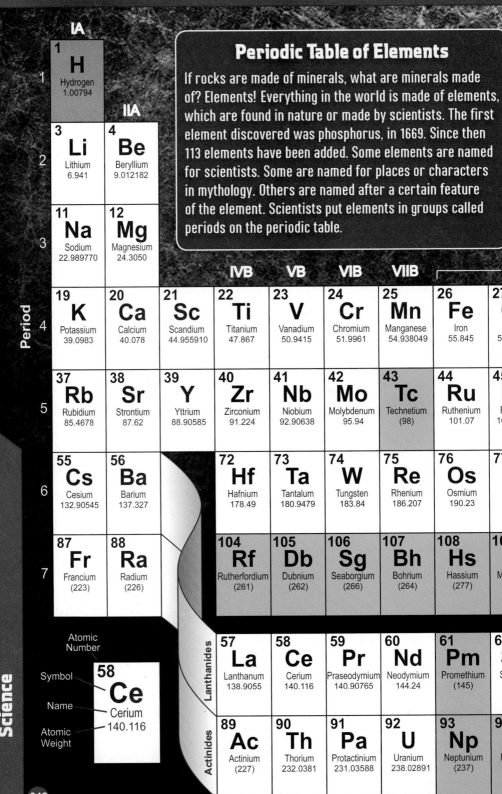

Periodic Table of Elements

If rocks are made of minerals, what are minerals made of? Elements! Everything in the world is made of elements, which are found in nature or made by scientists. The first element discovered was phosphorus, in 1669. Since then 113 elements have been added. Some elements are named for scientists. Some are named for places or characters in mythology. Others are named after a certain feature of the element. Scientists put elements in groups called periods on the periodic table.

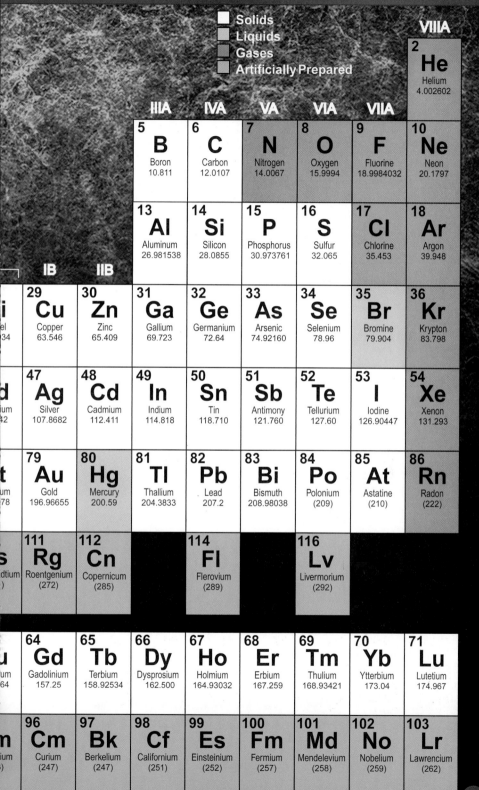

Solids
Liquids
Gases
Artificially Prepared

VIIIA	
	2 **He** Helium 4.002602

IIIA	IVA	VA	VIA	VIIA	
5 **B** Boron 10.811	6 **C** Carbon 12.0107	7 **N** Nitrogen 14.0067	8 **O** Oxygen 15.9994	9 **F** Fluorine 18.9984032	10 **Ne** Neon 20.1797
13 **Al** Aluminum 26.981538	14 **Si** Silicon 28.0855	15 **P** Phosphorus 30.973761	16 **S** Sulfur 32.065	17 **Cl** Chlorine 35.453	18 **Ar** Argon 39.948

IB	IIB						
29 **Cu** Copper 63.546	30 **Zn** Zinc 65.409	31 **Ga** Gallium 69.723	32 **Ge** Germanium 72.64	33 **As** Arsenic 74.92160	34 **Se** Selenium 78.96	35 **Br** Bromine 79.904	36 **Kr** Krypton 83.798
47 **Ag** Silver 107.8682	48 **Cd** Cadmium 112.411	49 **In** Indium 114.818	50 **Sn** Tin 118.710	51 **Sb** Antimony 121.760	52 **Te** Tellurium 127.60	53 **I** Iodine 126.90447	54 **Xe** Xenon 131.293
79 **Au** Gold 196.96655	80 **Hg** Mercury 200.59	81 **Tl** Thallium 204.3833	82 **Pb** Lead 207.2	83 **Bi** Bismuth 208.98038	84 **Po** Polonium (209)	85 **At** Astatine (210)	86 **Rn** Radon (222)
111 **Rg** Roentgenium (272)	112 **Cn** Copernicum (285)		114 **Fl** Flerovium (289)		116 **Lv** Livermorium (292)		

64 **Gd** Gadolinium 157.25	65 **Tb** Terbium 158.92534	66 **Dy** Dysprosium 162.500	67 **Ho** Holmium 164.93032	68 **Er** Erbium 167.259	69 **Tm** Thulium 168.93421	70 **Yb** Ytterbium 173.04	71 **Lu** Lutetium 174.967
96 **Cm** Curium (247)	97 **Bk** Berkelium (247)	98 **Cf** Californium (251)	99 **Es** Einsteinium (252)	100 **Fm** Fermium (257)	101 **Md** Mendelevium (258)	102 **No** Nobelium (259)	103 **Lr** Lawrencium (262)

Before

NO STANDING
EXCEPT
COMMERCIAL VEHICLES
METERED PARKING
3 HOUR LIMIT
7AM - 6PM
MON THRU FRI

6PM - MIDNIGHT
MON THRU FRI
METERED PARKING
6 HOUR LIMIT
⟷

8AM - MIDNIGHT
SATURDAY
METERED PARKING
6 HOUR LIMIT
⟷

SP-273E   DEPT OF TRANSPORTATION

After

3 hour
metered
parking
COMMERCIAL
VEHICLES ONLY
OTHERS NO STANDING
Monday - Friday
7am - 6pm
⟷

6 hour
metered
parking
Monday - Friday
6pm - Midnight

Saturday
8am - Midnight
⟷

Dept of Transportation   SP-515E

Signs & Symbols

BREAKING NEWS

Signs should communicate clearly, but drivers in New York City complained that parking signs were unclear and confusing. In January 2013, the city announced it was replacing the signs with new ones designed to be easier to read and understand. Look at the old sign and the new one. Can you spot the differences?

Basic Signs

Fire extinguisher

Women's room

Men's room

First aid

Elevator

Information

Disabled (parking, restrooms, access)

Bus

Recycle

Fallout shelter

No smoking

No admittance

No parking

Danger

Poison

Stop

Yield

Do not enter

No left turn

Falling rock

Stop ahead

Bicycle path

Traffic light ahead

Railroad crossing

Pedestrian crossing

Intersection ahead

Left turn

Right turn

Two-way traffic

Slippery when wet

American Sign Language

In the manual alphabet of the hearing impaired, the fingers of the hand are moved to positions that represent the letters of the alphabet. Whole words and ideas are also expressed in sign language.

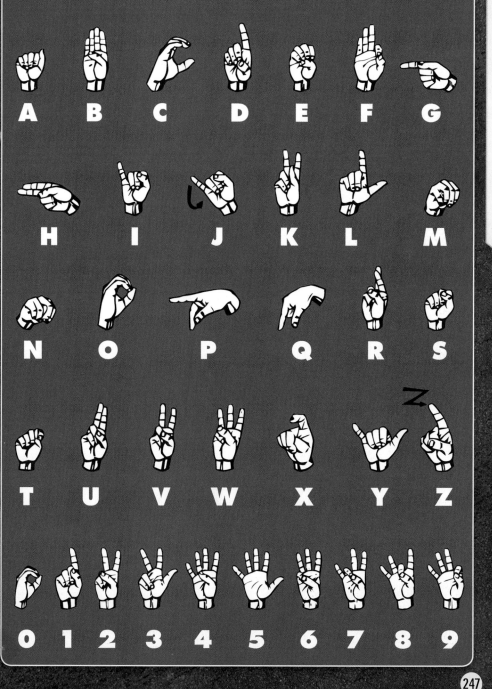

Space

STAY
TUNED

On February 15, 2013, a meteor the size of a large bus entered Earth's atmosphere and blew up above Chelyabinsk, Russia, injuring 1,200 people below. Hours later, an asteroid flew by Earth. Scientists are developing meteor-mapping and asteroid-detection systems so earthlings can have more warning next time. The first system could be ready by 2015.

The Solar System
(with distances from the Sun*)

Mars
141.6 million miles
(227.9 million km)

Earth
92.9 million miles
(149.6 million km)

Venus
67.2 million miles
(108.2 million km)

Mercury
36.0 million miles
(57.9 million km)

SUN

*Distances rounded to nearest tenth

Neptune
2.8 billion miles
(4.5 billion km)

Uranus
1.8 billion miles
(2.9 billion km)

Saturn
885.9 million miles
(1.4 billion km)

Jupiter
483.7 million miles
(778.4 million km)

CHECK
IT OUT
!

Space Rocks!

- **Asteroid**: Rocky object that orbits the Sun
- **Comet**: Ball of dirt and ice with a tail that orbits the Sun
- **Meteoroid**: Small particle from an asteroid or comet
- **Meteor**: Meteoroid that enters Earth's atmosphere, burns up, and is visible as a streak of light
- **Meteorite**: Meteoroid that falls to Earth

In February 2013, 13-year-old Jansen Lyons found a 2-lb. meteorite near his New Mexico home, using a homemade metal detector. Experts at nearby University of New Mexico estimate the space object landed 10,000 years ago.

Basic Facts About the Planets in Our Solar System

Planet	Average distance from Sun	Rotation period (hours)	Period of revolution (in Earth days)	Diameter relative to Earth	Average surface or effective temperature	Planetary satellites (moons)
Mercury	36.0 million miles (57.9 million km)	1,407.5 hours	88 days	38.2%	332°F (166°C)	0
Venus	67.2 million miles (108.2 million km)	5,832.2 hours*	224.7 days	94.9%	864°F (462°C)	0
Earth	92.9 million miles (149.6 million km)	23.9 hours	365.24 days	100%	59°F (15°C)	1
Mars	141.6 million miles (227.9 million km)	24.6 hours	687 days	53.2%	-80°F (-62°C)	2
Jupiter	483.7 million miles (778.4 million km)	9.9 hours	4,330.6 days	1,121%	-234°F (-148°C)	66
Saturn	885.9 million miles (1.4 billion km)	10.7 hours	10,755.7 days	944%	-288°F (-178°C)	at least 62
Uranus	1.8 billion miles (2.9 billion km)	17.2 hours*	30,687.2 days	401%	-357°F (-216°C)	at least 27
Neptune	2.8 billion miles (4.5 billion km)	16.1 hours	60,190 days	388%	-353°F (-214°C)	at least 13

Space

*Retrograde rotation; rotates backward, or in the opposite direction from most other planetary bodies.

Basic Facts About the Sun

Position in the solar system	center
Average distance from Earth	92,955,820 miles (149,597,891 km)
Distance from center of Milky Way galaxy	27,710 light-years
Rotation Period	25.38 days
Equatorial diameter	864,400 miles (1,391,117 km)
Diameter relative to Earth	109 times larger
Temperature at core	27,000,000°F (15,000,000°C)
Temperature at surface	10,000°F (5,538°C)
Main components	hydrogen and helium
Expected life of hydrogen fuel supply	6.4 billion years

Top 10 Largest Bodies in the Solar System

Ranked by size in equatorial diameter

1. Sun
864,400 miles
(1,391,117 km)

2. Jupiter
88,846 miles
(142,984 km)

3. Saturn
74,898 miles
(120,536 km)

4. Uranus
31,764 miles
(51,118 km)

5. Neptune
30,776 miles
(49,528 km)

6. Earth
7,926 miles
(12,755 km)

7. Venus
7,521 miles
(12,104 km)

8. Mars
4,222 miles
(6,794 km)

9. Ganymede
(moon of Jupiter)
3,280 miles
(5,262 km)

10. Titan
(moon of Saturn)
3,200 miles
(5,149 km)

Astronomy Terms and Definitions

Light-year (distance traveled by light in one year)	5.880 trillion miles (9.462 trillion km)
Velocity of light (speed of light)	186,000 miles/second (299,338 km/s)
Mean distance, Earth to Moon	238,855 miles (384,400 km)
Radius of Earth (distance from Earth's center to the equator)	3,963.19 miles (6,378 km)
Equatorial circumference of Earth (distance around the equator)	24,901 miles (40,075 km)
Polar circumference of Earth (distance around the poles)	24,860 miles (40,008 km)
Earth's mean velocity in orbit (how fast it travels)	18.5 miles/second (29.8 km/sec)

Fast Facts About the Moon

Age	4.6 billion years
Location	solar system
Mean distance from Earth	238,855 miles (384,400 km)
Diameter	2,160 miles (3,476 km)
Period of revolution	27 Earth days

Interesting features:
The Moon has no atmosphere or magnetic field. Most rocks on the surface of the Moon seem to be between 3 and 4.6 billion years old. Thus the Moon provides evidence about the early history of our solar system.

Top 10 Known Closest Comet Approaches to Earth Prior to 2013

5. Biela
December 9, 1805
3,402,182.5 miles
(5,475,282 km)

6. Comet of 1743
February 8, 1743
3,625,276.5 miles
(5,834,317 km)

4. Halley
April 10, 837
3,104,724.0 miles
(4,996.569 km)

7. Pons-Winnecke
June 26, 1927
3,662,458.7 miles
(5,894,156 km)

3. IRAS-Araki-Alcock
May 11, 1983
2,900,221.5 miles
(4,667,454 km)

8. Comet of 1014
February 24, 1014
3,783,301.1 miles
(6,088,633 km)

2. Tempel-Tuttle
October 26, 1366
2,128,687.8 miles
(3,425,791 km)

9. Comet of 1702
April 20, 1702
4,062,168.8 miles
(6,537,427 km)

1. Lexell
July 1, 1770
1,403,632.1 miles
(2,258,927 km)

10. Comet of 1132
October 7, 1132
4,155,124.7 miles
(6,687,025 km)

The Phases of the Moon

The Moon's appearance changes as it moves in its orbit around Earth.

First quarter

Waxing gibbous

Waxing crescent

Full moon

New moon

Waning gibbous

Waning crescent

Last quarter

Major Constellations

Latin	English	Latin	English
Aries	Ram	Lynx	Lynx
Camelopardalis	Giraffe	Lyra	Harp
Cancer	Crab	Microscopium	Microscope
Canes Venatici	Hunting Dogs	Monoceros	Unicorn
Canis Major	Big Dog	Musca	Fly
Canis Minor	Little Dog	Orion	Orion
Capricornus	Goat	Pavo	Peacock
Cassiopeia	Queen	Pegasus	Pegasus
Centaurus	Centaur	Phoenix	Phoenix
Cetus	Whale	Pictor	Painter
Chamaeleon	Chameleon	Pisces	Fish
Circinus	Compass	Piscis Austrinus	Southern Fish
Columba	Dove	Sagitta	Arrow
Corona Australis	Southern Crown	Sagittarius	Archer
Corona Borealis	Northern Crown	Scorpius	Scorpion
Corvus	Crow	Sculptor	Sculptor
Crater	Cup	Scutum	Shield
Crux	Southern Cross	Serpens	Serpent
Cygnus	Swan	Sextans	Sextant
Delphinus	Dolphin	Taurus	Bull
Dorado	Goldfish	Telescopium	Telescope
Draco	Dragon	Triangulum	Triangle
Equuleus	Little Horse	Triangulum Australe	Southern Triangle
Gemini	Twins	Tucana	Toucan
Grus	Crane	Ursa Major	Big Bear
Hercules	Hercules	Ursa Minor	Little Bear
Horologium	Clock	Virgo	Virgin
Lacerta	Lizard	Volans	Flying Fish
Leo	Lion	Vulpecula	Little Fox
Leo Minor	Little Lion		

Galaxies Nearest to the Sun

1. Canis Major Dwarf Galaxy
25,000 light-years

2. Sagittarius Dwarf Elliptical Galaxy
70,000 light-years

3. Large Magellanic Cloud
179,000 light-years

4. Small Magellanic Cloud
210,000 light-years

It would take the spacecraft *Voyager* about 749,000,000 years to get to Canis Major Dwarf Galaxy, the closest galaxy to ours.

CHECK OUT!

Stars Closest to Earth *

1. Proxima Centauri
4.22 light-years

2. Alpha Centauri A and B
4.35 light-years

3. Barnard's Star
5.9 light-years

4. Wolf 359
7.6 light-years

5. Lalande 21185
8.0 light-years

6. Sirius A and B
8.6 light-years

7. Luyten 726-8A and 726-8B
8.9 light-years

*besides the Sun

SAVE THE DATE

Sochi, Russian Federation, will host back-to-back world-class athletic competitions in 2014. The Winter Olympics will take place from February 7 to February 23, followed by the Paralympic Games, March 7-16. Keep up to date on both at www.sochi2014.com. Read about the Olympics on pages 266 and 267.

Sports

League Leaders 2012

Passing Yards
Drew Brees, New Orleans Saints — 5,177

Rushing Yards
Adrian Peterson, Minnesota Vikings — 2,097

Receiving Yards
Calvin Johnson, Detroit Lions — 1,964

Touchdowns
Arian Foster, Houston Texans — 17

Kick Returns
David Wilson, New York Giants — 57 returns/1,533 yards

Super Bowl XLVII

On February 3, 2013, the National Football League staged its championship pro football game, Super Bowl XLVII, between National Football Conference (NFC) leaders San Francisco 49ers and American Football Conference (AFC) leaders Baltimore Ravens at Mercedes-Benz Superdome in New Orleans, Louisiana. The Ravens won 34—31. Ravens QB Joe Flacco was named MVP. He completed 22 of 33 passes for 287 yards and three touchdowns and no interceptions. Action was halted for 34 minutes when an electrical relay device failed and caused a blackout.

Baltimore Ravens (AFC) 34
San Francisco 49ers (NFC) 31

The Pittsburgh Steelers made NFL history in February 2009 when Pittsburgh won the Super Bowl for the sixth time—the most Super Bowl victories by any single team. They claimed the Lombardi Trophy in Super Bowls IX, X, XIII, XIV, XL, and XLIII. The San Francisco 49ers (XVI, XIX, XXIII, XXIV, XXIX) and the Dallas Cowboys (VI, XII, XXVII, XXVIII, XXX) are the other league leaders, with five championships each.

CHECK IT OUT!

Sports

Bowl Championship Series (BCS)

National Championship Game 2012
Alabama 42, Notre Dame 14

Major Bowl Games 2012–2013

Game	Location	Teams/Score
Capital One Bowl	Orlando, FL	Georgia 45, Nebraska 31
Chick-fil-A Bowl	Atlanta, GA	Clemson, 25, LSU 24
Russell Athletic Bowl	Orlando, FL	VA Tech 13, Rutgers 10
Fiesta Bowl	Glendale, AZ	Oregon 35, Kansas St 17
Gator Bowl	Jacksonville, FL	Northwestern 34, Miss St 20
Outback Bowl	Tampa, FL	S Carolina 33, Michigan 28
Cotton Bowl	Arlington, TX	Texas A&M 41, Oklahoma 13
Orange Bowl	Miami, FL	Florida St 31, N Illinois 10
Rose Bowl	Pasadena, CA	Stanford 20, Wisconsin 14
Sugar Bowl	New Orleans, LA	Louisville 33, Florida 23

Heisman Trophy 2012

Johnny Manziel of the Texas A&M Aggies is the 33rd quarterback to receive the Heisman Memorial Trophy as the most outstanding college football player in the nation. He is also the first freshman ever to win. Manziel completed 273 of 400 passes this year for 3,419 yards and 24 touchdowns, only throwing 8 interceptions. He is the second Heisman Trophy winner from Texas A&M.

Top Players 2012

Rookies of the Year
American League — Mike Trout, Los Angeles Angels
National League — Bryce Harper, Washington Nationals

Managers of the Year
American League — Bob Melvin, Oakland Athletics
National League — Davey Johnson, Washington Nationals

Most Valuable Player Awards
American League — Miguel Cabrera, Detroit Tigers
National League — Buster Posey, San Francisco Giants

Cy Young Awards
American League — David Price, Tampa Bay Rays
National League — R.A. Dickey, New York Mets

Gold Glove Winners 2012
(selected by managers and players)

American League

	Jeremy Hellickson, Tampa Bay Rays
Pitcher	Jake Peavy, Chicago White Sox
Catcher	Matt Wieters, Baltimore Orioles
First Baseman	Mark Teixeira, New York Yankees
Second Baseman	Robinson Canó, New York Yankees
Third Baseman	Adrián Beltré, Texas Rangers
Shortstop	J. J. Hardy, Baltimore Orioles
	Alex Gordon, Kansas City Royals
	Adam Jones, Baltimore Orioles
Outfielders	Josh Reddick, Oakland Athletics

National League

Pitcher	Mark Buehrle, Miami Marlins
Catcher	Yadier Molina, St. Louis Cardinals
First Baseman	Adam LaRoche, Washington Nationals
Second Baseman	Darwin Barney, Chicago Cubs
Third Baseman	Chase Headley, San Diego Padres
Shortstop	Jimmy Rollins, Philadelphia Phillies
	Carlos González, Colorado Rockies
	Andrew McCutchen, Pittsburgh Pirates
Outfielders	Jason Heyward, Atlanta Braves

Sports

League Leaders 2012

American League

Batting Average	Miguel Cabrera, Detroit Tigers
Home Runs	Miguel Cabrera, Detroit Tigers
Runs Batted In	Miguel Cabrera, Detroit Tigers
Wins	David Price, Tampa Bay Rays
Earned Run Average	David Price, Tampa Bay Rays
Saves	Jim Johnson, Baltimore Orioles

National League

Batting Average	Buster Posey, San Francisco Giants
Home Runs	Ryan Braun, Milwaukee Brewers
Runs Batted In	Chase Headley, San Diego Padres
Wins	Gio Gonzalez, Washington Nationals
Earned Run Average	Clayton Kershaw, Los Angeles Dodgers
Saves	Craig Kimbrel, Atlanta Braves

World Series 2012

On October 28, 2012, the San Francisco Giants beat the Detroit Tigers 4–3, winning their fourth straight game to sweep the best-of-seven series. Only four other National League teams have swept the series in the past 105 years. Pablo Sandoval, Giants third baseman, was named MVP. He hit .500 with three home runs, a double, and four RBIs in 16 at-bats. The Giants have won two of the past three World Series.

Little League World Series 2012

Tokyo Kitasuna Little League of Tokyo, Japan, defeated Goodlettsville Baseball Little League of Goodlettsville, Tennessee, 12–2 to cap the title in the Little League World Series, played in South Williamsport, PA, August 16–August 26. Noriatsu Osaka had three home runs and a triple. Starting Tokyo pitcher Kotaro Kiyomiya, a thirteen-year-old with a fastball clocked in the high 70s, struck out eight players in four innings and added an RBI single.

NBA Championship Finals 2012

On June 21, 2012, the Miami Heat clinched the National Basketball championship in game 5 with a 121–106 win over the Oklahoma City Thunder in the best-of-seven series played at AmericanAirlines Arena in Miami, FL. LeBron James was named MVP, scoring 26 points, 13 assists, and 11 rebounds.

NBA Top Scorers 2012

NAME	TEAM	GAMES	AVG. POINTS
1. Carmelo Anthony	NYK	64	28.6
2. Kevin Durant	OKC	78	28.3
3. Kobe Bryant	LAL	77	27.3
4. LeBron James	MIA	74	26.9
5. James Harden	HOU	74	25.9

WNBA Championship Finals 2012

On October 21, 2012, the Indiana Fever faced the Minnesota Lynx at the Bankers Life Fieldhouse in Indianapolis, IN, and won 87–78 to capture the Women's National Basketball (WNBA) title. It is the first WNBA championship for the Fever. Tamika Catchings was named MVP, scoring 25 points.

WNBA Top Scorers 2012

NAME	TEAM	GAMES	AVG. POINTS (per game)
1. Angel McCoughtry	Atlanta Dream	24	21.4
2. DeWanna Bonner	Phoenix Mercury	32	20.6
3. Cappie Pondexter	New York Liberty	34	20.4
4. Epiphanny Prince	Chicago Sky	26	18.1
5. Tina Charles	Connecticut Sun	33	18.0

Sports

COLLEGE BASKETBALL

NCAA Men's Division I Championship 2013

The Louisville Cardinals beat the Michigan Wolverines to win the National Collegiate Athletic Association (NCAA) championship on April 8, 2013, at the Georgia Dome in Atlanta, GA. The Cardinals came from behind in the second half to win 82–76, capturing Louisville's first men's basketball title since 1986. Louisville captain Luke Hancock scored 22 points and was named Most Outstanding Player of the Final Four. After a season in which he averaged under 2 points a game, Wolverine guard Spike Albrecht thrilled fans by scoring 17 points and was named Most Valuable Player of the championship game. Cardinals reserve guard Kevin Ware, who suffered a broken leg in the regional final against Duke on March 31, watched the game propped up on crutches, and then was given the honor of cutting down the nets.

NCAA Men's Championship Game Leaders

	LOUISVILLE		MICHIGAN	
Points	Luke Hancock	22	Trey Burke	24
Rebounds	Chane Behanan	12	Mitch McGary	6
Assists	Gorgui Dieng	6	Tim Hardaway Jr.	4

NCAA Women's Division I Championship 2013

In the women's division of the NCAA, the University of Connecticut Huskies defeated the Louisville Cardinals 93–60 on April 9, 2013, to win the national championship game played at the New Orleans Arena in New Orleans, LA. It was the eighth time the UConn women, led by Coach Geno Auriemma, have made it to the finals—and the eighth time they've won. Freshman star Breanna Stewart scored 23 points and was named Most Outstanding Player of the Final Four.

London 2012 Summer Olympics

The 2012 Summer Olympics took place in London, England, from July 27-August 12. More than 200 buildings were knocked down to make way for construction of Olympic stadiums, arenas, and other venues. Two thousand newts and more than one hundred toads living in the construction area were relocated to new habitats.

> **26 sports**
> **302 medal events**
> **8.8 million tickets**
> **About 10,500 athletes**

The Aquatics Center was at the heart of some of the most-watched events. To reduce the amount of water used in the Aquatics Center, pool water was reused to flush the Center's toilets.

Medal Count Leaders

Country	Gold	Silver	Bronze	Total
United States	46	29	29	104
China	38	27	23	88
Russian Federation	24	26	32	82
Great Britain	29	17	19	65
Germany	11	19	14	44
Japan	7	14	17	38
Australia	7	16	12	35
France	11	11	12	34
South Korea	13	8	7	28
Italy	8	9	11	28
Netherlands	6	6	8	20
Ukraine	6	5	9	20
Hungary	8	4	5	17
Brazil	3	5	9	17
Spain	3	10	4	17
Cuba	5	3	6	14
Kazakhstan	7	1	5	13

Sports

Locations of the Modern-Day Olympics

Year	Location	Year	Location
1896	Athens, Greece	1972	Munich, Germany
1900	Paris, France	1972	Sapporo, Japan
1904	St. Louis, Missouri, USA	1976	Montreal, Canada
1906	Athens, Greece	1976	Innsbruck, Austria
1908	London, UK	1980	Moscow, USSR
1912	Stockholm, Sweden	1980	Lake Placid, New York, USA
1916	Canceled	1984	Los Angeles, California, USA
1920	Antwerp, Belgium	1984	Sarajevo, Yugoslavia
1924	Chamonix, France	1988	Seoul, South Korea
1924	Paris, France	1988	Calgary, Alberta, Canada
1928	Amsterdam, Holland	1992	Barcelona, Spain
1928	St. Moritz, Switzerland	1992	Albertville, France
1932	Los Angeles, California, USA	1994	Lillehammer, Norway
1932	Lake Placid, New York, USA	1996	Atlanta, Georgia, USA
1936	Berlin, Germany	1998	Nagano, Japan
1936	Garmisch-Partenkirchen, Germany	2000	Sydney, Australia
1940	Canceled	2002	Salt Lake City, Utah, USA
1944	Canceled	2004	Athens, Greece
1948	London, UK	2006	Turin, Italy
1948	St. Moritz, Switzerland	2008	Beijing, China
1952	Helsinki, Finland	2010	Vancouver, Canada
1952	Oslo, Norway	2012	London, UK
1956	Melbourne, Australia	2014	Sochi, Russian Federation
1956	Cortina d'Ampezzo, Italy	2016	Rio de Janeiro, Brazil
1960	Rome, Italy	2018	Pyeong Chang, South Korea
1960	Squaw Valley, California, USA		
1964	Tokyo, Japan		
1964	Innsbruck, Austria		
1968	Mexico City, Mexico		
1968	Grenoble, France		

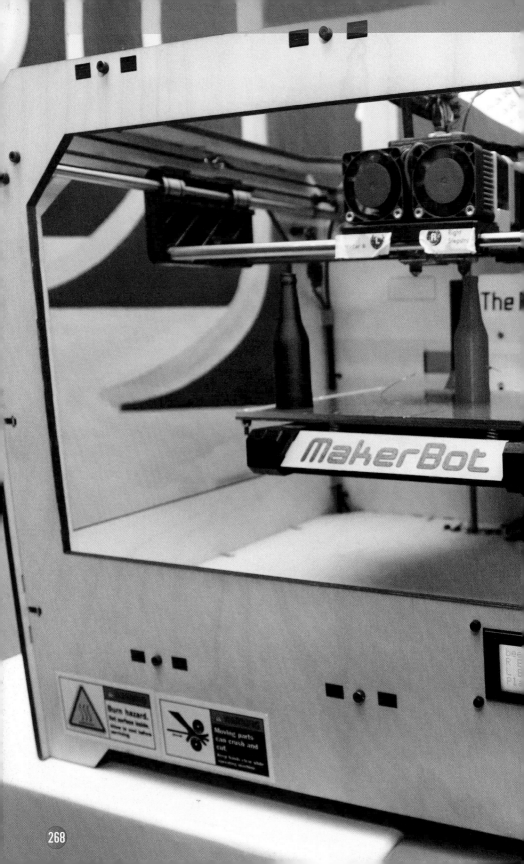

Technology & Computers

What can you make on a printer? Nowadays, just about anything—including a miniature model of yourself. New 3-D printing technology uses plastic instead of paper to create real, physical objects instead of flat paper copies.

Handcuffs made by a 3-D printer

Number of Internet Users in the United States in 2012

As of 2012, an estimated 273.79 million Americans had Internet access. This is an increase from 245.2 million in 2011. The graph shows increases since 2001.

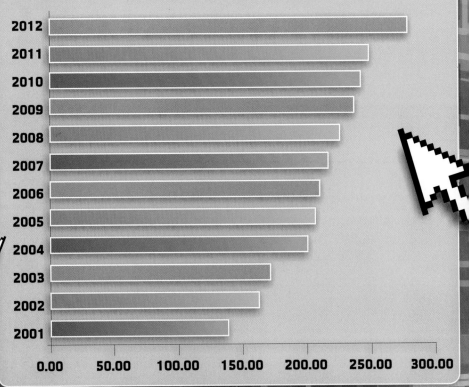

Top U.S. Internet Activities

According to the Nielsen Corporation, the top individual reason Americans go online is to use social networks and blogs.*

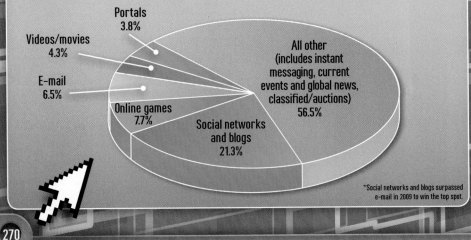

Portals
3.8%

Videos/movies
4.3%

E-mail
6.5%

Online games
7.7%

Social networks
and blogs
21.3%

All other
(includes instant
messaging, current
events and global news,
classified/auctions)
56.5%

*Social networks and blogs surpassed
e-mail in 2009 to win the top spot.

Top 10 Worldwide Internet Users

Country	Internet Users (millions)	Users per 1,000 Population	% of Worldwide Users
China	439.62	324.3	19.45%
United States	263.33	840.7	11.65%
India	165.68	137.9	7.33%
Japan	106.85	844.8	4.73%
Brazil	71.72	352.4	3.17%
Germany	65.72	799.0	2.91%
Russia	55.35	398.8	2.45%
United Kingdom	50.37	819.7	2.23%
Indonesia	49.53	201.6	2.19%
France	48.63	774.0	2.15%

Top 10 U.S. Internet Destinations

1. Google sites (YouTube, Blogger)
2. Yahoo! sites (Flickr, Rivals.com)
3. Microsoft sites (Bing, Xbox Live)
4. Facebook.com (Instagram)
5. AOL Inc. (Moviefone, Patch, Huffington Post)
6. Amazon sites (Zappos, Audible, IMDb)
7. Ask Network (Dictionary, Mindspark, Pronto)
8. Wikipedia Foundation sites (Wikipedia)
9. Glam Media (Glam, Brash)
10. Apple Inc. (iTunes)

Top 10 World Internet Destinations

1. Google sites (YouTube, Blogger)
2. Microsoft sites (Bing, Xbox Live)
3. Facebook.com
4. Yahoo! sites (Yahoo! Voices, Rivals.com, Flickr)
5. Wikipedia Foundation sites (Wikipedia)
6. Amazon sites (Zappos, Audible, IMDb, LoveFilm)
7. Apple Inc. (iTunes)
8. Federated Media Publishing (Imgur, Boing Boing)
9. Tencent Inc. (QQ)
10. Ask Network

Top 5 U.S. E-mail Websites

Website	Visitors (in thousands)
Yahoo! Mail	84,198
Google Gmail	68,581
Windows Live Hotmail	40,230
AOL Email	24,628
Comcast.net WebMail	9,213

*Number of persons age 2 and older in any U.S. location, in thousands, who visited the website at least once in Apr.–June 2012.

Top 5 Search and Navigation Websites

Website	Searches (millions)	Searchers (in thousands)*	% of Searches
Google sites	36,540	192,415	65
Yahoo! sites	8,569	105,836	15
Microsoft sites	8,421	93,015	15
Ask Network	1,548	71,488	3
AOL, Inc.	804	16,205	1

*Number of persons age 2 and older in any U.S. location, in thousands, who visited the website at least once in Apr.–June 2012.

CHECK IT OUT!

Emoticons are symbols formed from computer characters and used to show the sender's feelings in texts and e-mails. The first emoticon was invented in 1982 by Scott Fahlman, a professor at Carnegie Mellon University in Pittsburgh, PA. Fahlman used three keystrokes to create a smiley face. : -)

Screen Time, Anytime

Once, the only way to watch news, movies, and favorite programs was on a TV set. Now we can watch and interact with video content almost anytime we want, using Blu Ray devices, mobile phones, game consoles, and the Internet. Here's a look at how much time young Americans spend on different devices every week.

	Ages 2–11 Hours: Minutes	Ages 12–17 Hours: Minutes
Traditional TV	24:32	21:28
Time-shifted TV	2:03	1:37
DVD/Blu Ray	2:01	1:05
Game console	2:15	3:27
Internet	0:43	1:37
Mobile phone	--	0:24

Top 5 Most-Visited U.S. Video Sites

Website	Visitors (in thousands)
Google sites (YouTube)	154,609
Yahoo! sites	54,273
Vevo	47,980
Facebook.com	45,870
Microsoft site (Xbox Live)	41,770

*Number of persons age 2 and older in any U.S. location, in thousands, who visited the website at least once in Apr.-June 2012.

CHECK IT OUT!

YouTube by the numbers:
- More than 1 billion unique visits (not counting multiple visits by the same user) each month
- Over 4 billion hours of video watched each month
- 72 hours of video uploaded every *minute*

Mobile Internet

According to StatCounter, an international company that does research on Internet statistics, Internet usage through mobile devices was 14.3% as of February 2013. That percentage is up from 8.5% in 2012. Apple is the top supplier of mobile operating systems in the United States and the United Kingdom while Android leads globally.

America Gets Smart(phones)

As of December 2012, about 125.9 million people, or about 54% of people who own mobile phones, own smartphones. Here are the leading types of smartphones and the percentage of cell phone owners for each one.

Smartphone	% of Smartphone Owners
Android	53.4%
Apple	36.3%
BlackBerry	8.4%

What Do People Do on Their Mobile Devices?

Activity	% of Cell Phone Owners Who Use Their Phone to:
Take pictures	82
Send or receive text messages	80
Access the Internet	56
Send or receive e-mails	50
Record videos	44
Download apps	43
Look for health or medical info online	31
Check bank account balance or do online banking	29

Americans spent more than twice the amount of time on mobile apps in 2012 as they did in 2011.

CHECK IT OUT!

All About Apps

More than a million apps (applications) are available for download on mobile devices. Apple users (iPhone, iPad, and iPhone) have downloaded the most.

Device	Total Number of Free and Costing App Downloads*
Apple products	40 billion
Android	25 billion
BlackBerry	3 billion

*Apple figure as of January 2013, Android as of September 2012, BlackBerry as of July 2012

Free iPhone Apps:
Top Downloaded Apps of 2012

YouTube
Instagram
Draw Something
Flashlight
Facebook
Pandora
Temple Run
Pinterest
Twitter

According to *PC World*, Instagram, a photo sharing site, went from 30 million accounts in April 2012 to 90 million monthly active users in January 2013.

CHECK IT OUT!

275

America's Social Life

Social media is becoming a bigger and bigger part of American daily life, as new networks appear and existing websites add social features. The number of ways to connect is growing too, as technology creates new devices.

How Are We Connecting to Social Networks?

Device	Percentage of Users
Computer	94%
Mobile phone	46%
Tablet	16%
Handheld music player	7%
Game console	4%
Internet-enabled TV	4%
E-reader	3%

10 Top Social Networks

Facebook
Blogger
Twitter
WordPress
LinkedIn
Pinterest
Google+
Tumblr
MySpace
Wikia

Teens and Technology: Connecting 24/7

According to the Pew Research Center, 93% of young people 12–17 own or have use of a computer, and 95% of teens are online—more than any other age group except 18–29. More and more, teens are using their mobile devices to connect anytime they want.

Percent of all teens

78%	Have a cell phone
37%	Have a smartphone
23%	Have a tablet computer
74%	Occasionally go online with a mobile device
25%	Mostly go online with a mobile device

According to a survey of 13–17-year-olds by Commonsense Media, teens love to text and connect with friends through social media. But almost half of respondents said their favorite way to communicate is face-to-face.

Percent of respondents

90%	Have used social media
68%	Text every day
51%	Visit social network sites every day
23%	Visit at least two different social sites a day
11%	Send or receive tweets at least once a day
49%	Prefer to communicate in person
33%	Prefer to communicate by text
7%	Prefer to communicate by social networks
4%	Prefer to communicate by talking on the phone

U.S. Government

SAVE THE DATE President Abraham Lincoln delivered his Gettysburg Address on November 19, 1863, at the Pennsylvania battlefield where more than 50,000 Confederate and Union soldiers had died a few months earlier. The famous speech is inscribed in the Lincoln Memorial in Washington, DC. Events honoring the 150th anniversary of the Gettysburg Address were scheduled for most of 2013. Read about Abraham Lincoln and all the other American presidents beginning on page 289.

The Branches of Government

Executive

The President

- Symbol of our nation and head of state
- Shapes and conducts foreign policy and acts as chief diplomat
- Chief administrator of federal government
- Commander-in-chief of armed forces
- Has authority to pass or veto congressional bills, plans, and programs
- Appoints and removes nonelected officials
- Leader of his or her political party

Legislative

The Congress:
The Senate
The House of Representatives

- Chief lawmaking body
- Conducts investigations into matters of national importance
- Has power to impeach or remove any civil officer from office, including the president
- Can amend Constitution
- The Senate is made up of 100 senators—2 from each state
- The House of Representatives is made up of 435 congressional representatives, apportioned to each state according to population

Judicial

The Supreme Court

- Protects Constitution
- Enforces commands of executive and legislative branches
- Protects rights of individuals and shields citizens from unfair laws
- Defines laws of our nation
- Can declare laws unconstitutional

U.S. Government

Highest Federal Salaries

Official	Salary
President	$400,000
Vice President	$231,900
Speaker of the House	$224,600
Chief Justice of the Supreme Court	$223,500
Associate justices	$213,900
President Pro Tempore of the Senate	$194,400
Senate majority and minority leaders	$194,400
House majority and minority leaders	$194,400
Appeals court judges	$184,500
Senators	$174,000
Representatives	$174,000
District judges	$174,000

CHECK IT OUT!

For most of the years between 1789 and 1855, members of Congress received no yearly salary at all. Instead they were paid $6.00 to $8.00 a day when Congress was in session. Benjamin Franklin proposed that elected government officials not be paid anything for their service, but his proposal didn't win much support.

How a Bill Introduced in the House of Representatives Becomes a Law

How a Bill Originates

The executive branch inspires much legislation. The president usually outlines broad objectives in the yearly State of the Union address.

Members of the president's staff may draft bills and ask congresspersons who are friendly to the legislation to introduce them.

Other bills originate independently of the administration, perhaps to fulfill a campaign pledge made by a congressperson.

How a Bill Is Introduced

Each bill must be introduced by a member of the House. The Speaker then assigns the bill to the appropriate committee.

The committee conducts hearings during which members of the administration and others may testify for or against the bill.

If the committee votes to proceed, the bill goes to the Rules Committee, which decides whether to place it before the House.

The House Votes

A bill submitted to the House is voted on, with or without a debate. If a majority approves it, the bill is sent to the Senate.

Senate Procedure

The Senate assigns a bill to a Senate committee, which holds hearings and then approves, rejects, rewrites, or shelves the bill.

If the committee votes to proceed, the bill is submitted to the Senate for a vote, which may be taken with or without a debate.

Results

If the Senate does not change the House version of the bill and a majority approves it, the bill goes to the president for signing.

If the bill the Senate approves differs from the House version, the bill is sent to a House-Senate conference for a compromise solution.

If the conference produces a compromise bill and it is approved by both the House and Senate, the bill goes to the president for signing.

When a Bill Becomes Law

The bill becomes law if the president signs it. If the president vetoes the bill, two-thirds of both the House and Senate must approve it again before it can become law. If the bill comes to the president soon before Congress adjourns, the president may not do anything at all. If the bill is not signed before Congress adjourns, the bill dies. This is called the president's "pocket veto."

U.S. Government

(A similar procedure is followed for bills introduced in the Senate.)

State and Federal Court Systems

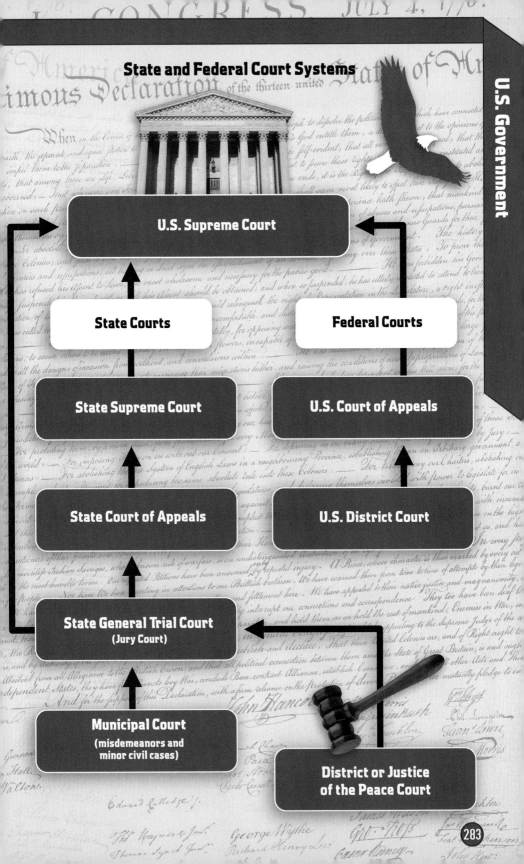

U.S. Supreme Court

State Courts

Federal Courts

State Supreme Court

U.S. Court of Appeals

State Court of Appeals

U.S. District Court

State General Trial Court
(Jury Court)

Municipal Court
(misdemeanors and minor civil cases)

District or Justice of the Peace Court

The Sequence of Presidential Succession

If the president dies, resigns, is removed from office, or can't carry out his or her duties, the vice president assumes the president's duties. If the vice president dies or becomes unable to serve, who is next in line? The order of presidential replacements is below.

1. Vice President
2. Speaker of the House
3. President Pro Tempore of the Senate
4. Secretary of State
5. Secretary of the Treasury
6. Secretary of Defense
7. Attorney General
8. Secretary of the Interior
9. Secretary of Agriculture
10. Secretary of Commerce
11. Secretary of Labor
12. Secretary of Health and Human Services
13. Secretary of Housing and Urban Development
14. Secretary of Transportation
15. Secretary of Energy

Voting

Basic Laws and Requirements

- You must be 18 years of age or older before an election in order to vote in it.
- You must be an American citizen to vote.
- You must register before voting.
- You must show proof of residence in order to register.

How to Register

- Registering often only requires filling out a simple form.
- It does not cost anything to register.
- You need not be a member of any political party to register.
- To find out where to register, you can call your town hall or city board of elections.
- You can find out more about voting and registering at:

www.eac.gov/voter

Voter Turnout: 1960–2012

Year	Percent of citizens who voted
2012*	53.6%
2010	37.8%
2008*	56.8%
2000	51.3%
1990	36.5%
1980*	52.6%
1970	46.6%
1960*	63.1%

*Presidential election year

The Electoral College

Although people turn out on Election Day and cast their votes for president, the president and vice president are only indirectly elected by the American people. In fact, the president and vice president are the only elected federal officials not chosen by direct vote of the people. These two officials are elected by the Electoral College, which was created by the framers of the Constitution.

Here is a basic summary of how the Electoral College works:
- There are 538 electoral votes.
- The votes are divided among the 50 states and the District of Columbia. The number of votes that each state has is equal to the number of senators and representatives for that state. (California has 53 representatives and 2 senators; it has a total of 55 electoral votes.)
- During an election, the candidate who wins the majority of popular votes in a given state wins all the electoral votes from that state.
- A presidential candidate needs 270 electoral votes to win.

You may have heard that it is possible for a presidential candidate who has not won the most popular votes to win an election. This can happen if a candidate wins the popular vote in large states (ones with lots of electoral votes) by only a slim margin and loses the popular votes in smaller states by a wide margin.

Electoral Votes for President

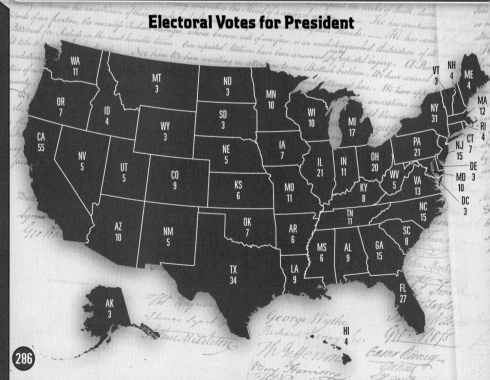

U.S. Government

U.S. Presidents with the Most Electoral Votes

President		Year	Number of electoral votes
Ronald Reagan	🐘	1984	525
Franklin D. Roosevelt	🫏	1936	523
Richard Nixon	🐘	1972	520
Ronald Reagan	🐘	1980	489
Lyndon B. Johnson	🫏	1964	486
Franklin D. Roosevelt	🫏	1932	472
Dwight D. Eisenhower	🐘	1956	457
Franklin D. Roosevelt	🫏	1940	449
Herbert Hoover	🐘	1928	444
Dwight D. Eisenhower	🐘	1952	442

🐘 = Republican
🫏 = Democrat

U.S. Presidents with the Most Popular Votes

President		Year	Number of popular votes
Barack Obama	🫏	2008	69,498,000
Barack Obama	🫏	2012	62,611,000
George W. Bush	🐘	2004	61,837,000
Ronald Reagan	🐘	1984	54,167,000
George W. Bush	🐘	2000	50,465,000
George H. W. Bush	🐘	1988	48,643,000

287

Who Is on Our Paper Money?

$1
George Washington

$2
Thomas Jefferson

$5
Abraham Lincoln

$10
Alexander Hamilton

$20
Andrew Jackson

$50
Ulysses S. Grant

$100
Benjamin Franklin

$500*
William McKinley

$1,000*
Grover Cleveland

$5,000*
James Madison

$10,000*
Salmon P. Chase

$100,000*
Woodrow Wilson

*Bills above $100 are no longer made.

Who Is on Our Coins?

Dime:
Franklin D. Roosevelt

Half-dollar:
John F. Kennedy

Penny:
Abraham Lincoln

Nickel:
Thomas Jefferson

Quarter:
George Washington

Dollar:
Sacagawea

Presidents of the United States

1. George Washington
Born: Feb. 22, 1732, Wakefield, Virginia
Died: Dec. 14, 1799, Mount Vernon, Virginia
Term of office: April 30, 1789—March 3, 1797
Age at inauguration: 57
Party: Federalist
Vice President: John Adams
First Lady: Martha Dandridge Custis Washington

2. John Adams
Born: Oct. 30, 1735, Braintree (now Quincy), Massachusetts
Died: July 4, 1826, Braintree, Massachusetts
Term of office: March 4, 1797—March 3, 1801
Age at inauguration: 61
Party: Federalist
Vice President: Thomas Jefferson
First Lady: Abigail Smith Adams

3. Thomas Jefferson
Born: April 13, 1743, Shadwell, Virginia
Died: July 4, 1826, Monticello, Virginia
Term of office: March 4, 1801—March 3, 1809
Age at inauguration: 57
Party: Democratic Republican
Vice President: Aaron Burr, George Clinton
First Lady: Martha Skelton Jefferson

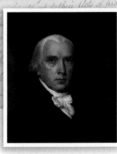

4. James Madison
Born: March 16, 1751, Port Conway, Virginia
Died: June 28, 1836, Orange, Virginia
Term of office: March 4, 1809—March 3, 1817
Age at inauguration: 57
Party: Democratic Republican
Vice President: George Clinton, Elbridge Gerry
First Lady: Dolley Todd Madison

CHECK IT OUT!

George Washington is the only president who was unanimously elected. He received every single vote!

5. James Monroe

Born: April 28, 1758, Westmoreland County, Virginia
Died: July 4, 1831, New York City, New York
Term of office: March 4, 1817—March 3, 1825
Age at inauguration: 58
Party: Democratic Republican
Vice President: Daniel D. Tompkins
First Lady: Elizabeth Kortright Monroe

6. John Quincy Adams

Born: July 11, 1767, Braintree, Massachusetts
Died: Feb. 23, 1848, Washington, DC
Term of office: March 4, 1825—March 3, 1829
Age at inauguration: 57
Party: Democratic Republican
Vice President: John C. Calhoun
First Lady: Louisa Johnson Adams

7. Andrew Jackson

Born: March 15, 1767, Waxhaw, South Carolina
Died: June 8, 1845, Nashville, Tennessee
Term of office: March 4, 1829—March 3, 1837
Age at inauguration: 61
Party: Democrat
Vice President: John C. Calhoun, Martin Van Buren
First Lady: Rachel Robards Jackson

8. Martin Van Buren

Born: Dec. 5, 1782, Kinderhook, New York
Died: July 24, 1862, Kinderhook, New York
Term of office: March 4, 1837—March 3, 1841
Age at inauguration: 54
Party: Democrat
Vice President: Richard M. Johnson
First Lady: Hannah Hoes Van Buren

9. William Henry Harrison
Born: Feb. 9, 1773, Berkeley, Virginia
Died: April 4, 1841, Washington, DC*
Term of office: March 4, 1841—April 4, 1841
Age at inauguration: 68
Party: Whig
Vice President: John Tyler
First Lady: Anna Symmes Harrison

10. John Tyler
Born: March 29, 1790, Greenway, Virginia
Died: Jan. 18, 1862, Richmond, Virginia
Term of office: April 6, 1841—March 3, 1845
Age at inauguration: 51
Party: Whig
Vice President: (none)**
First Lady: Letitia Christian Tyler,
Julia Gardiner Tyler†

11. James Knox Polk
Born: Nov. 2, 1795, Mecklenburg, North Carolina
Died: June 15, 1849, Nashville, Tennessee
Term of office: March 4, 1845—March 3, 1849
Age at inauguration: 49
Party: Democrat
Vice President: George M. Dallas
First Lady: Sarah Childress Polk

12. Zachary Taylor
Born: Nov. 24, 1784, Orange County, Virginia
Died: July 9, 1850, Washington, DC*
Term of office: March 5, 1849—July 9, 1850
Age at inauguration: 64
Party: Whig
Vice President: Millard Fillmore
First Lady: Margaret (Peggy) Smith Taylor

CHECK IT OUT!

William Henry Harrison had the longest inauguration speech and the shortest term of any president. After giving a speech lasting 105 minutes in the cold rain, he developed pneumonia and died 32 days later.

* Died in office, natural causes
** Vice President Tyler took over the duties of the president when William Henry Harrison died in office, leaving the vice presidency vacant.
† President Tyler's first wife died in 1842. He remarried in 1844.

13. Millard Fillmore
Born: Jan. 7, 1800, Cayuga County, New York
Died: March 8, 1874, Buffalo, New York
Term of office: July 10, 1850—March 3, 1853
Age at inauguration: 50
Party: Whig
Vice President: (none)*
First Lady: Abigail Powers Fillmore

14. Franklin Pierce
Born: Nov. 23, 1804, Hillsboro, New Hampshire
Died: Oct. 8, 1869, Concord, New Hampshire
Term of office: March 4, 1853—March 3, 1857
Age at inauguration: 48
Party: Democrat
Vice President: William R. King
First Lady: Jane Appleton Pierce

15. James Buchanan
Born: April 23, 1791, Mercersburg, Pennsylvania
Died: June 1, 1868, Lancaster, Pennsylvania
Term of office: March 4, 1857—March 3, 1861
Age at inauguration: 65
Party: Democrat
Vice President: John C. Breckenridge
First Lady: (none)**

16. Abraham Lincoln
Born: Feb. 12, 1809, Hardin, Kentucky
Died: April 15, 1865, Washington, DC[†]
Term of office: March 4, 1861—April 15, 1865
Age at inauguration: 52
Party: Republican
Vice President: Hannibal Hamlin, Andrew Johnson
First Lady: Mary Todd Lincoln

* When Zachary Taylor died, Millard Fillmore became the second vice president to inherit the presidency, leaving the vice presidency vacant.
** Buchanan was the only president who never married. A favorite niece, Harriet Lane, acted as White House hostess during his administration.
† Assassinated

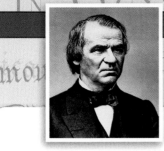

17. Andrew Johnson
Born: Dec. 29, 1808, Raleigh, North Carolina
Died: July 31, 1875, Carter Station, Tennessee
Term of office: April 15, 1865—March 3, 1869
Age at inauguration: 56
Party: Democrat (nominated by Republican Party)
Vice President: (none)*
First Lady: Eliza McCardle Johnson

18. Ulysses Simpson Grant
Born: April 27, 1822, Point Pleasant, Ohio
Died: July 23, 1885, Mt. McGregor, New York
Term of office: March 4, 1869—March 3, 1877
Age at inauguration: 46
Party: Republican
Vice President: Schuyler Colfax, Henry Wilson
First Lady: Julia Dent Grant

19. Rutherford Birchard Hayes
Born: Oct. 4, 1822, Delaware, Ohio
Died: Jan. 17, 1893, Fremont, Ohio
Term of office: March 4, 1877—March 3, 1881
Age at inauguration: 54
Party: Republican
Vice President: William A. Wheeler
First Lady: Lucy Webb Hayes

20. James Abram Garfield
Born: Nov. 19, 1831, Orange, Ohio
Died: Sept. 19, 1881, Elberon, New Jersey**
Term of office: March 4, 1881—Sept. 19, 1881
Age at inauguration: 49
Party: Republican
Vice President: Chester A. Arthur
First Lady: Lucretia Rudolph Garfield

CHECK IT OUT!

On March 1, 1872, Ulysses S. Grant established Yellowstone as the country's first national park.

* Andrew Johnson became president when Abraham Lincoln was assassinated, leaving the vice presidency vacant.
** Assassinated

21. Chester Alan Arthur
Born: Oct. 5, 1829, Fairfield, Vermont
Died: Nov. 18, 1886, New York City, New York
Term of office: Sept. 20, 1881—March 3, 1885
Age at inauguration: 51
Party: Republican
Vice President: (none)*
First Lady: Ellen Herndon Arthur

22. Grover Cleveland
Born: March 18, 1837, Caldwell, New Jersey
Died: June 24, 1908, Princeton, New Jersey
Term of office: March 4, 1885—March 3, 1889
Age at inauguration: 47
Party: Democrat
Vice President: Thomas A. Hendricks
First Lady: Frances Folsom Cleveland

23. Benjamin Harrison
Born: Aug. 20, 1833, North Bend, Ohio
Died: March 13, 1901, Indianapolis, Indiana
Term of office: March 4, 1889—March 3, 1893
Age at inauguration: 55
Party: Republican
Vice President: Levi P. Morton
First Lady: Caroline Scott Harrison
(died in 1892)

24. Grover Cleveland
Born: March 18, 1837, Caldwell, New Jersey
Died: June 24, 1908, Princeton, New Jersey
Term of office: March 4, 1893—March 3, 1897
Age at inauguration: 55
Party: Democrat
Vice President: Adlai E. Stevenson
First Lady: Frances Folsom Cleveland

CHECK IT OUT!

Grover Cleveland is the only president elected to two nonconsecutive terms.

*Chester Alan Arthur became president when James Garfield was assassinated, leaving the vice presidency vacant.

25. William McKinley

Born: Jan. 29, 1843, Niles, Ohio
Died: Sept. 14, 1901, Buffalo, New York*
Term of office: March 4, 1897—Sept. 14, 1901
Age at inauguration: 54
Party: Republican
Vice President: Garret A. Hobart,
Theodore Roosevelt
First Lady: Ida Saxton McKinley

26. Theodore Roosevelt

Born: Oct. 27, 1858, New York City, New York
Died: Jan. 6, 1919, Oyster Bay, New York
Term of office: Sept. 14, 1901—March 3, 1909
Age at inauguration: 42
Party: Republican
Vice President: Charles W. Fairbanks
First Lady: Edith Carow Roosevelt

27. William Howard Taft

Born: Sept. 15, 1857, Cincinnati, Ohio
Died: March 8, 1930, Washington, DC
Term of office: March 4, 1909—March 3, 1913
Age at inauguration: 51
Party: Republican
Vice President: James S. Sherman
First Lady: Helen Herron Taft

28. (Thomas) Woodrow Wilson

Born: Dec. 28, 1856, Staunton, Virginia
Died: Feb. 3, 1924, Washington, DC
Term of office: March 4, 1913—March 3, 1921
Age at inauguration: 56
Party: Democrat
Vice President: Thomas R. Marshall
First Lady: Ellen Axon Wilson,
Edith Galt Wilson**

*Assassinated
**Wilson's first wife died early in his administration and he remarried before leaving the White House.

29. Warren Gamaliel Harding

Born: Nov. 2, 1865, Corsica (now Blooming Grove), Ohio
Died: Aug. 2, 1923, San Francisco, California*
Term of office: March 4, 1921—Aug. 2, 1923
Age at inauguration: 55
Party: Republican
Vice President: Calvin Coolidge
First Lady: Florence Kling De Wolfe Harding

30. (John) Calvin Coolidge

Born: July 4,1872, Plymouth Notch, Vermont
Died: Jan. 5, 1933, Northampton, Massachusetts
Term of office: Aug. 3, 1923—March 3, 1929
Age at inauguration: 51
Party: Republican
Vice President: Charles G. Dawes
First Lady: Grace Goodhue Coolidge

31. Herbert Clark Hoover

Born: Aug. 10, 1874, West Branch, Iowa
Died: Oct. 20, 1964, New York City, New York
Term of office: March 4, 1929—March 3, 1933
Age at inauguration: 54
Party: Republican
Vice President: Charles Curtis
First Lady: Lou Henry Hoover

32. Franklin Delano Roosevelt

Born: Jan. 30, 1882, Hyde Park, New York
Died: April 12, 1945, Warm Springs, Georgia*
Term of office: March 4, 1933—April 12, 1945
Age at inauguration: 51
Party: Democrat
Vice President: John N. Garner, Henry A. Wallace, Harry S Truman
First Lady: Anna Eleanor Roosevelt

CHEC IT OU !

Two presidents, John Adams and Thomas Jefferson, died on the same day—July 4, 1826. Another president, James Monroe, died on July 4, 1831. A fourth, Calvin Coolidge, was born on July 4, 1872.

*Died in office, natural causes

33. Harry S Truman
Born: May 8, 1884, Lamar, Missouri
Died: Dec. 26, 1972, Kansas City, Missouri
Term of office: April 12, 1945—Jan. 20, 1953
Age at inauguration: 60
Party: Democrat
Vice President: Alben W. Barkley
First Lady: Elizabeth (Bess) Wallace Truman

34. Dwight David Eisenhower
Born: Oct. 14, 1890, Denison, Texas
Died: March 28, 1969, Washington, DC
Term of office: Jan. 20, 1953—Jan. 20, 1961
Age at inauguration: 62
Party: Republican
Vice President: Richard M. Nixon
First Lady: Mamie Doud Eisenhower

35. John Fitzgerald Kennedy
Born: May 29, 1917, Brookline, Massachusetts
Died: Nov. 22, 1963, Dallas, Texas*
Term of office: Jan. 20, 1961—Nov. 22, 1963
Age at inauguration: 43
Party: Democrat
Vice President: Lyndon B. Johnson
First Lady: Jacqueline Bouvier Kennedy

36. Lyndon Baines Johnson
Born: Aug. 27, 1908, Stonewall, Texas
Died: Jan. 22, 1973, San Antonio, Texas
Term of office: Nov. 22, 1963—Jan. 20, 1969
Age at inauguration: 55
Party: Democrat
Vice President: Hubert H. Humphrey
First Lady: Claudia (Lady Bird) Taylor Johnson

*Assassinated

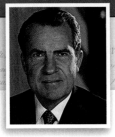

37. Richard Milhous Nixon

Born: Jan. 9, 1913, Yorba Linda, California
Died: April 22, 1994, New York City, New York
Term of office: Jan. 20, 1969—Aug. 9, 1974*
Age at inauguration: 56
Party: Republican
Vice President: Spiro T. Agnew (resigned), Gerald R. Ford
First Lady: Thelma (Pat) Ryan Nixon

38. Gerald Rudolph Ford

Born: July 14, 1913, Omaha, Nebraska
Died: Dec. 26, 2006, Rancho Mirage, California
Term of office: Aug. 9, 1974—Jan. 20, 1977
Age at inauguration: 61
Party: Republican
Vice President: Nelson A. Rockefeller
First Lady: Elizabeth (Betty) Bloomer Warren Ford

39. James Earl (Jimmy) Carter

Born: Oct. 1, 1924, Plains, Georgia
Term of office: Jan. 20, 1977—Jan. 20, 1981
Age at inauguration: 52
Party: Democrat
Vice President: Walter F. Mondale
First Lady: Rosalynn Smith Carter

40. Ronald Wilson Reagan

Born: Feb. 6, 1911, Tampico, Illinois
Died: June 5, 2004, Los Angeles, California
Term of office: Jan. 20, 1981—Jan. 20, 1989
Age at inauguration: 69
Party: Republican
Vice President: George H. W. Bush
First Lady: Nancy Davis Reagan

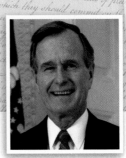

41. George Herbert Walker Bush

Born: June 12, 1924, Milton, Massachusetts
Term of office: Jan. 20, 1989—Jan. 20, 1993
Age at inauguration: 64
Party: Republican
Vice President: James Danforth (Dan) Quayle
First Lady: Barbara Pierce Bush

CHECK IT OUT!

There have been two father-son presidential combinations: John Adams and John Quincy Adams, and George H. W. Bush and George W. Bush. In addition, President William Henry Harrison was the grandfather of President Benjamin Harrison.

U.S. Government

*Resigned

42. William Jefferson (Bill) Clinton

Born: Aug. 19, 1946, Hope, Arkansas
Term of office: Jan. 20, 1993–Jan. 20, 2001
Age at inauguration: 46
Party: Democrat
Vice President: Albert (Al) Gore Jr.
First Lady: Hillary Rodham Clinton

43. George Walker Bush

Born: July 6, 1946, New Haven, Connecticut
Term of office: Jan. 20, 2001–Jan. 20, 2009
Age at inauguration: 54
Party: Republican
Vice President: Richard B. (Dick) Cheney
First Lady: Laura Welch Bush

44. Barack Hussein Obama Jr.

Born: Aug. 4, 1961, Honolulu, Hawaii
Term of office: Jan. 20, 2009–
Age at inauguration: 47
Party: Democrat
Vice President: Joseph R. (Joe) Biden Jr.
First Lady: Michelle Robinson Obama

President Barack Obama was born in Honolulu, Hawaii, to a white mother who had grown up in Kansas and a black father from Kenya, Africa. As a young child, Obama was one of only a few black students at his school. He became an outstanding student at college and at Harvard Law School. After law school he worked to help poor families in Chicago, Illinois, get better health care and more educational programs. In 1996, he became an Illinois state senator, and in 2004, he was elected to the U.S. Senate. In 2008, Obama won the Democratic nomination for president and became the first African American to be elected to the highest office in the country. In 2012, President Obama defeated Mitt Romney to win reelection.

In 1955, an African American woman named Rosa Parks refused to give up her seat on a Montgomery, Alabama, city bus to a white passenger. Her brave act helped start the Civil Rights movement. In 2013, the United States honored the 100th anniversary of her birth with a special stamp. The bus Rosa Parks was riding is on display at the Henry Ford Museum in Dearborn, Michigan.

2013

USA FOREVER

Rosa Parks

> **Also at the Henry Ford**

> The Wright Brothers' bicycle shop
> Abraham Lincoln's rocking chair
> Limousines of five presidents
   George Washington's camp chest and bed

Visit online at www.henryfordmuseum.org.

U.S. History

| c. 1000 | Viking explorer Leif Ericson explores North American coast and founds temporary colony called Vinland. |

| 1492 | On first voyage to America, Christopher Columbus lands at San Salvador Island in Bahamas. |

| 1513 | Juan Ponce de León discovers Florida. Vasco Nuñez de Balboa crosses Panama and sights Pacific Ocean. |

| 1520 | Ferdinand Magellan, whose ships were first to circumnavigate world, discovers South American straits, later named after him. |

| 1521 | Hernán Cortéz captures Mexico City and conquers Aztec Empire. |

| 1534–1539 | Jacques Cartier of France explores coast of Newfoundland and Gulf of St. Lawrence. Hernando de Soto conquers Florida and begins three-year trek across Southeast. |

| 1540 | Francisco Vásquez de Coronado explores Southwest, discovering Grand Canyon and introducing horses to North America. |

| 1541 | Hernando de Soto discovers Mississippi River. |

1572	Sir Francis Drake of England makes first voyage to Americas, landing in Panama.
1585	Sir Walter Raleigh establishes England's first American colony at Roanoke.
1603	Samuel de Champlain of France explores St. Lawrence River, later founds Quebec.
1607	First permanent English settlement in America established at Jamestown, Virginia. Capt. John Smith imprisoned by Native Americans and saved by Pocahontas, daughter of Chief Powhatan.
1609	Henry Hudson sets out in search of Northwest Passage. Samuel de Champlain sails into Great Lakes.
1620	Pilgrims and others board *Mayflower* and travel to Plymouth, Massachusetts. They draw up Mayflower Compact.
1626	Dutch colony of New Amsterdam founded on Manhattan Island, bought from Native Americans for about $24.
1675	Thousands die in King Philip's War between New Englanders and five Native American tribes.
1692	Witchcraft hysteria breaks out in Salem, Massachusetts, leading to 20 executions.

U.S. History Highlights: 1700s–1800s

1754	French and Indian War begins.
1763	Treaty of Paris ends French and Indian War.
1765	Parliament passes Stamp Act (tax on newspapers, legal documents, etc.) and Quartering Act (requiring housing of British soldiers in colonists' homes).
1770	Five Americans, including Crispus Attucks, a black man said to be the leader, perish in Boston Massacre (March 5).
1773	British Parliament passes Tea Act, leading to Boston Tea Party (Dec. 16).
1775	American Revolution begins with battles of Lexington and Concord (April 19). Second Continental Congress appoints George Washington as commander of Continental Army.
1776	Second Continental Congress approves Declaration of Independence on July 4.
1777	Congress adopts Stars and Stripes flag and endorses Articles of Confederation. Washington's army spends winter at Valley Forge, Pennsylvania.
1783	Treaty of Paris signed, officially ending American Revolution (Sept. 3).
1787	Constitution accepted by delegates to Constitutional Convention in Philadelphia on Sept. 17.
1803	Louisiana Purchase from France doubles size of United States.

1804	Lewis and Clark expedition sets out from St. Louis, Missouri. New Jersey begins gradual emancipation of slaves. Alexander Hamilton killed in duel with Aaron Burr.
1812	War of 1812 with Britain begins by close vote in Congress.
1815	War of 1812 ends.
1825	Erie Canal opens.

1846	Mexican War begins when U.S. troops are attacked in disputed Texas territory.
1849	Gold Rush brings hundreds of thousands to California. Elizabeth Blackwell is first American woman to receive medical degree.
1860	Democratic Party splits into Northern and Southern wings. South Carolina is first Southern state to secede from Union after election of Abraham Lincoln.
1861	Civil War begins with attack on Ft. Sumter in South Carolina (April 12).
1862	Pres. Lincoln issues Emancipation Proclamation, freeing slaves in ten states.
1865	Gen. Lee surrenders to Gen. Grant at Appomattox Court House, Virginia (April 9). Pres. Lincoln assassinated by John Wilkes Booth in Washington, DC.
1870	Fifteenth Amendment, guaranteeing right to vote for all male U.S. citizens, is ratified (Feb. 3).
1898	After mysterious explosion of battleship *Maine* in Havana harbor (Feb. 15), Spanish-American War breaks out (April 25).

1903	Orville and Wilbur Wright conduct first powered flight near Kitty Hawk, NC (Dec. 17).
1909	Expedition team led by Robert E. Peary and Matthew Henson plants American flag at North Pole (April 6). W. E. B. DuBois founds National Association for the Advancement of Colored People (NAACP).
1917	Congress declares war on Germany (April 6) and Austria-Hungary (Dec. 7), bringing United States into World War I.
1918	Armistice Day ends World War I (Nov. 11).
1920	Nineteenth Amendment establishes women's right to vote (Aug. 26).
1927	Charles Lindbergh completes nonstop solo flight from New York to Paris (May 20–21).
1929	Stock market crash on "Black Tuesday" ushers in Great Depression (Oct. 29).
1932	Amelia Earhart is first woman to fly solo across Atlantic.
1941	Japanese planes attack Pearl Harbor, Hawaii, killing 2,400 U.S. servicemen and civilians (Dec. 7). United States declares war on Japan (Dec. 8). Germany and Italy declare war on United States (Dec. 11). United States declares war on Germany and Italy (Dec. 11).
1945	Germany surrenders, ending war in Europe (May 7). Atomic bombs dropped on Hiroshima (Aug. 6) and Nagasaki (Aug. 9); Japan surrenders, ending World War II (Aug. 14).
1950	North Korea invades South Korea, beginning Korean War (June 25).
1954	Supreme Court orders school desegregation in Brown v. Board of Education decision (May 17).
1958	In response to Soviet launch of Sputnik, United States launches Explorer I, first American satellite.
1962	Lt. Col. John H. Glenn Jr. is first American to orbit Earth.
1963	Dr. Martin Luther King Jr. delivers his "I Have a Dream" speech in Washington, DC (Aug. 28). Pres. Kennedy assassinated in Dallas, Texas (Nov. 22).

1965	Black nationalist Malcolm X assassinated in New York City (Feb. 21). Pres. Johnson orders U.S. Marines into South Vietnam (March 8).
1968	Dr. Martin Luther King Jr. is assassinated by James Earl Ray in Memphis, Tennessee (April 4). After winning California presidential primary, Sen. Robert F. Kennedy of New York is assassinated by Sirhan Sirhan in Los Angeles, California (June 5).
1969	Neil Armstrong and Edwin "Buzz" Aldrin of *Apollo 11* are first men to walk on Moon (July 20).
1972	Congress debates Equal Rights Amendment.
1974	Pres. Nixon resigns, elevating Vice Pres. Ford to presidency (Aug. 9).
1981	*Columbia* completes first successful space shuttle mission (April 12–13). Sandra Day O'Connor becomes first female Justice of Supreme Court.
1983	Sally Ride, aboard space shuttle *Challenger*, is first American female astronaut.
1986	Space shuttle *Challenger* explodes in midair over Florida.
1991	U.S. sends aircraft, warships, and 400,000 troops to Persian Gulf to drive Iraq's armed forces from Kuwait in Operation Desert Storm (Jan. 17). Ground war begins six weeks later and lasts only 100 hours (Feb. 24–28).
2001	On Sept. 11, hijackers overtake four U.S. planes, crashing two of them into World Trade Center in New York City. In all, 2,977 lives are lost.
2003	Suspecting weapons of mass destruction, United States declares war on Iraq (March 20). Official combat ends May 1.
2009	Sen. Barack Obama, first African American major presidential candidate, is inaugurated as president.
2011	Last U.S. troops leave Iraq in December. Occupy Wall Street protest movement spreads to 100 U.S. cities and around the world.
2012	Mass shootings in Colorado, Wisconsin, and Connecticut prompt debate about gun control.
2013	Barack Obama is inaugurated for a second term as president.

DECLARATION OF INDEPENDENCE

(Phrases in red are key ideas.)

IN CONGRESS, JULY 4, 1776

THE UNANIMOUS DECLARATION OF THE THIRTEEN UNITED STATES OF AMERICA

When in the Course of human events, it becomes necessary for one people to dissolve the political bands which have connected them with another, and to assume among the powers of the earth, the separate and equal station to which the Laws of Nature and of Nature's God entitle them, a decent respect to the opinions of mankind requires that they should declare the causes which impel them to the separation.

We hold these truths to be self-evident, that all men are created equal, that they are endowed by their Creator with certain unalienable Rights, that among these are Life, Liberty and the pursuit of Happiness. —That to secure these rights, Governments are instituted among Men, deriving their just powers from the consent of the governed, —That whenever any Form of Government becomes destructive of these ends, it is the Right of the People to alter or to abolish it, and to institute new Government, laying its foundation on such principles and organizing its powers in such form, as to them shall seem most likely to effect their Safety and Happiness. Prudence, indeed, will dictate that Governments long established should not be changed for light and transient causes; and accordingly all experience hath shown, that mankind are more disposed to suffer, while evils are sufferable, than to right themselves by abolishing the forms to which they are accustomed. But when a long train of abuses and usurpations, pursuing invariably the same Object evinces a design to reduce them under absolute Despotism, it is their right, it is their duty, to throw off such Government, and to provide new Guards for their future security. —Such has been the patient sufferance of these Colonies; and such is now the necessity which constrains them to alter their former Systems of Government. The history of the present King of Great Britain is a history of repeated injuries and usurpations, all having in direct object the establishment of an absolute Tyranny over these States. To prove this, let Facts be submitted to a candid world.

He has refused his Assent to Laws, the most wholesome and necessary for the public good.

He has forbidden his Governors to pass Laws of immediate and pressing importance, unless suspended in their operation till his Assent should be obtained; and when so suspended, he has utterly neglected to attend to them.

He has refused to pass other Laws for the accommodation of large districts of people, unless those people would relinquish the right of Representation in the Legislature, a right inestimable to them and formidable to tyrants only.

He has called together legislative bodies at places unusual, uncomfortable, and distant from the depository of their public Records, for the sole purpose of fatiguing them into compliance with his measures.

He has dissolved Representative Houses repeatedly, for opposing with manly firmness his invasions on the rights of the people.

He has refused for a long time, after such dissolutions, to cause others to be elected; whereby the Legislative powers, incapable of Annihilation, have returned to the People at large for their exercise; the State remaining in the mean time exposed to all the dangers of invasion from without, and convulsions within.

He has endeavoured to prevent the population of these States; for that purpose obstructing the Laws for Naturalization of Foreigners; refusing to pass others to encourage their migrations hither, and raising the conditions of new Appropriations of Lands.

He has obstructed the Administration of Justice, by refusing his Assent to Laws for establishing Judiciary powers.

He has made Judges dependent on his Will alone, for the tenure of their offices, and the amount and payment of their salaries.

He has erected a multitude of New Offices, and sent hither swarms of Officers to harrass our people, and eat out their substance.

He has kept among us, in times of peace, Standing Armies without the Consent of our legislatures.

He has affected to render the Military independent of and superior to the Civil power.

He has combined with others to subject us to a jurisdiction foreign to our constitution, and unacknowledged by our laws; giving his Assent to their Acts of pretended Legislation:

For Quartering large bodies of armed troops among us:

For protecting them, by a mock Trial, from punishment for any Murders which they should commit on the Inhabitants of these States:

For cutting off our Trade with all parts of the world:

For imposing Taxes on us without our Consent:

For depriving us in many cases, of the benefits of Trial by Jury:

For transporting us beyond Seas to be tried for pretended offences:

For abolishing the free System of English Laws in a neighbouring Province, establishing therein an Arbitrary government, and enlarging its Boundaries so as to render it at once an example and fit instrument for introducing the same absolute rule into these Colonies:

For taking away our Charters, abolishing our most valuable Laws, and altering fundamentally the Forms of our Governments:

For suspending our own Legislatures, and declaring themselves invested with power to legislate for us in all cases whatsoever.

He has abdicated Government here, by declaring us out of his Protection and waging War against us.

He has plundered our seas, ravaged our Coasts, burnt our towns, and destroyed the lives of our people.

He is at this time transporting large Armies of foreign Mercenaries to compleat the works of death, desolation and tyranny, already begun with circumstances of Cruelty & perfidy scarcely paralleled in the most barbarous ages, and totally unworthy the Head of a civilized nation.

He has constrained our fellow Citizens taken Captive on the high Seas to bear Arms against their Country, to become the executioners of their friends and Brethren, or to fall themselves by their Hands.

He has excited domestic insurrections amongst us, and has endeavoured to bring on the inhabitants of our frontiers, the merciless Indian Savages, whose known rule of warfare, in an undistinguished destruction of all ages, sexes and conditions.

In every stage of these Oppressions We have Petitioned for Redress in the most humble terms: Our repeated Petitions have been answered only by repeated injury. A Prince whose character is thus marked by every act which may define a Tyrant, is unfit to be the ruler of a free people.

Nor have We been wanting in attentions to our Brittish brethren. We have warned them from time to time of attempts by their legislature to extend an unwarrantable jurisdiction over us. We have reminded them of the circumstances of our emigration and settlement here. We have appealed to their native justice and magnanimity, and we have conjured them by the ties of our common kindred to disavow these usurpations, which, would inevitably interrupt our connections and correspondence. They too have been deaf to the voice of justice and of consanguinity. We must, therefore, acquiesce in the necessity, which denounces our Separation, and hold them, as we hold the rest of mankind, Enemies in War, in Peace Friends.

We, therefore, the Representatives of the united States of America, in General Congress, Assembled, appealing to the Supreme Judge of the world for the rectitude of our intentions, do, in the Name, and by Authority of the good People of these Colonies, solemnly publish and declare, That these United Colonies are, and of Right ought to be Free and Independent States; that they are Absolved from all Allegiance to the British Crown, and that all political connection between them and the State of Great Britain, is and ought to be totally dissolved; and that as Free and Independent States, they have full Power to levy War, conclude Peace, contract Alliances, establish Commerce, and to do all other Acts and Things which Independent States may of right do. And for the support of this Declaration, with a firm reliance on the protection of divine Providence, we mutually pledge to each other our Lives, our Fortunes and our sacred Honor.

THE BILL OF RIGHTS

(Phrases in red are key ideas.)

THE FIRST 10 AMENDMENTS TO THE CONSTITUTION

(The first 10 amendments, known collectively as the Bill of Rights, were adopted in 1791.)

AMENDMENT I

Congress shall make no law respecting an establishment of religion, or prohibiting the free exercise thereof; or abridging the freedom of speech, or of the press; or the right of the people peaceably to assemble, and to petition the Government for a redress of grievances.

AMENDMENT II

A well regulated Militia, being necessary to the security of a free State, the right of the people to keep and bear Arms, shall not be infringed.

AMENDMENT III

No Soldier shall, in time of peace be quartered in any house, without the consent of the Owner, nor in time of war, but in a manner to be prescribed by law.

AMENDMENT IV

The right of the people to be secure in their persons, houses, papers, and effects, against unreasonable searches and seizures, shall not be violated, and no Warrants shall issue, but upon probable cause, supported by Oath or affirmation, and particularly describing the place to be searched, and the persons or things to be seized.

AMENDMENT V

No person shall be held to answer for a capital, or otherwise infamous crime, unless on a presentment or indictment of a Grand Jury, except in cases arising in the land or naval forces, or in the Militia, when in actual service in time of War or public danger; nor shall any person be subject for the same offence to be twice put in jeopardy of life or limb; nor shall be compelled in any criminal case to be a witness against himself, nor be deprived of life, liberty, or property, without due process of law; nor shall private property be taken for public use, without just compensation.

AMENDMENT VI

In all criminal prosecutions, the accused shall enjoy the right to a speedy and public trial, by an impartial jury of the State and district wherein the crime shall have been committed, which district shall have been previously ascertained by law, and to be informed of the nature and cause of the accusation; to be confronted with the witnesses against him; to have compulsory process for obtaining witnesses in his favor, and to have the Assistance of Counsel for his defence.

AMENDMENT VII

In Suits at common law, where the value in controversy shall exceed twenty dollars, the right of trial by jury shall be preserved, and no fact tried by jury, shall be otherwise re-examined in any Court of the United States, than according to the rules of the common law.

AMENDMENT VIII

Excessive bail shall not be required, nor excessive fines imposed, nor cruel and unusual punishments inflicted.

AMENDMENT IX

The enumeration in the Constitution, of certain rights, shall not be construed to deny or disparage others retained by the people.

AMENDMENT X

The powers not delegated to the United States by the Constitution, nor prohibited by it to the States, are reserved to the States respectively, or to the people.

Important Supreme Court Decisions

Marbury v. Madison (1803)
The Court struck down a law "repugnant to the Constitution" for the first time and set the precedent for judicial review of acts of Congress.

Dred Scott v. Sanford (1857)
Dred Scott, a Missouri slave, sued for his liberty after his owner took him into free territory. The Court ruled that Congress could not bar slavery in the territories. This decision sharpened sectional conflict about slavery.

Plessy v. Ferguson (1896)
This case was about the practice of segregating railroad cars in Louisiana. The Court ruled that as long as equal accommodations were provided, segregation was not discrimination and did not deprive black Americans of equal protection under the Fourteenth Amendment. This decision was overturned by Brown v. Board of Education (1954).

Brown v. Board of Education (1954)
Chief Justice Earl Warren led the Court to decide unanimously that segregated schools violated the equal protection clause of the Fourteenth Amendment. Efforts to desegregate Southern schools after the Brown decision met with massive resistance for many years.

Miranda v. Arizona (1966)
The Court ruled that Ernesto Miranda's confession to certain crimes was not admissible as evidence because he had been denied his right to silence and to legal counsel. Now police must advise suspects of their "Miranda rights" when they're taken into custody.

Roe v. Wade (1973)
In a controversial decision, the Court held that state laws restricting abortion were an unconstitutional invasion of a woman's right to privacy.

Chief Justices of the U.S. Supreme Court

Chief Justice	Tenure	Appointed by
John Jay	1789–1795	George Washington
John Rutledge	1795	George Washington
Oliver Ellsworth	1796–1800	George Washington
John Marshall	1801–1835	John Adams
Roger B. Taney	1836–1864	Andrew Jackson
Salmon P. Chase	1864–1873	Abraham Lincoln
Morrison R. Waite	1874–1888	Ulysses S. Grant
Melville W. Fuller	1888–1910	Grover Cleveland
Edward D. White	1910–1921	William H. Taft
William H. Taft	1921–1930	Warren G. Harding
Charles E. Hughes	1930–1941	Herbert Hoover
Harlan F. Stone	1941–1946	Franklin D. Roosevelt
Fred M. Vinson	1946–1953	Harry S Truman
Earl Warren	1953–1969	Dwight D. Eisenhower
Warren E. Burger	1969–1986	Richard M. Nixon
William H. Rehnquist	1986–2005	Ronald Reagan
John G. Roberts Jr.	2005–	George W. Bush

Weather

BREAKING RECORDS

In 2012, the United States suffered the worst drought since the 1950s and some of the hottest temperatures in U.S. history. The hot, dry conditions ruined crops, cracked highways, and sparked wildfires that roared across millions of acres.

U.S. Weather Extremes

The numbers below are based on 30-year averages of temperature, wind, snowfall, rainfall, and humidity at weather stations in the 48 continental states (not Alaska and Hawaii).

5 Driest Places

Location	Annual Precipitation
Yuma, AZ	3.01 in. (7.65 cm)
Las Vegas, NV	4.49 in. (11.40 cm)
Bishop, CA	5.02 in. (12.75 cm)
Bakersfield, CA	6.49 in. (16.48 cm)
Alamosa, CO	7.25 in. (18.41 cm)

5 Wettest Places

Location	Annual Precipitation
Mount Washington, NH	101.91 in. (258.85 cm)
Quillayute, WA	101.72 in. (258.37 cm)
Astoria, OR	67.13 in. (170.51 cm)
Mobile, AL	66.29 in. (168.38 cm)
Pensacola, FL	64.28 in. (163.27 cm)

5 Coldest Places

Location	Average Temperature
Mount Washington, NH	27.2°F (-2.66°C)
International Falls, MN	37.4°F (3.00°C)
Marquette, MI	38.7°F (3.72°C)
Duluth, MN	39.1°F (3.94°C)
Caribou, ME	39.2°F (4.00°C)

5 Hottest Places

Location	Average Temperature
Key West, FL	78.1°F (25.61°C)
Miami, FL	76.7°F (24.83°C)
Yuma, AZ	75.3°F (24.05°C)
West Palm Beach, FL	75.3°F (24.05°C)
Fort Wayne, FL	74.9°F (23.83°C)

CHECK IT OUT!

The line where cold and warm air masses collide is called a front. A cold front occurs when cold air pushes warm air out of its way. Cold fronts can bring stormy and even severe weather. A warm front occurs when warm air pushes away cold air, and it can bring gray, drizzly weather. (On a weather map, a cold front is indicated by a blue line with triangles below. Warm fronts are shown as red lines with half-circles above.)

Worldwide Weather Extremes

Highest Recorded Temperatures by Continent

Temperature	Continent	Location	Date
131°F (55°C)	Africa	Kebili, Tunisia	July 7, 1931
134°F (56.7°C)	North America	Death Valley, California, United States	July 10, 1913
129.2°F (54°C)	Asia	Tirat Tsvi, Israel	June 21, 1942
123°F (50.5°C)	Australia	Oodnadatta, South Australia	January 2, 1960
120°F (48.9°C)	South America	Rivadavia, Argentina	December 11, 1905
118.4°F (48°C)	Europe	Athens, Greece (and Elefsina, Greece)	July 10, 1977
59°F (15°C)	Antarctica	Vanda Station	May 1, 1974

Lowest Recorded Temperatures by Continent

Temperature	Continent	Location	Date
-129°F (-89.4°C)	Antarctica	Vostok Station	July 21, 1983
-90°F (-67.8°C)	Asia	Oimekon, Russia	February 6, 1933
-90°F (-67.8°C)	Asia	Verkhoyansk, Russia	February 5 and 7, 1892
-81.4°F (-63°C)	North America	Snag, Yukon Territory, Canada	February 3, 1947
-72.6°F (-58.1°C)	Europe	Ust-Shchugor, Russia	December 31, 1978
-27°F (-32.8°C)	South America	Sarmiento, Argentina	June 1, 1907
-11°F (-23.9°C)	Africa	Ifrane, Morocco	February 11, 1935
-9.4°F (-23.0°C)	Australia	Charlotte Pass, New South Wales	June 29, 1994

Highest Average Annual Precipitation by Continent

Amount	Continent	Location
467.4 in. (1,187.2 cm)	Asia	Mawsynram, India
405.0 in. (1,028.7 cm)	Africa	Debundscha, Cameroon
354.0 in. (899.2 cm)	South America	Quibdo, Colombia
316.3 in. (803.4 cm)	Australia	Bellenden Ker, Queensland, Australia
276.0 in. (700.0 cm)	North America	Henderson Lake, BC, Canada
183.0 in. (464.8 cm)	Europe	Crkvica, Bosnia and Herzegovina

Lowest Average Annual Precipitation by Continent

Amount	Continent	Location
0.03 in. (0.08 cm)	South America	Arica, Chile
0.08 in. (0.20 cm)	Antarctica	Amundsen-Scott South Pole Station
0.10 in. (0.25 cm)	Africa	Wadi Halfa, Sudan
1.20 in. (3.05 cm	North America	Batagues, Mexico
1.80 in. (4.57 cm)	Asia	Aden, Yemen
4.05 in. (10.28 cm)	Australia	Mulka (Troudaninna), South Australia
6.40 in. (16.26 cm)	Europe	Astrakhan, Russia

STAY TUNED In Canada, it costs 1.6 cents to make one penny. That's a big reason Canada decided to take the penny out of circulation, beginning February 2013. It costs 2.4 cents to make a penny in the United States, and using pennies for purchases takes extra time. Does it make sense for us to lose our cents, too?

Weights & Measures

Simple Metric Conversion Table

To convert	To	Multiply by
centimeters	feet	0.0328
centimeters	inches	0.3937
cubic centimeters	cubic inches	0.0610
degrees	radians	0.0175
feet	centimeters	30.48
feet	meters	0.3048
gallons	liters	3.785
grams	ounces	0.0353
inches	centimeters	2.54
kilograms	pounds	2.205
kilometers	miles	0.6214
knots	miles/hour	1.151
liters	gallons	0.2642
liters	pints	2.113
meters	feet	3.281
miles	kilometers	1.609
ounces	grams	28.3495
pounds	kilograms	0.4536

Converting Household Measures

To convert	To	Multiply by
dozens	units	12
baker's dozens	units	13
teaspoons	milliliters	4.93
teaspoons	tablespoons	0.33
tablespoons	milliliters	14.79
tablespoons	teaspoons	3
cups	liters	0.24
cups	pints	0.50
cups	quarts	0.25
pints	cups	2
pints	liters	0.47
pints	quarts	0.50
quarts	cups	4
quarts	gallons	0.25
quarts	liters	0.95
quarts	pints	2
gallons	liters	3.79
gallons	quarts	4

Temperature Conversions

Fahrenheit	Celsius
475	246.1
450	232.2
425	218.3
400	204.4
375	190.6
350	176.7
325	162.8
300	148.9
275	135.0
250	121.1
225	107.2
212	100.0
110	43.3
105	40.6
100	37.8
95	35.0
90	32.2
85	29.4
80	26.7
75	23.9
70	21.1
65	18.3
60	15.6
55	12.8
50	10.0
45	7.2
40	4.4
35	1.7
32	0.0
30	−1.1
25	−3.9
20	−6.7
15	−9.4
10	−12.2
5	−15.0
0	−17.8
−5	−20.6
−10	−23.3
−15	−26.1
−20	−28.9
−25	−31.7
−30	−34.4
−35	−37.2
−40	−40.0
−45	−42.8

Weights & Measures

Fractions and Their Decimal Equivalents

1/2	0.5000	2/7	0.2857	5/9	0.5556
1/3	0.3333	2/9	0.2222	5/11	0.4545
1/4	0.2500	2/11	0.1818	5/12	0.4167
1/5	0.2000	3/4	0.7500	6/7	0.8571
1/6	0.1667	3/5	0.6000	6/11	0.5455
1/7	0.1429	3/7	0.4286	7/8	0.8750
1/8	0.1250	3/8	0.3750	7/9	0.7778
1/9	0.1111	3/10	0.3000	7/10	0.7000
1/10	0.1000	3/11	0.2727	7/11	0.6364
1/11	0.0909	4/5	0.8000	7/12	0.5833
1/12	0.0833	4/7	0.5714	8/9	0.8889
1/16	0.0625	4/9	0.4444	8/11	0.7273
1/32	0.0313	4/11	0.3636	9/10	0.9000
1/64	0.0156	5/6	0.8333	9/11	0.8182
2/3	0.6667	5/7	0.7143	10/11	0.9091
2/5	0.4000	5/8	0.6250	11/12	0.9167

Length or Distance
U.S. Customary System

1 foot (ft.)	=	12 inches (in.)				
1 yard (yd.)	=	3 feet	=	36 inches		
1 rod (rd.)	=	5½ yards	=	16 ½ feet		
1 furlong (fur.)	=	40 rods	=	220 yards	=	660 feet
1 mile (mi.)	=	8 furlongs	=	1,760 yards	=	5,280 feet

An international nautical mile has been defined as 6,076.1155 feet.

Six Quick Ways to Measure If You Don't Have a Ruler

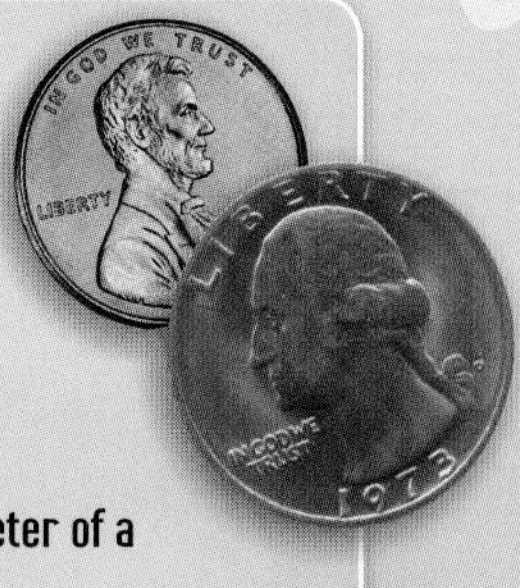

1. Most credit cards are 3⅜ inches by 2⅛ inches.
2. Standard business cards are 3½ inches long by 2 inches tall.
3. Floor tiles are usually manufactured in 12-inch squares.
4. U.S. paper money is 6⅛ inches wide by 2⅝ inches tall.
5. The diameter of a quarter is approximately 1 inch, and the diameter of a penny is approximately ¾ of an inch.
6. A standard sheet of paper is 8½ inches wide and 11 inches long.

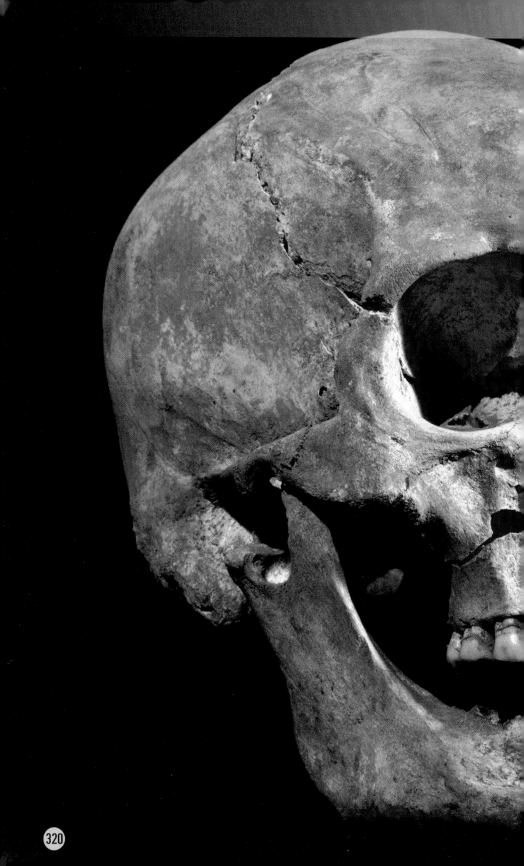

World History

STAY TUNED

In February 2013, scientists identified a skull and skeleton buried under a British parking garage as the remains of Richard III, England's king from 1483 to 1485. History has generally cast Richard in the role of a wicked, ruthless villain, but his supporters claim he was actually a good ruler who introduced fair laws and reforms. They hope this discovery will lead to new truths to set Richard's record straight.

Ancient History Highlights

Date	Event
4.5 billion BCE	Planet Earth forms.
3 billion BCE	First signs of life (bacteria and green algae) appear in oceans.
3.2 million BCE	*Australopithecus afarensis* roams Earth (remains, nicknamed Lucy, found in Ethiopia in 1974).
1.8 million BCE	*Homo erectus* ("upright man"). Brain size twice that of *australopithecine* species.
100,000 BCE	First modern *Homo sapiens* live in east Africa.
4500–3000 BCE	Sumerians in Tigris and Euphrates valleys develop city-state civilization. First phonetic writing.
3000–2000 BCE	Pharaonic rule begins in Egypt with King Menes. Great Sphinx of Giza constructed. Earliest Egyptian mummies created.
2000–1500 BCE	Israelites enslaved in Egypt.
1500–1000 BCE	Ikhnaton develops monotheistic religion in Egypt (circa 1375 BCE). His successor, Tutankhamun, returns to earlier gods. Moses leads Israelites out of Egypt into Canaan. Ten Commandments. End of Greek civilization in Mycenae with invasion of Dorians.
800–700 BCE	First recorded Olympic Games (776 BCE). Legendary founding of Rome by Romulus (753 BCE).
700–600 BCE	Founding of Byzantium by Greeks (circa 660 BCE). Building of Acropolis in Athens by Solon, Greek lawmaker (630–560 BCE).
600–500 BCE	Confucius (551–479 BCE) develops philosophy of Confucianism in China. Siddhartha Gautama or Buddha (563–483 BCE) founds Buddhism in India.
300–241 BCE	First Punic War (264–241 BCE). Rome defeats Carthaginians and begins domination of Mediterranean. Invention of Mayan calendar in Yucatán (more exact than older calendars). First Roman gladiatorial games (264 BCE). Archimedes, Greek mathematician (287–212 BCE).
250–201 BCE	Construction of Great Wall of China begins.
149–146 BCE	Third Punic War. Rome destroys Carthage.
100–51 BCE	Julius Caesar (100–44 BCE) invades Britain and conquers Gaul (France). Spartacus leads slave revolt against Rome (73 BCE). Birth of Jesus (variously given 7 BCE to 4 BCE).

World History

People of Ancient History

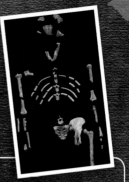

Lucy

In 1974, in Hadar, Ethopia, scientists discovered a nearly complete skeleton of an *Australopithecus afarensis*, or early human being, which they named Lucy. The skeleton provided scientists with critical insight into the history of humans.

Tutankhamun

Tutankhamun, or King Tut, was one of the most famous pharaohs, or rulers, of ancient Egypt. He began ruling at age 10 and died at 19. There are no written records about his life. Until recently, most of the information known came from what Howard Carter discovered in King Tut's tomb in 1922. In 2010, results of a two-year study including DNA tests and CT scans of King Tut's mummy revealed the probable cause of his death as a leg injury complicated by bone disease and malaria.

Confucius

Confucius was a thinker and educator in ancient China. His beliefs and teachings about the way a person should live and treat others greatly influenced the Chinese culture and inspired the Ru school of Chinese thought. Later his beliefs spread to other parts of the world, and his type of belief system came to be known as Confucianism.

Buddha

Siddhartha Gautama was born the son of a wealthy ruler in what is modern-day Nepal. One day he was confronted with the suffering of people outside his kingdom, and he left his life of privilege. Siddhartha searched for enlightenment through meditation and eventually found his own path of balance in the world. He earned the title Buddha, or "Enlightened One," and spent the rest of his life helping others to reach enlightenment.

Julius Caesar

As a great politician, military leader, and dictator, Julius Caesar expanded the Roman Empire. He led Rome in conquering Gaul (France), ended the civil war, and instituted many social reforms. His rule ended with his assassination by many of his fellow statesmen on March 15, the Ides of March.

World History Highlights: 1–1499 CE

Date	Event
1–49 CE	Crucifixion of Jesus Christ (probably 30 CE).
312–337	Under Constantine the Great, eastern and western Roman empires reunite and new capital, Constantinople, is established.
350–399	Huns (Mongols) invade Europe (circa 360).
622–637	Muhammad flees from Mecca to Medina. Muslim empire grows (634). Arabs conquer Jerusalem (637).
c. 900	Vikings discover Greenland.
c. 1000	Viking raider Leif Ericson discovers North America, calls it Vinland. Chinese invent gunpowder.
1211–1227	Genghis Khan invades China, Persia, and Russia.
1215	King John of England forced by barons to sign Magna Carta, limiting royal power.
1231–1252	Inquisition begins as Pope Gregory IX creates special court to locate and punish heretics. Torture used (1252).
1251	Kublai Khan comes to prominence in China.
1271–1295	Marco Polo of Venice travels to China.
c. 1325	Renaissance begins in Italy.
1337–1453	English and French fight for control of France in Hundred Years' War.
1347–1351	About 25 million Europeans die from "Black Death" (bubonic plague).
1368	Ming dynasty begins in China.
1429	Joan of Arc leads French against English.
1452	Leonardo da Vinci, painter of *Mona Lisa* and other masterpieces, born near Florence, Italy.
1492–1498	Columbus discovers Caribbean Islands and Americas, returns to Spain (1493). Second voyage to Dominica, Jamaica, Puerto Rico (1493–1496). Third voyage to Orinoco (1498).
1497	Vasco da Gama sails around Africa and discovers sea route to India (1498). John Cabot, employed by England, explores Canadian coast.

World History

People of 1–1499 CE

Constantine

Known as Constantine the Great, he served as the emperor of Rome from 312 to 337. He created a "new" Rome by bringing religious tolerance to the empire and laying a foundation for Western culture. He moved the center of the empire from Rome to the Greek colony of Byzantium, which he renamed Constantinople.

Muhammad

As a prophet from Mecca, Muhammad worked to restore the faith of Abraham. He spread the religion of Islam and the belief in one true God, Allah. His teachings were recorded in the Koran. As his teachings spread, many aristocrats in Mecca began to oppose him. Muhammad fled to Medina, an event that marks the beginning of the Muslim calendar. In 629, he won over his opposition in Mecca. By the time he died in 632, most of the Arabian Peninsula followed his political and religious ideas.

Genghis Khan

Born around 1162 in Mongolia, Genghis Khan was a warrior and ruler who united the tribes of Mongolia and founded the Mongol Empire. He spent his life establishing and increasing his empire by conquering China, Russia, and parts of Persia.

Joan of Arc

At the age of thirteen, Joan of Arc heard the voices of saints telling her to help the French king defeat the English. She presented herself to the king and led the French army to victory at Orléans, forcing the English out of the region. She was later captured by the English, accused of heresy, and burned at the stake. Joan of Arc was hailed as a hero in France for her bravery and made a saint.

Leonardo da Vinci

Italian-born Leonardo da Vinci was one of the most farsighted, multitalented, and relentless thinkers of the time. He was a great artist, inventor, engineer, mathematician, architect, scientist, and musician whose works and insights influenced generations.

World History Highlights: 1500–1899

Date	Event
1509	Henry VIII becomes king of England.
1513	Juan Ponce de León explores Florida and Yucatán Peninsula for Spain.
1517	Martin Luther pins his 95 theses on door of Wittenberg Castle Church in Wittenberg, Germany, starting Protestant Reformation.
1520	Ferdinand Magellan discovers Straits of Magellan and Tierra del Fuego for Spain.
1547	Ivan IV, known as Ivan the Terrible, crowned czar of Russia.
1558	Elizabeth I, Henry VIII's daughter, becomes queen of England.
1585–1587	Sir Walter Raleigh's men reach Roanoke Island, Virginia.
1588	Spanish Armada attempts to invade England and is defeated.
1609	Henry Hudson explores Hudson River and Hudson Bay for England.
1632	Italian astronomer Galileo Galilei is first person to view space through a telescope and confirms belief that Earth revolves around Sun.
1687	Sir Isaac Newton publishes his theories on gravity and his laws of motion.
1721	Peter I, known as Peter the Great, crowned czar of Russia.
1756	Seven Years' War breaks out, involving most European countries.
1778	James Cook sails to Hawaii.
1789	Parisians storm Bastille prison, starting French Revolution.
1804	Scottish explorer John Ross begins expedition to find Northwest Passage in Arctic.
1821	Mexico gains its independence from Spain.
1845	Irish potato crops are ruined by blight, or fungus, creating famine that causes millions to starve to death or emigrate to America.
1859	Charles Darwin publishes On the Origin of Species.
1898	Spanish-American War begins.

People of 1500–1899

Ferdinand Magellan

As a Portuguese explorer, Magellan sailed under both the Portuguese and Spanish flags. To find a route to India by sailing west, he sailed around South America to the Pacific Ocean, discovering the Strait of Magellan along the way. Although he was killed in the Philippines and did not complete the journey, his ships made it back to Spain and were the first to circumnavigate the globe.

Elizabeth I

Queen Elizabeth I ruled England, leading her country through war with wisdom and courage. She was a beloved queen who brought prosperity and a rebirth of learning to England, making the country a major European power. For this reason, the era in which she ruled became known as the Elizabethan Age.

Galileo

Galileo Galilei was a great Italian thinker whose contributions in philosophy, astronomy, and mathematics shaped the way we view the world. He helped develop the scientific method and establish the mathematical laws of falling motion. He advanced the development of the telescope to the point where he could use it to view objects in space and prove that Earth revolved around the Sun. His findings and beliefs were radical at the time and led to his excommunication from the Catholic Church.

Sir Isaac Newton

The contributions of this English physicist and mathematician laid the foundation of many modern sciences. Newton's discovery of white light and its composition of colors paved the way for studies in modern optics. His laws of motion gave a basis to modern physics and his law of universal gravity created a framework for classic mechanics.

Peter the Great

Crowned czar of Russia at the age of ten, Peter ruled jointly with his half brother until his brother's death. As sole ruler, Peter expanded the Russian empire to reclaim access to the Baltic Sea and establish trade with Europe. He reorganized government, founding the city of St. Petersburg as the new capital of Russia and creating the Russian army and navy.

World History Highlights: 1900–Present

Date	Event
1905	Albert Einstein formulates his theory of relativity.
1911	Marie Curie wins Nobel Prize for chemistry.
1914	Archduke Franz Ferdinand, heir to Austrian-Hungarian throne, assassinated in Sarajevo, setting off events that lead to World War I.
1918	Massive worldwide flu epidemic kills more than 20 million people.
1919	Treaty of Versailles signed, ending World War I.
1927	American Charles Lindbergh is first to fly solo across Atlantic Ocean.
1939	Germany invades Poland, sparking World War II. Britain and France declare war on Germany. United States remains neutral.
1941	Japan attacks United States by bombing American ships at Pearl Harbor, Hawaii. United States declares war on Japan and enters World War II.
1945	Germany surrenders. United States drops atomic bombs on two Japanese cities, Hiroshima and Nagasaki. World War II ends. United Nations, international peacekeeping organization, formed.
1948	Israel proclaims its independence. Gandhi, nonviolent leader of Indian Nationalist movement against British rule, assassinated.
1950	North Korea invades South Korea, starting Korean War.
1964	United States begins sending troops to Vietnam to assist South Vietnam during Vietnamese civil war.
1973	Paris Peace Accords signed, ending Vietnam War.
1989	Chinese army shoots and kills protestors in China's Tiananmen Square. Berlin Wall, separating East and West Germany, torn down.
1991	President Frederik Willem de Klerk negotiates to end apartheid in South Africa. Union of Soviet Socialist Republics (USSR) dissolved into independent states.
1994	Nelson Mandela elected president of South Africa in first free elections.
1997	Mother Teresa, champion of poor in Calcutta, India, dies.
2006	Iraqi dictator Saddam Hussein captured and killed for crimes against humanity.
2011	Protests in Tunisia, Egypt, and Libya lead to the removal or death of longtime dictators. Osama bin-Laden, leader of Al-Qaeda and mastermind of the September 11, 2001, attacks on the United States, is killed by U.S. forces in Pakistan.
2012	Egyptians voted in the country's first-ever democratic election.

World History

People of 1900–Present

Albert Einstein

Called the greatest scientist of the 20th century, physicist Albert Einstein developed revolutionary theories about how the world works, especially the connection between matter and energy. Einstein's knowledge was applied to the development of the atomic bomb, which he said saddened him. Today calling somebody an "Einstein" means that he or she is a genius, but young Albert Einstein was known more for playing tricks in school than for getting good grades.

Marie Curie

Polish-French chemist Marie Curie is best known for discovering the radioactive element radium, for which she won a Nobel Prize. She also discovered an element called polonium, named for her birthplace, Poland. Although radium is used to treat and diagnose diseases, repeated or excessive exposure can cause serious illness and even death. After years of working with radium, Marie Curie died in 1934 from radiation poisoning.

Mohandas Gandhi

To the people of India, Mohandas Gandhi was the Mahatma, or Great Soul. Gandhi believed in tolerance for all religious beliefs. He led peaceful protests to bring about social change and freedom from British rule. India was granted freedom in 1947, but fighting between Hindus and Muslims continued. Gandhi spoke out against the fighting, angering many and resulting in his assassination. In America, Dr. Martin Luther King Jr. modeled his nonviolent strategy of fighting racism on Gandhi's methods.

Nelson Mandela

In 1994, Nelson Mandela was elected the first black president of South Africa. That was the first year in which South Africans of all races could vote, thanks to of the end of the government's previous policy of racial segregation, called apartheid. Mandela had served many years in prison for leading protests against apartheid and became a world-famous symbol of racial injustice. After his release from prison, he led discussions with white leaders that led to the end of apartheid and to a nonracial form of government.

Mother Teresa

Born Agnes Gonxha Bojaxhiu, Mother Teresa was a Roman Catholic nun who became known as the "Saint of the Gutters" for her work with poor people. She founded a religious order in India to provide food, schools, health care, and shelters for the poor, sick, and dying. Mother Teresa received numerous awards for her work, including the Nobel Peace Prize. In 2003, Pope John Paul II approved the first step toward declaring Mother Teresa a saint in the Roman Catholic Church.

Homework Helpers

Use the tips, guides, definitions, examples, and ideas on the next four pages to help you ace spelling, writing, and every homework assignment.

Parts of Speech

Picking Up the Pieces

Pieces of a jigsaw puzzle need to be correctly connected to form a complete picture. Words need to be correctly connected to form a sentence. The part each word plays in a sentence is called its part of speech.

Part of Speech	Definition	Example
Noun	A person, place, or thing	kids, plates, spaghetti, meatballs
Pronoun	A word that replaces a noun	they
Adjective	A word that modifies a noun (*A*, *an*, and *the* are special types of adjectives called articles)	the, hungry
Verb	An action word	devoured, exclaimed
Adverb	A word that modifies a verb	quickly, loudly
Conjunction	A word like *but* or *and* that joins together groups of words or sentences	and
Preposition	A word like *in* or *of* that shows the relationship between one noun and another noun, verb, or, adverb	of
Interjection	An exclamation, usually a short part of speech that shows emotion or emphasis	Yum!

The hungry kids quickly devoured plates of spaghetti and meatballs. "Yum!" they exclaimed loudly.

Tip: A proper noun is a word for a particular person, place, or thing. Always use capital letters for proper nouns. Examples: Abraham Lincoln, Australia, Fourth of July

Vocabulary

Prefixes

A prefix is a group of letters that starts a word. If you know common prefixes, you can figure out meanings of new words and expand your spoken and written vocabulary. (Some prefixes have more than the one meaning given below.)

Prefix	Meaning	Example
anti–	against	antibacterial
circum–	around	circumnavigate
co–	with	copilot
dis–	not	disappear
ex–	away from	expel
in–	not	incomplete
inter–	between	intersection
micro–	small	microchip
pre–	before	prefix
sub–	under	submarine
trans–	across	transform

Roots

Hidden within many words are parts of words called roots, which come from the Greek and Latin languages. Word roots can appear at the beginning, middle, or end of a word, but they always mean the same thing.

Root	Meaning	Example
audi	hear	audition
auto	self	automatic
bene	good	benefit
bio	life	biology
chrono	time	chronicle
dict	say	dictate
phil	love	philosophy
port	carry	portable
spec	see	spectacle
terr	earth	terrain

Spelling
Sounds Wrong to Me

Homophones are words that sound the same but have different spellings and meanings, like *know* and *no* and *bare* and *bear*. Avoid making these common homophone mistakes.

There Their They're

There is an adverb meaning a place.
Their is a pronoun that shows possession.
They're is a contraction that stands for "they are."

They're riding *their* bikes over *there*.

To Too Two

To is a preposition that shows direction.
Too is an adverb meaning "also."
Two is a number.

You *two* can come *to* the party, *too*.

Its It's

Its is a pronoun that shows possession.
It's is a contraction of "it is" or "it has."

It's a road known for *its* dangerous curves.

Punctuation
Use Your Comma Sense

Teachers say using commas incorrectly is the mistake students make most frequently. Here are three rules to remember:

1. Don't use a comma between the subject and verb.

Wrong:
Jennie, picked some flowers for her grandma.

Right:
Jennie picked some flowers for her grandma.

2. Use a comma before a conjunction to join two complete thoughts (independent clauses).

Jennie picked some flowers for her grandma, and then she put them in a vase.

3. Use commas around extra information (nonrestrictive clauses).

Jennie picked some flowers for her grandma, who was visiting, and then she put them in a vase.

Research and Study Skills
Book It

Got a report to write? The help you need to craft a perfect paper is as near as the library.

- Use an atlas to find maps of continents, countries, states, or cities.
- Use encyclopedias and almanacs for facts, figures, stats, and other information.
- Use a dictionary to find out a word's meaning and pronunciation, its origin, and its part of speech.
- Use a thesaurus to find synonyms (words that mean the same as other words) and antonyms (words that mean the opposite of other words).
- Ask a librarian (nicely, of course) for help if you get stuck. Librarians know a tremendous amount of information and are eager to point kids in the right direction.

Cool Tools Online

Dictionaries, thesauruses, and other reference materials are available online as well as in book form. In fact, you can find out almost anything you want to know online—the catch is, not all the information is correct. You can trust the information on these websites to be accurate, up to date, and especially good for kids.

Site: www.ipl.org
What you'll find: Information about almost everything, from animals to sports to school cancellations! Plus a chance to e-mail a librarian or connect with other kids

Site: www.nal.usda.gov/awic/pubs/scifair.htm
What you'll find: Science fair topics

Site: www.kids.gov
What you'll find: Information about U.S. history, government, the states, and more

Site: www.nasa.gov/audience/forstudents/index.html
What you'll find: Information on the planets, the stars, space research, and missions

Site: www.scholastic.com/kids/homework
What you'll find: Tips on writing, research, test-taking, and study skills

Site: www.ala.org
What you'll find: Keyword "great websites for kids" for a terrific assortment of sites, reviewed and selected by librarians

Tip: Don't copy and paste material directly from the Internet. Print it out and rewrite it in your own words to avoid plagiarism, which is using someone else's ideas and words as your own. Another tip: Use more than one source whenever you do research.

333

What's Next?

BREAKTHROUGH

Paris Luckowski, of Newark, NJ, was too sick to go to school for months, so he sent a replacement: a four-foot-tall robot with motorized wheels named VGo. Paris controlled VGo's movements through his home computer, just like playing a video game. Through wireless video, Paris's classmates and teachers could see and hear him, and he could see and hear them. These tele-presence robots are keeping sick kids in several states from missing classwork and missing fun with friends.

SUPER SENSES

Today's computers and smartphones have microphones and cameras to help us see and hear. According to researchers at International Business Machines Corporation (IBM) and other experts, technology will bring super new powers to all five senses—touch, hearing, smell, taste, and sight—by the year 2017.

Feels Like a Bargain
Online shoppers will have more than pictures on a screen to help them make buying decisions. They'll be able to reach out and touch clothing and other items. At least, it will seem that way. Tiny vibrations built into mobile devices will copy textures such as smoothness and softness and transmit them when you touch the screen.

What's That Sound?
Super sensors will be able to "hear" cracks in a bridge before they appear. Sensors will also be able to figure out from the sound of a baby's cry whether he or she is hungry, sick, or just wants attention.

Makes Scents
Smell technology will let officials discover problems like a failing city sewage system before it's obvious to the human nose. Medical professionals will be able identify warning signs of certain diseases by smelling someone's breath.

What's Cooking, Computer?
Computers will have "digital taste buds" that will let them create meals that taste delicious and are super healthy. They'll tap into huge databases to find ingredients people might not think of themselves.

Eye Spy
Long letter-and-number passwords will be outdated. Computers and smartphones will use facial recognition software and eye scans to make an ID.

On the Right Track

GPS (Global Positioning Satellite) systems do everything from forecasting weather to making cell phones work. New uses for GPS are being developed every day. Visit www.gps.gov/applications to learn more.

New computerized headsets from Golden-i use GPS to help firefighters and other first responders find victims trapped in buildings.

GPS built into a new tracking collar from Tracker Technologies works with a smartphone app to let you build a virtual fenced area for your dog and get a text alert if your pet wanders away.

SMARTER AND KINDER

Popular Mechanics magazine recently made more than 100 predictions about ways technology will change the world. Some of their predictions are being tested or already exist, and many point to a smarter, kinder, and safer world ahead.

Smart Cars
Cars will "talk" with traffic lights and other vehicles to prevent accidents and keep traffic moving. Software will predict traffic jams an hour before they happen so drivers can switch to another route.

Smart Clothes and Buildings
So long, laundry detergent and water! Clothes made of fabric coated with titanium dioxide will need only sunlight to become clean and fresh. Titanium dioxide on metal buildings will change air pollution particles into a harmless film that will wash away in the rain.

Safer for People, Animals, and Other Living Things
Sensors will help rescuers find disaster victims by detecting chemicals in breath, sweat, and skin. Drugs will be tested on silicon chips designed to work like human organs instead of animals. Synthetic meat will help feed a growing world population, reducing the need to raise more animals for food.

Index

Index

Photo Credits

Animals
pp. 6-7: loggerhead turtle, © idreamphoto/Shutterstock; p. 11: giant tortoise, © Daniel Wilson/Shutterstock; p. 15: small dinosaur, © Ralf Juergen Kraft/Shutterstock; p. 16: firefly, © Dr. Morley Read/Shutterstock; p. 20: dromedary camel, © PardoY/Shutterstock; humpback whale, © Ethan Daniels/Shutterstock; killer whale, © Condor 36/Shutterstock; p. 21: shrew, © Miroslav Hlavko/Shutterstock; p. 28: amur leopard, © Eduard Kyslynskyy/Shutterstock; p. 29: cows, sxc.hu, © Watje; oysters, sxc.hu, © Samuel Rosa; kangaroos, sxc.hu, © Charlie Lawrence; p. 31: poodle, sxc.hu, © Bethan Hazell; Labrador retriever, sxc.hu, © Marcelo Britofilho; Persian cat, sxc.hu, © bonvivant

Birthdays
pp. 32-33: Kyla Ross, © Jae C. Hong/AP Photo; p. 34: Victoria Justice, © s_bukley/Shutterstock; p. 35: David Beckham, © Photo Works/Shutterstock

Books & Literature
pp. 38-39: Wimpy Kid balloon, © Charles Sykes/AP Photo

Buildings & Landmarks
pp. 42-43: Singapore Flyer Ferris wheel, © Dmitry Berkut/Shutterstock; p. 46: Channel Tunnel (Chunnel), © Bloomberg via Getty Images; p. 47: Mausoleum of Halicarnassus, © EvrenKalinbacak/Shutterstock; p. 48: Tacoma Narrows Bridge, © kathmanduphotog/Shutterstock; p. 49: Burj Khalifa, © Rahhal/Shutterstock.com; p. 50: Exploratorium, © Exploratorium; Guggenheim Bilbao, © A.B.G./Shutterstock; p. 51: Metropolitan Museum of Art, © ChameleonsEye/Shutterstock

Calendars & Holidays
pp. 52-53: © Pam Lockeby/Daytona Beach News Journal/AP Photo

Crime
pp. 66-67: © zimmytws/Shutterstock

Disasters
pp. 70-71: © Wayne Parry/AP Photo; p. 72: rescue dog, © fotostory/Shutterstock; p. 73: Mt. Mayon, © Katerina Sysoeva/Shutterstock

Environment
pp. 76-77: Aerial global shot, Earth Hour, © NASA Earth Observatory/NOAA NGDC; p. 77: lightbulb, © ducu59us/Shutterstock; p. 78: paper and paperboard, sxc.hu © Tim Meijer; p. 81: Tucson, AZ, © You Touch Pix of EuToch/Shutterstock

Flags & Facts, Countries of the World
pp. 86-87: Panama Canal, © Bettmann/Corbis; pp. 88-89: world map, © stockmaps.com, GeoNova Publishing, Inc.; p. 90: birds, sxc.hu, © Rainer Schmied; p. 92: Bengal tiger, sxc.hu, © Thad Zajdowicz; p. 96: emerald bracelet, sxc.hu, © Lavinia Marin; p. 97: Lego blocks, sxc.hu, © Craig Rodway; p. 98, Great Pyramid of Khufu, sxc.hu, © James Farmer; p. 100: Cologne Cathedral, sxc.hu, © Dirk Ziegener; p. 101: cashews, sxc.hu, © Sonny Leon; guinea pig, sxc.hu, © Kim Andre Silkebaekken; p. 102: geyser, sxc.hu, © Dr. Zsolt Zatrok; Taj Mahal, sxc.hu, © Dr. Zsolt Zatrok; p. 104: Koran, sxc.hu, © Ramzi Hashisho; p. 107, fishing on the Niger River, sxc.hu, © Dennis Hunink; p. 108: sugar cane, sxc.hu, © clix; p. 114: fruit pie, sxc.hu, © Erica Bressan; p. 115: sailing ship, sxc.hu, © Stella Levi; p. 118: porcelain statue, sxc.hu, © clix

Flags & Facts, States of the United States

pp. 122-123: © EpicStockMedia/Shutterstock; p. 128: woolly mammoth, sxc.hu, © Lavinia Marin; p. 131: surfer, sxc.hu, © Michelle Dennis; p. 136: deer, sxc.hu, © B Creavis; p. 138: Carlsbad Caverns, © Galyna Andrushko/Shutterstock; Empire State Building, © Marc Venema/Shutterstock; p. 139: bullfrog, © Chrystal Bilodeau/Shutterstock; p. 140: beaver, © BMJ/Shutterstock; p. 142: bluebonnets, © Belozorova Elena/Shutterstock; p. 144: Devils Tower, © Wildnerdpix/Shutterstock

Games

pp. 146-147: © Jason DeCrow/Invision for Hasbro/AP Images; p. 149: teen on tablet, © Pressmaster/Shutterstock

Geography

pp. 150-151: © Stewart Smith Photography/Shutterstock; p. 157: Tokyo, Japan: sxc.hu, © Dan Price (ishnaf); p. 176: Mt. McKinley, © Richard A McMillin/Shutterstock

Health & Wellness

pp. 182-183: © Larry St. Pierre/Shutterstock; p. 187: fishing, sxc.hu, © Benjamin Earwicker, www.garrisonphoto.org/sxc

Inventors & Inventions

pp. 188-189: © Blaz Kure/Shutterstock

Languages

pp. 192-193: © isaxar/Shutterstock

Math

pp. 198-199: © usgs.gov

Military

pp. 206-207: © koh sze kiat/Shutterstock

Movies & TV

pp. 210-211: Darth Vader (*Star Wars*), © nevenm/Shutterstock; stars (background), © Cardens Design/Shutterstock; p. 212: Daniel Day-Lewis, © Joe Seer/Shutterstock; p. 213: Johnny Depp, © cinemafestival/Shutterstock; Emma Stone, © DFree/Shutterstock; p. 214: Mark Harmon, © Featureflash/Shutterstock; Ross Lynch, © Joe Seer/Shutterstock

Music

pp. 216-217: Fifth Harmony, © Frank Micelotta/Invsion/AP Photo; p. 218: One Direction, © Featureflash/Shutterstock; p. 219: Justin Bieber, © WireImage; Carly Rae Jepsen, © Featureflash/Shutterstock

Plants

pp. 220-221: © NASA

Population

pp. 224-225: © Jorg Hackemann/Shutterstock; p. 226: penguin on ice floe, sxc.hu, © Jan Will; p. 226: Vatican, © Banauke/Shutterstock; p. 229: Los Angeles, CA, © Andrey Bayda/Shutterstock; p. 231: Miami, FL, © Songquan Deng/Shutterstock

Religion

pp. 232-233: © prasit chansareekorn/Shutterstock; p. 235: Pope Benedict, © miqu77/Shutterstock

Science

pp. 236-237: © Red Bull Content Pool/AP Photo

Signs & Symbols

pp. 244-245: yellow cab in Times Square, © Stuart Monk/Shutterstock; p. 244: NYC parking signs, © Ron Leighton Design

Space

pp. 248-249: © Alin Brotea/Shutterstock

Sports

pp. 258-259: © Haslam Photography/Shutterstock; p. 260: Joe Flacco, © Action Sports Photography/Shutterstock; p. 261: Johnny Manziel, © Black Russian Studio/Shutterstock; p. 263: Pablo Sandoval, © Photo Works/Shutterstock; p. 265: Kevin Ware, © David E. Klutho/Sports Illustrated/Getty Images; p. 266: London Aquatics Center, © David Burrows/Shutterstock; p. 267: girls' Olympic gymnastics team, © lev radin/Shutterstock

Technology & Computers

pp. 268-269: 3-D printer, © Imaginechina via AP Images; p. 269: handcuffs, © Jeffrey Rutzky/Ron Leighton Design; p. 272: smiley emoticon, © Gelpi JM/Shutterstock; p. 275: girl with mobile phone, © Denis Kuvaev/Shutterstock; p. 276: social networks icon, © gst/Shutterstock; social media network connection concept, © Cienpies Design/Shutterstock; p. 277: © gezzeg/shutterstock.com

U.S. Government

pp. 278-279: © Lane V. Erickson/Shutterstock; p. 280: Supreme Court, © Mesut Dogan/Shutterstock; p. 283: gavel, © Neamov/Shutterstock

U.S. History

p. 300: Rosa Parks stamp (inset), © catwalker/Shutterstock; pp. 300-301: President Obama on bus, © Pete Souza/Whitehouse.gov

Weather

pp. 312-313: © EmiliaUngur/Shutterstock; p. 314: Mt. Washington, © Liz Van Steenburgh/Shutterstock

Weights & Measures

pp. 316-317: © Jonathan Hayward/The Canadian Press/AP Photo

World History

pp. 320-321: skeleton, © UOL/Splash News/Corbis; p. 321: facial reconstruction of Richard III, © London News Pictures/Rex Features via AP Images; p. 322: Great Wall of China, © Joan Ho

What's Next?

pp. 334-335: school hallway, © Matty Symons/Shutterstock; robot, © 2013 VGo Communications; p. 337: dog tracking collar, © Tracker Technologies; Golden-i headset, © Golden-i

Cover

top left: Fruit Ninja Sensei slicing orange, Courtesy Half Brick; top right: Shawn White, © PNC/Corbis; center: english bulldog, © WilleeCole/Shutterstock, Inc.; bottom left: Beyonce, © Gilbert Carrasquillo/Getty Images; bottom right: crocodile, ©Alexander Cherednichenko/Shutterstock, Inc.